Amy Lee; or, Without and Within

George Canning Hill

BIBLIOLIFE

AMY LEE;

OR,

WITHOUT AND WITHIN.

"SWEET ARE THE USES OF ADVERSITY."
SHAKSPEARE.

BY THE AUTHOR OF "OUR PARISH."

BOSTON:
BROWN, BAZIN, AND COMPANY.
1856.

CONTENTS.

CONTENTS.   ▼

CHAPTER XXIII.
1 *

AMY LEE.

CHAPTER I.

A WRECK OF A MAN.

THE fire shone in the shovel, the tongs, and the poker, sending its pleasant glow over the room. Though the carpet was somewhat faded and worn, its figures brightened a good deal in the light, and made the little apartment look unusually cheerful.

A small table was drawn out into the middle of the floor, and spread with a white napkin. Before the bright coal fire that burned in the grate stood a large easy chair, stuffed, and covered with a dull chintz, within whose broad arms half reclined the wasted and weary figure of a man. Now he lifted his hands from the sides of his chair, and employed them as screens for his eyes; now he let them fall again into their old places, and dropped back his head exhaustingly, as if there were no more strength left in him.

"Amy," said he, in a tone of querulousness that seemed his habit, "when are we going to have supper? It's always so *late*, when I want it early."

"Why, it's not yet quite six o'clock, father," answered a very sweet voice from another part of the room. "We always have it sent in at six, you know. Are you hungry to-night, father?"

"No; but I want my supper."

"O, well, I guess it will be along very soon now. They're generally pretty punctual with our meals, I think. Sometimes, you know, they have more to do. I would try and be as patient as I could, father."

And the daughter began a gentle bustle about the room, thinking that thus he might feel that *something* was being done to hasten the preparations for his evening meal. She moved the chairs, replaced the little stand, dusted the table under the glass, went round picking up threads and frayed ends of cloth from the carpet, stirred the fire with the poker, set a chair for herself near the little stand opposite that of her father, and finally brushed out the imaginary wrinkles from her apron, and smoothed down her abundant hair with the palms of both hands. All the time her father kept whining and groaning; and when at last she stood before him with her hands on her head, her face expressive of such unbounded gratefulness and pleasure, his eyes studied her features with a look that should have betrayed the most searching self-condemnation.

It was near the end of winter, a very rough and trying one to poor people every where, and unpleasantly long and tedious even to those whose circumstances had heaped all comforts and luxuries around them. Fuel had been scarce, and provisions very high, and every thing else went up in price correspondingly. Many a blue lip had begged along the streets during the last three months for help, and many a poverty-stricken family had wondered day after day where the next meal was to come from, when the one at which they sat should be over.

In a retired part of Boston, where a short and narrow street branched off from a much more populous and busy one, was the respectable boarding house kept by Mrs. Dozy. Not often were carriages to be seen passing through this street, for it was much out of the way of the railroad stations, and nothing was to be gained by so circuitous a route of travel. Occasionally drays and heavy carts, with a file of stalwart horses drawing them, would rattle through, filling the place with sharp echoes of wheels, and hoofs, and noisy shouts; but as a general thing it was an uncommonly quiet street, given up to the use and enjoyment of nervous old ladies and profoundly contemplative old gentlemen. There was a small druggist's shop on the corner, and half way down hung out the sign of a modest shoemaker. A great many men passed through, in the course of the day, with little tin pails swinging in their hands, the bright and unmistakable proofs of industrious day laborers.

Amy Lee had been home herself but a little while, and in that time she had done much to calm the shattered nervous system of her poor father. The moment she had thrown off her bonnet and shawl, she was at his side, inquiring after his wants and his happiness. And even while she stooped down to take out the numbness from her fingers in the blaze, he began his usual whining complaints, and she her customary offices of patience and love.

"O, well, father," said she, after hearing him a moment, "I'm sure I wouldn't mind it. You'll soon get over these bad feelings, you know, and then you will laugh to think what little things troubled you so. Come, cheer up, father. The winter's most over, you know, and it will soon be spring, and then we are going out a little in the country, on the warm days. Won't that be grand?" And she shrugged her shoulders, and suffered a smile to break over her face that should have melted the heart of a cynic.

"I don't know," groaned her parent. "I'm sure I don't know. Why, Amy, what are we coming to? *I* can't understand. You can't go on in this way, and work all the time, year in and year out."

"Why not, I want to know? I *have* done it, and I can *keep on* doing it. What is easier than that?"

"Yes, but we ought to — ought to have something to *depend* upon. Only your hands, — how little *that* is! We ought to have something in the bank; — and how shall we find it there? — or when?"

"You don't look at the bright side, father. What have we to do with the bank? I can teach my few scholars in their music lessons, and that is quite enough to support us here. What more do we either of us need than a *living*? You borrow fears, I am afraid, father. You shouldn't do that. Here I am right by your side, and here I will stay as long as you live. While I can earn any thing, you shall be cared for. And when I can't —— " She stopped without meaning to.

"What then? When you *can't!* When you *can't!*" eagerly broke in her dejected parent, hastening to catch up this unhappy possibility.

"We can still trust in God," calmly answered Amy, "even as we do now."

"Ah, but — ah, but — but it's not such a pleasant thing to be a beggar, now. If I could only work myself, Amy. But I *can't;* no, I can't. I really don't believe I ever shall again. O, O, O!" and with these words he threw back his head in the great chair, let fall his thin and almost fleshless hands, and the tears followed each other down his cheeks as fast as if they ran from the eyes of a very child. It was amazing to behold the mastery that disease had acquired over him. He had no strength, no hope, no energy. He looked up to that single girl with as much trust as to a power that he already confessed vastly his superior. In her white hands lay his very means of existence, and on her happy face slept the pictures in which he found all his daily enjoyment.

The moment she saw to what a state of prostration his nervous system was reduced, she drew up a little stool to his side, and taking his hand in her own, began the task of quieting him. She appealed to every feeling of his heart to bring him out of this situation; assuring him that there was no need whatever that he should go to work again, for her own receipts were amply sufficient to take care of them both. And she bade him try and compose himself, begging him not to give up so readily to these changeable moods, but to resist them with all bravery till he should succeed in conquering them forever.

A tender sight it was to see this young girl, thus supporting and steadying her father. She had strength enough and courage enough, to endure the trials that might be put upon both. Frail as she was at best, she could nevertheless bear up stoutly under trouble. Because she did not rely on herself. She knew well that she was on all sides surrounded with a Power, faithful trust in whom was never betrayed. And though afflictions might multiply upon her a hundred fold, still her trust would never be shaken; and with her heart thus disposed, for her there was no such thing as affliction, or perplexity, or fear, or despair. It is a blessed condition, indeed, into which any humble and simple soul may enter.

Amy's father had been in his day a very respectable member of the legal profession. His business was extensive, and he seemed to prosper. While Amy was not more than three years old he had lost his wife, who left only this dear child to him in remembrance of their brief but happy union. He never married again, but seemed from that time to centre all his affections on little Amy.

She grew up in the enjoyment of excellent advantages, entering at the best schools, and going through their several courses with marked credit. He gave her opportunities to perfect herself in music; and now, when she had reached her nineteenth year, — for our story finds her just entering upon it, — it happened that this musical skill of hers was exactly the thing that was to provide subsistence for both of them.

A wretched habit, that he seemed totally unable either to control or break away from, had brought her father to his present lamentable condition; and now that he was no longer permitted to gratify his appetite as regularly as before, and only at such times as he could furtively appropriate, he had sunk down like a dying flame into a state almost of bodily and intellectual paralysis, and given himself up to perpetual fretfulness and dejection. It was certainly a great care for any one to watch all his changing moods and minister faithfully to his many frivolous wants; but he was blessed with a child who stood ever ready to perform both these duties, and esteemed it an inestimable privilege, too, to be the means of providing a livelihood for them both. It was an example of a pure devotion.

Amy's father was a confirmed opium eater. Little by little the habit had stolen over him, sullying one bright

2

point of his character after another, till the whole was blackened with the most lamentable darkness. While the powerful drug was kept from him, he showed signs of returning vigor, but they were generally not much more than signs. His mental energies had been gradually undermined, till now there was nothing left for them to lean upon, and they too fell with the rest of his qualities, making a wide and complete ruin.

Whenever he could manage, however, to get a taste of the destroying drug, for the time it brightened up his faculties, and shed a fitful and artificial light over his usual gloom. This was the more lamentable to witness, inasmuch as it brought out in brighter relief the wasted spots of his cankered nature, and invariably suggested the profounder darkness and gloom that would follow the indulgence very speedily after.

At this time, he had been without any stimulus of this character for several weeks. The weather had been severely cold, and forbade his going out of his room; and sitting there in his chair gazing into the fire, and brooding gloomily over the glowing coals, he had by slow degrees grown to be so very weak and childish, that he needed in truth more attention than ever. Amy saw that his strength was gradually failing him, and had seriously asked herself if it were not best to consult a physician. Still there was nothing alarming in any of his symptoms, or apparent reason for more fear than was customary.

She sat by his side, holding his wasted hand, and trying gently to soothe him.

" If I had any *strength*, Amy," said he, looking vacantly about the room.

" What would you do then, father ? " she inquired.

" *You* shouldn't work so."

" Ah, but I know you worry yourself too much about that. Now just suppose I had nothing at all to do — couldn't *find* any thing to do, when I most needed it ; shouldn't we be worse off then, father, than we are now ? There *are* people more wretched than even you and I are. I've seen them with my own eyes, this very winter. But I had only pity and sympathy for them. That might not have been very *much*, but it was all I had ; it was my poor little *mite*."

" I wish *I* had a poor little mite, Amy, to throw into *our* treasury."

" You have — you have, father ; and not such a little one, either. Don't you know you have ? "

" What is it ? What ? I should be glad to cast it in, Amy."

" It's your love for me, father. That makes me richer every day than all else. O, if I could tell you, and if you could understand, what a satisfaction it is for me to be useful to you, when you have done so much all my life for me ! "

The father threw his other hand across her shoulder, and uttered a groan. It sounded as if it really came from the depths of his heart.

Just then Mrs. Dozy's servant girl brought in the

supper on a tray, and placed it on tl.e little stand. Then inquiring of Amy if there was any thing more wanting, she went out of the room and shut the door behind her. And this little family of two — father and daughter — drew up to the board, while she poured the tea from their miniature pot, and he sipped it and tried as hard as he could for a moment to seem altogether happy.

CHAPTER II.

THE BESETTING SIN.

Such were the conditions on which Amy and her father lived in the house of Mrs. Dozy, that it was quite the same as if they were keeping house alone by themselves. Amy hired a couple of rooms, and it was stipulated that their meals should be regularly sent in to them. This latter arrangement helped along that feeling of independence which her father so much desired to cherish, besides securing to both of them an amount of quiet that they otherwise might not in such a position have been able to find. And it relieved Amy of considerable anxiety, too, as Mrs. Dozy was always quite willing, when the former was absent with her pupils, to drop in occasionally upon her father, and see that he was in every respect comfortable and wanted for nothing.

A few days only after the evening scene selected for opening the story, Amy took leave of her father as usual, and went out to her labor. It was after dinner, and the air was much blander and sunnier than it had lately been, possibly giving distant and indistinct hints of the coming spring.

2 *   (17)

"Now you'll make yourself as easy as you can, father," were her last words to him, as she stooped down and left a child's kiss on his cheek. "If you want any thing while I am gone, you can just step into the other room, you know, and Mrs. Dozy will wait on you. Good by, father. I shall hurry back to read to you, you know.".

"Yes, yes, yes," said her father, in a voice that lacked the slightest betrayal either of energy or feeling. And so sinking his head back in the chair, he commenced rubbing his hands together, and gave up to the sluggish courses of his thought.

Amy tripped down the stairs and lightly along the street. She had three lessons to give that afternoon, and they would occupy her about an hour each. The people she met seemed to wear pleasanter faces than usual, and she imagined it must be from the secret influence of the weather. There are such days and half days sometimes in every winter, that fairly cheat one's senses out of the thraldom of the season's bleakness, and warm the heart as with the most genial sunshine.

For an hour, perhaps, her father sat quietly in his chair after she had gone, drifting slowly and idly along whithersoever the changing tides of his feeling carried him. He looked in the fire of coals; he looked at his thin hands; he looked up at the papered wall; and he looked into the fire again. This was listlessness, surely, if any thing was, and even his weakened intellect could not fail so to behold it.

Tired at length with the recurrence of these same old shades of feeling, he got up from his chair and began to pace slowly up and down the room. Now and then he stopped to look in the little glass that hung over the bureau ; and when he did so, he brushed his gray hair lightly off from his temples with one hand, saying in a loud whisper to himself the while — " Getting to be old ! getting to be old ! " And then he crossed both hands behind him, and fell into his slow walk again.

Finally, as he came up before the window once more, he paused to look out. When he stopped he meant only to gratify the moment's idle whim ; but that single little moment made a great change in his destiny. The pleasant sun was shining down the sides of the houses over the way, and lay in irregular strips here and there along the street, furnishing shadows of the chimneys, and parapets, and gables, that surmounted some of the dwellings in that vicinity. The street was exceedingly quiet, scarcely a stray dustman's cart rattling lightly over the stones, and only a few doves fluttering about from one spot to another in quest of such chance provender as their bright red eyes could espy.

" So still ! " said he to himself, looking out meditatively. " It carries me back — carries me back ! Those doves now, over there, how happy they are ! how happy ! Why can't *I* be happy, too ? I *can be*, if I like, I know. *Dreams* bring happiness, and I know what *makes* dreams ! I can sit here by this window, though I *am* alone, and be

as happy as they. Who can hinder? It will all be in
this brain," — he touched his hand to his forehead, —
"in this brain."

That moment he had fallen again.

For, turning swiftly away from where he was standing,
he began to walk the floor much more excitedly, and went
straight at last to the drawers of Amy in her little room.
The opium fiend had seized him. He was ready to go
wherever it bade him follow.

"If she has left her key in the drawer," said he,
doubtingly. "Yes, she has! she has!" And he pulled
out the drawer with the haste of a man who was a much
more violent robber than he.

As soon as he had opened it, he proceeded to rummage
for her purse. He handled a very various assortment
indeed of things alternately useful and ornamental, and
at last laid his hand upon the object most desired.
Taking the purse from the corner, he felt of its two
pockets, and stood and leisurely made his calculation.

"Perhaps if I take out what silver change I want,"
said he to himself, "it will never be missed at all;
whereas, if I should go to robbing her of a bank bill, she
could not *help* finding it out the first time she goes to her
purse. *Robbing* her, did I say? It's not robbing her at
all. Isn't she my daughter — my own child? Doesn't
she labor for *me* as well as for *herself*? Isn't this just as
much *my* money as it is *hers*? No, no, indeed; talk of
robbing, forsooth, when a man takes what he needs from

the purse of his own child! I'll help myself then. I am
so much in want of a little — only a little, just to console
me, and to bring together these shattered feelings, and to
raise the spirits to a healthier tone! I can't abide this
way of living long. I don't think I can get through
another day, unless I have opium."

Thinking thus to silence the feeble protests of his con-
science altogether, he set about emptying his daughter's
purse of all its contents, spreading them around on the
top of her little dresser. As his eyes caught the bewildering brightness of the hoarded heap of silver, and ran
over the figures that fixed the value to her little wad of
bank notes, his brain became suddenly dizzy, and he
assumed an air of strength that seemed in him almost
preternatural.

"There! there! there!" whispered he, picking out
with a great deal of care one piece of money after another;
"I think that will be enough; and if I should buy a
little *over*, why, how handy it will be for me, shut up here
alone, to help me spin out these long hours of the day
when *she* is gone."

So he replaced the notes, slipped back the remainder
of the silver into the other side of the purse, put the latter into the drawer, pushed in the drawer quietly, and
hurried back into the next room. All this sudden manœu-
vring had sufficed to bring a flush to his cheeks, that
was a perfect telltale of his guilt. Again he stepped before the window and looked out. The sun was as pleasant
as before, and the street exactly as quiet.

" *Why* can't I go out, such a day as this, I would like
to know? Who tells me I am not able? Besides, it's to
be only a few minutes, a very few minutes, and I am
right back again. I shall try it, I think, at any rate."

With this he looked around for his shoes and his fur-
lined overshoes, — for on pleasant afternoons Amy very
often accompanied him herself on a short walk down the
street, — and hurried to put them on, first taking the pre-
caution, however, to turn the key in the door, lest Mrs.
Dozy might happen in on one of her neighborly errands.
Then he took down his fur cap and cloak, and putting on the
one and carefully wrapping the other around him, reported
to himself that he was ready for his most rash adventure.

Cautiously he turned back the lock again, dreading to
catch the slightest sound, and involuntarily making his
mouth work itself round with the movement of the key.
At first he dared open the door but the width of a narrow
crack; then, as he heard no sign of a noise in the hall,
he essayed a still wider aperture, so that he could thrust
out his head and look around for himself. Seeing no
person in his way, he stepped forth quickly into the hall,
and glided with an astonishingly swift motion down the
stairs.

The latch of the outer door happened to be lifted; so
there would be no difficulty about his getting in again
without a key. He accordingly placed his hand upon the
knob, and effected a passage immediately into the open
street. As he went along so skulkingly down the walk,

wrapping his cloak up about his throat and face, and hugging to the wall closely, he could not help congratulating himself that he had succeeded so easily in effecting his escape ; and if his features could have been seen by any one, they would have appeared distorted to an almost unrecognizable degree.

Stealthily as a depredating cat he paced along over the pavements in his soft overshoes, until he had reached the corner of a street quite distant from the place of his residence. There he stops and looks for a moment thoughtfully all around him. The whim takes him that he will go up this other street, and he pursues his way in that direction.

Finally he felt his spirits much elated, on standing before a shop window in which were displayed great globes of colored mixtures, the certain indications of a druggist's establishment. Seeing these, he entered without any further consideration.

There happened to be only a boy-clerk in the shop, who advanced from behind the counter to wait on his new customer. The misguided man still kept his cloak drawn carefully about his mouth, determined to disguise himself with all the means of concealment he could command. He inquired the price of opium. The boy told him, looking all the time straight in his eyes. The other's gaze, however, was equal to the trial, especially as the inward fires of his old appetite sent up wild and dazzling flames into his eyes continually. Accordingly he told him how

much he would have, and laid the money with one hand
on the counter, still holding the cloak about his mouth
and face with the other. The boy picked up the silver,
counted it, rattled it chinkingly in his hand, and gazed at
his customer again.   It was evident that he wished to be
as well satisfied as he could of the character of the person
with whom he was dealing.

"I wish you would be as quick as you can," said the
father of Amy, turning half around and assuming an air
of perfect carelessness.   Perhaps he dreaded to see the
door open and another person walk in.

The clerk thereupon made haste to do his errand, and
in a short time laid upon the counter the money's worth
of the drug wrapped in a clean white paper. Mr. Lee
picked it up, made a hurried half bow, and left the place.
He stepped on the pavement again with the lightness of
one who felt himself already travelling in dreams.

Now back again by the way he had come. He walked
as if his feet were winged. He took no heed of space,
and thought not of whom he might meet. Placing the
opium in his side pocket with wonderful care, he folded
his cloak with both arms about him, and paced rapidly on.

O, the tyranny of appetite. O, the sorrowful sight of
a poor being, fashioned and endowed even as the very
highest of us all, groping like a slave along the dark
chambers of this god's gloomy palace, and seeking and
praying — not to come at the light, not to reach the open
air and sky, but — to penetrate into darker and still

darker recesses continually. He treasured the drug as if
it had been gold. His thoughts gloated over it, like the
thought of an eager money-digger over a newly-found
fortune. Imagination was already at work, sketching her
beautiful pictures of the blissful enjoyment the eating
would bring, and coloring them all over with the most
gorgeous and bewildering hues. His feelings stretched
themselves to much more than the feelings of the poor
dwarfed creatures he met on his way, and took into their
all-surrounding embrace all men, and nations, and king-
doms, and conditions. These grand and overpowering
delights he had tasted often enough to understand somewhat of their meaning; the woe that followed he tried to
forget, and for the moment did succeed in forgetting.

When he arrived home he found that he was quite out
of breath, and able to climb the stairs but slowly. He
opened and shut the outer door with all care, hoping
earnestly that no one would discover his absence. There
was nobody to be seen in the hall, and he passed into his
own room quietly. Amy had not yet come home; there
was no danger of that. Had Mrs. Dozy been in? For a
moment the inquiry staggered him. "At all events,"
said he to himself, "she'll not fail to call again very soon,
if she has, and ask me where I've been." But no Mrs.
Dozy came to inquire where he had been, and his heart
was at rest. The purloining of the silver from Amy's
purse, — that gave him no thought, and of course no
uneasiness; the fiend of appetite controlled and over-

3

shadowed all his better feelings, eradicating almost those
that are supposed capable of being rooted out only with
nature itself.

Taking off his cloak and cap with all despatch, he hung
them in their accustomed places, and then slipped off his
overshoes; and as he seated himself so quietly again in
his great chair, he could not help feeling the utter prostration and languor that now settled upon him, by way of
compensation for his very imprudent and exciting walk.

" Ah, but I'll come out of this," said he, with a dull
smile playing faintly about his mouth; " these moods
shall not control me in this way." And drawing forth
the paper of opium from his side pocket, he administered
to his depraved and destroying appetite a large enough
dose for its present wants, and went and hid the rest
hurriedly about his bed.

" When I go to bed," said he again, " I shall know
where to find more. This lying awake so nights —— "
He did not stop to finish the sentence, but threw himself
once more into an easy posture in his chair, and let the
subtile poison work its secret way through his brain.

The fire was beautifully bright, and he looked into it
for an hour. The sunshine and the doves in the street he
had quite forgotten; nothing now was present with him
but the opium and the blaze. With an eager longing did
he wait for the moment when he should stand giddy on
the brilliant portal of his dreams.

CHAPTER III.

THE END OF IT.

AMY came home after a time, and accosted her father in her usual pleasant way. She found him sitting in his chair still, apparently wrapped in the cloak of his quiet thoughts. But the instant he looked up in her face, and made an attempt to reply to her, his eye kindled with a new and a strangely tremulous light, and his articulation immediately betrayed him.

"Such a *glorious* time as I'm having here, Amy!" said he. "Why, you haven't been gone a quarter of an hour, have you? How the time does fly away!."

She saw without hesitation that he had stealthily managed to indulge in his old habit again, and her heart for a moment sank within her. But recollecting that it would not mend the matter at all to put a bad face upon it in his presence, she answered him as nearly as she could in her usual pleasant way, and began to set about her customary preparations for the evening. Still there was a burden at her heart that she bore about with her sorrowfully. Though she concealed her feelings from him, who would be likely at such a time as this to cherish suspicions not at all calculated to add to their happiness, she was still unable to cheat herself out of her most wretched and despondent convictions. If her father would but break away from this habit! He had promised, and for a long time his promise had been kept; but where and what was he now? It made her heart sick to think where all this might end; she shuddered at the idea of pursuing such thoughts whither they must lead her.

The visions were gathering about her father, and he talked incessantly. Now he sat and dreamed aloud in a soft and low voice, as in a happy soliloquy. Now he rose suddenly in his chair, and turning his face around upon Amy, reeled off his long and involute sentences to her till he was weary. Scarcely for a whole minute would his excited condition permit him to keep silence. His tongue was going continually.

Amy would have gone and sat lovingly by his side and tried to compose him, but she too well knew that would be useless now. If it were *himself* by whose side she was to sit down, it had been a different matter. But to go and attempt to reason with the wild demon that possessed him would be to waste her strength and wear away her heart.

"But do you know, Amy," said her father, half turning about again, in his controlling delirium, — "do you know what a splendid afternoon we have had? and how I have stood at the window and watched the fluttering doves, and followed that glorious, glorious sunshine back to the

source whence it comes? and how like new creatures all
the people have seemed that passed in the street? Do
you know what castles all those houses are on the opposite side of the way, with their turrets, and battlements,
and pinnacles, and spires? and what gay people inhabit
them, too — far brighter than any I ever read of in the
old romances, or than were ever celebrated in the flowing
numbers of the Minnesingers? and how I can see long
galleries running round and round their fine castles, and
then high galleries through and through them, hung
about with so many beautiful pictures of men and women,
and lighted by that same yellow sunlight that streamed
soft through the most golden mists?

"Ah, what royalty this life of ours is!" And he
turned back and looked into the fire. "What a grand
affair it all is! Who can measure it? Who can sound it?
Who can go all around and tell its infinite circumference?
And to tie ourselves down so to these little matters of every-
day life, and get perplexed so by the swift trailing of the
few shadows over our heads, and grope and mope so
solemnly because we will not see the way, when the true
way is all the while so dazzling and glorious, — it's folly,
I say, and worse than folly; it's a slow and weary *death*.
Better die at once, and pass out of these shadows. But
to walk so loftily as one can, if only he *will*, — ah, that
is indeed a new and surpassing dream. There is nothing
to be compared with it for splendor. What may not one
finally know? How high may he not reach? Who can

3 *

tell how many bright worlds there are — sphere beyond
sphere, sphere beyond sphere, till even space itself is not
sufficient to more than hold and keep them all? Who
knows the beings that may live beyond us, far out of our
little short reach, away in the dim ether where God is,
and where mortal man is not and cannot exist?"

His dreams carried him in this manner on and on, till
he was completely lost in them. The web of them was
woven so subtilely and intricately by the power that was
upon him, he could not extricate himself from the mesh,
nor extend his bedazzled and bewildered vision beyond
their maze. His thoughts ascended to heights that in a
state of calm sanity he could never have comprehended;
and they sounded to deeps from which it would seem impossible for a rational mind ever to come away. He did
not walk on the earth; he flew with the wings of an
immortal. He saw not any shadows on the ground, or on
his soul; he lived and bathed his thoughts in the broad
and blazing sunlight that encircled and enveloped the
system of the universe. It was the wildest and most in-
explicable insanity that the mind of mortal could undergo.
While its influence was upon him, he seemed to live a
thousand hours in one. All the forces of his soul were
concentrated astonishingly. He was lifted up to a lofty
and dizzy height by the fearful power into whose hands
he had surrendered himself; but alas! only to be dashed
down the more fiercely into depths of dreary gloom, from
which return seemed almost impossible.

The girl came in at length with the supper, which Amy was thoughtful enough to receive at the door. Placing it herself on the little stand, she took her own seat as usual opposite her father, and asked him tenderly if he would not have tea.

" Tea! " exclaimed he, with a wild gesture, turning round suddenly upon her — " no, indeed. What do *I* want of so tame an herb as that — so innocent, — so like the drink you mix for children? No, give *me* the glorious *drug*, that makes one feel his immortality. Give me *that* and *you* may have the tea."

Tears stole into Amy's eyes in spite of all the strength of her resolution, and she felt that her hand trembled as she poured out the cup for herself. She was sad beyond measure. O, if but one single heart could have shared with her this weary, weary burden! But in the wide world where was that heart to be found? Yet she could support it alone; for she prayed for strength, and strength was always given her; she prayed for calmness and patience, and her soul was possessed and full. It was nothing but weak humanity that had brought the tears; they would dry up in the warmth of her heavenly Father's abounding love, and she would be stronger than ever again.

So she sat and tried to eat her supper alone. Her father's gaze was wild and staring, and when she happened to look up and catch his eye, her own was really bewildered with what she saw. Yet she managed to get through

with the meal, and felt somewhat refreshed. Her afternoon's tasks happened to have been unusually protracted
and tiresome, and when she came home she hoped to have
rest. But what rest? And how? And with whom?

The evening wore away drearily. All the time her
father kept up his persistent talk, dreaming his idle and
preposterous dreams, and wearying her beyond measure.
Still she did not offer any complaint. It would have been
idle in her to protest to him, for he would not have understood her. All that was left her was, simply to be patient
and endure in silence. She knew that he was wasting his
little remaining strength in a fearful manner; but what
help was there for it that she could command? She must
sit and watch him whom during the reign of the drug she
could not even call " father," and nurse her grief alone.

When at length it was time to retire, she so signified to
him, and withdrew with many childish misgivings into her
own apartment. Immediately she fell on her knees at the
foot of her bed and offered a prayer. It was only for
strength. She besought no selfish and temporal good.
She asked for faith to believe that all things were done
well. She begged for a perfect trust in the Providence
that is over all things, and in all, and through all, forever.
The whole of her petition could be summed up in the
single phrase, " Thy will be done."

And after many tears — inevitable signs only of the
prostration of nature — she fell asleep.

Of course she had had her suspicions of her father's

going out that afternoon, for she knew that he could not have been supplied with the means of gratifying his appetite if he had not left the house; but she knew the uselessness of putting to him any interrogatories in his present condition, and refrained from even alluding to the subject. As well, too, knew she that he must have taken what money he needed for his purpose from her purse; but she felt too sick at heart to go to it and count over her little hoard, that she might see how much had been abstracted. It made her downcast indeed to let her thoughts follow the subject along, and she heartily wished she could banish it from her mind altogether.

Scarcely had Amy withdrawn, when her father seemed to come to himself again. A luminous moment dawned on him. But the fiend claimed even that as his own, and put it into the victim's heart to consent to the sacrifice.

He remembered where he had secreted the deadly drug, and crept stealthily to the spot. With much cautiousness he withdrew it again from its hiding-place, and unrolled the paper. He gloated over it with wonderful joy. He felt as if he could hug the colossal spirit it imbodied to his excited breast.

Slowly he divided off from the whole lump what he thought he should need for the night. Then he rolled it all together in his palm, and said to himself that there was not enough; a little more, and he should be satisfied. So he divided from the lump an additional piece.

"Now I shall sleep, I guess," said he. "No more of

these terrible dreams, Amy. I will sleep as soundly as
even you." And he took down the whole of the prepa-
ration at a single dose. It was a very large one, for it was
administered not by a rational being, but by a man possessed of its own wild spirit. He threw off his clothes
without difficulty, and sought a night's long and unbro-
ken rest.

It would not come at once, however. The drug was
not potent enough for that. It rather dissipated and
drove off drowsy influences, than enticed and controlled
them. He lay, therefore, for a long time awaiting only the
approach of the balm that night rarely refuses to bring.
And late in the night, after the town clocks had struck
many hours in their lonely steeples, he sank away into a
deep and profound slumber.

As time passed, how profound and deep that slumber
grew! His breathing came and went in such short and
low swells of his lungs! His eyes were sunken as if
weights were pressing down their lids. A fearful sallow-
ness made his features seem still more unnatural, and gave
his face the aspect even of ghastliness and death. He
lay still — very still. There was scarcely any motion of
the bedclothes; no movement of uneasy limbs; no occasional drawings of longer and deeper breaths; no turning
over of the weary head upon the pillow. All was calm,
composed, and fearfully quiet. If he had not taken the
potion he had before entering upon this sleep, it would
have been so unnatural as to arouse the deepest fears.

Amy did not rest at all well. Two or three times she
got up and went to the door opening into the other
apartment, and listened carefully to see if he was quiet.
A needless anxiety; he lay as placid as a child. Still
her thoughts were much disturbed, and she could never
have told why. He caused great anxieties for her heart,
much as she nevertheless loved him. In truth it was
nothing but her love for him that permitted these anxieties
and fears. How long and how much would she not have
been glad to suffer for him, if only he could have become
free from his galling chains.

It was quite seven o'clock, however, before she rose;
and immediately after dressing she went into her father's
apartment to clear the grate and kindle the fire. On
tiptoe almost she stepped across the floor, unwilling to
awaken him from the slumber she thought his exhausted
nature must need. Little by little she shook down the
ashes through the bars into the pan, and cleared away the
refuse that remained from the last day's combustion.

She stepped to the closet to get the hod of soft coal,
and laid it on the papers she had torn and twisted for the
purpose of kindling it. And next she brought out the
anthracite, and silently laid on the shining pieces one by
one with the tongs. And finally, after touching the paper
underneath with a lighted match, she placed the blower
before all, and went about setting both that room and her
own " to rights."

She had made her bed, swept her floor a little, and

arranged her dress for the morning; and now she went
back to see to the fire. Taking down the heated blower,
she found the grate within a mass of glowing coals. She
added yet more anthracite, and put the hods away in the
closet. Amy was a pattern of order and neatness, as the
reader must already conclude; few girls could be found
that would surpass her. And having made a cheerful fire
and swept the hearth, she proceeded to commence her
arrangements for their breakfast.

Her eyes went searchingly over to the bed where her
father lay. There was not the least motion discoverable
about him. He slept profoundly indeed. His limbs
were still. His head lay buried deeply in the pillow.
There was no working of his features, although that
corner of the room was shaded, and she might not hence
be so well able to discover it.

Thinking it best now to awaken him that he might
make ready for breakfast, she called to him, standing
where she was by the hearth. But to no purpose. Again
she called, and watched to see some slight symptom of
waking; but none as yet.

"Father," said she, advancing a step or two towards
the bed. Still he had not a word of reply for her.

"Father," and a step or two still nearer.

Finding that he slept so deeply, she went to his bedside and looked in his face.

O, such a shock as went through her soul, when her
eyes rested on those thin and pinched features! Such a

feeling as thrilled her entire being, rendering her for the moment speechless, nerveless, motionless, lost altogether! She felt as if she must fall to the floor.

His eyes were shut tightly, and his mouth was a very little way open. He did not breathe at all. There was no breath to be felt, no sound of breathing to be heard, no motion in the least perceptible. Like a corpse he lay in the bed, in the stillness of an everlasting sleep.

Amy did not cry out when she felt herself suddenly recovering. Never seemed she so perfectly possessed of all her faculties. She placed a hand under each shoulder, and gently lifted him up. She laid her mouth close to his ear, and spoke to him again. She listened to catch his lightest breathing. She put her hand upon his forehead to trace any lurking warmth that would assert the possession of life. But no syllable of answer to her call, no movement as of breathing, no remaining warmth to testify that life still held its shattered and long-besieged citadel.

He was dead and cold.

And the tyrant drug had done its work there, leaving only this poor wreck in witness of the sure and certain destruction that follows fast after its fascinating tyranny.

Amy sat down on the bedside, and burying her face in her hands, wept and moaned, — O, no heart in the world can tell how bitterly.

4

CHAPTER IV.

ABOUT THE FUTURE.

THE servant girl came in with the breakfast, and placed it on the stand in the greatest alarm, for Amy weeping was, to her eyes, a new and unexpected sight. She stood a single moment dumbly regarding her, and immediately hurried out of the room to acquaint her mistress with her strange discovery.

Presently Mrs. Dozy herself entered, looking wildly every where about the apartment, until she espied Amy at the bedside. Then going straight up to her, she gently put her hand on her shoulder, and asked her what was the matter.

" Why, Miss Lee, Miss Lee," she ejaculated. " What *has* happened to you ? "

Amy could not speak, and she could not look up. It seemed as if her heart was deep in the slough of a very sore and dark distress.

The servant stood looking through the half-open door, her face expressing the most decided marks of sympathy and alarm.

From regarding Amy, Mrs. Dozy's gaze fell upon the

countenance of her father, and then in an instant she comprehended the whole of the great trouble.

"Why, he's dead! he's dead!" she exclaimed, with a sudden start, without thinking of the effect it must have on Amy.

The latter cried out in a voice of deep anguish, accompanying it with quick assenting motions of her head, "I know it, I know it. He's dead."

After a short lapse of time, needed as much for Mrs. Dozy to recover some degree of her equanimity as for Amy to quiet her sobbing, the former wound her arm affectionately about the poor girl's waist, and led her unresisting to a chair near the fire.

"Child, child," softly spake Mrs. Dozy, "you must not take on so. Try to be calm, just a little. It will be so much better for you. The trouble is a great one, I know; but you can bear it easier if you try to be calm."

Amy responded with little else than sobs, still burying her face in her hands. The kind woman, however, removed them gradually, and suffered her to lay her sick head against her breast.

"I wouldn't cry, dear child. I'm sure I wouldn't cry. How did he die? But you don't know, though. There, there, don't cry so, dear soul. You shall have every thing done that *can* be done, and if I am able, a good deal more. You was always such a *good* child. I really don't think you have any thing to reproach yourself for. You have been the very best of daughters to him, and every body knew it, and loved you the more for it. Only be quiet, dear. Be calm as you can. I know it's a great trial — a *great* trial indeed ; but we all of us have to go through with them at some time or other, and we must try and get reconciled.''

Thus she went on, essaying in her innocently simple way to bring balm to the freshly-opened wounds of the poor sufferer.

But it was the physical weakness chiefly of Amy's nature that caused the storm of her present distress. It would at length slowly abate, and she would be controlled only by those calm and translucent thoughts that furnished her happiness every day she lived. Little enough knew Mrs. Dozy, sympathizing as she really was too, of the true state of Amy's feelings. All she could see and understand was this outward sorrow. As it was violent, so she thought it must have unseated even the child's deeper and profounder sentiments. She was able to detect but little of the strong and abiding trust that held the girl's soul fast as by an anchor. She could discover scarce any of that all-pervading faith, that, after this short storm of pent-up feeling was over, would shine out over her youthful character like the sun bursting out of the rifted clouds.

Amy finally consented to be conducted into the other part of the house, away from the sights and the associations that wrought with such power upon her. Mrs. Dozy tried to prevail on her to take some nourishment, and after a time succeeded in her efforts. The girl was sent out to acquaint a few of the neighbors with the startling occurrence, and they came instantly to offer help and needed sympathy. Others, who heard of it, hurried breathlessly in the direction of the house to learn all the particulars, if so it might happen they could be the first to report them.

In the course of the day the coroner came, who on learning the circumstances of Mr. Lee's sickness and his whole case, concluded that it would be unnecessary to hold an inquest over the body, and afterwards left the house.

It is needless for me to narrate more particularly to the reader all the many little incidents that transpired subsequently to this ; how sad and dreary every thing looked to Amy about her room, now her father was dead ; what a strange feeling it caused her, to behold herself clad in a mourning suit for the first time ; what sensations the solemnization of the burial rite produced ; what friends came in to try (as they kindly thought) to console her ; what ideas possessed her mind about the future ; and how bitterly she thought of one to-morrow's following in quick and steady succession after another, and no father to whom to look, not for protection, it is true, but yet for daily companionship. Grief rolls a strong and turbid wave over every human heart. There are not those living who are at all times quite reconciled to the loss of their dearest friends, and quite ready to give them up forever. This

4 *

separation from those we love, with its attendant silence
and mystery, is, after all, the most trying ordeal through
which we are any of us called to pass; and happy indeed
is the one who at no single moment feels the rising of a
murmur, or the doubting interrogatories of reason, or the
most trifling weakness of his faith.   We can part with
· our limbs, and be stoics during the operation; but this
rending and tearing of all the subtler, and tenderer, and
more delicate fibres of the heart, — who, who in perfect
calmness is strong enough to abide it?

All the mournful ceremonies were at an end.   The last
surviving parent now slept the final sleep, and the little
apartments were quiet and lonely.   At first Amy thought
she *could not* go about her regular tasks at instruction again,
they would bring up so many associations of sorrow.
Then her thoughts turned and questioned themselves, and
sought to learn whence came this unquiet, and this practical murmuring.   And falling on her knees to beseech for
more faith, — for faith that would override and control
every circumstance, every feeling, every thought, and
every association, — she felt that a new strength had
entered into her heart and immediately taken full possession.

At once, therefore, she returned to her usual occupation,
carrying about a lighter frame of mind, and invigorated
even for any new trials that might be put upon her.   Her
old pupils found her all she had ever been to them, and
more.   A sweet incense seemed to have been crushed out

of her nature by the bereavement that had fallen so heavily. They studied furtively the heavenly expressions of her face as she talked with them, and wondered why she should seem so much happier than before. Poor children, they had the precious secret yet to learn for themselves. Not yet had they found the centre of all their existence in God.

But as time passed away, and these daily local associations continually presented themselves to her mind with a force that began to weary, if not to weaken her, she sat down seriously to ask herself if some way of relief might not be found. To remain continually where she now was, would be to become inclined to a morbid state of feeling. To go the same round, and battle against the same perplexing influences every day, was a life that not only offered her no resources for actual enjoyment, but had the effect even to shut out such as might from unseen quarters be willing to enter. She saw, the more she thought upon it, that it would be better for her to try and change the scene. Dear as this spot had once been, it was only draped about with the gloom of unhappy recollections now. If she could take into her feelings a new circle of objects, whether dearer or not than those around her now, it might bring a relief. .

And so she thought of the matter every day.

Spring had fast been coming along, though the bright season of flowers was not yet reached. It was the latter part of April already. Amy had made her arrange-

ments to leave the house of Mrs. Dozy by the first of
May, intending to retreat for the summer into one of the
quiet interior villages of Vermont ; there she was going to
open a little school, that would offer her many opportunities of enlarging and enriching her nature in doing
good, and furnish her besides with means of gaining an
independent subsistence. She resolved to give over her
music instruction for a while, and change not only the
scene but the occupation. Into her new work she would
be permitted to carry as much of her heart as she ever
could into the old, while its shifting and various items of
occupation would tend to refresh her by their very lightness. She would see *children*, and their natures would
instruct her own. From them she would learn greater
simplicity, and innocence, and faith. She was really rejoiced, to sum it all up, that the time for her departure
was so near at hand.

She was sitting in her room one afternoon, just as
twilight was gathering, thinking of the future. The bills
of her pupils had been collected, and all her own debts
properly paid. The balance remaining in her possession
was quite respectable. She could not help thinking how
much she would like to place it all, little as it was, at
the disposal of some dear friend.

Mrs. Dozy knocked gently on the door, and instantly
opened it. Finding Amy thus alone, she said she thought
she would run in and pass a few minutes with her, if for
nothing more than to inquire how she was.

Amy was very grateful for her thoughtfulness. Sometimes — she confessed — she *was* lonely; and often, too, that very feeling afforded her not a little pleasure. For during such hours she thought most of herself and her griefs, and they hallowed themselves afterwards in her memory.

"I think, after all," said her landlady, "that you will enjoy a great deal more this coming summer in the country. I was brought up in the country myself; and I could wish for nothing pleasanter than to get back again, I assure you."

"I promise myself much happiness there," replied Amy. "Yet I hardly know why I do, either. I have never lived much in the country, and know but little of the ways of such a life. But I sit here lately, and *dream* about it all; and I sketch such delightful pictures before my very eyes, I sometimes look around the room to see if they are not real. O, yes, but I am very sure I shall enjoy such sweet peace and quietude there."

"And perhaps you will not want ever to come back again. But we shall miss you bad enough here, I can tell you. Your room will be a lonely place to come into, I reckon. I hope, really, that you'll write me from where you are, after you get settled a little."

Amy assured her that she would, and added that none of the kindness shown her by Mrs. Dozy, or shown her father, either, would ever be forgotten.

"It's such a hard thing to lose a *good* boarder,"

exclaimed Mrs. Dozy, wiping her eyes as she went out of the room a few minutes later. "I've never yet made a friend that I really *like*, but something has come in of a sudden to separate us."

Yes, Mrs. Dozy; that is the way things always go in this world.

CHAPTER V.

A JOURNEY ALONE.

At last the day was at hand that was to begin Amy's changed life. It was a beautiful morning, and the balminess of May was diffusing itself over all nature. Even the choked and narrow town streets could not refuse to acknowledge by their pleasanter look the great change that was working with such magic every where. Children went gayly trooping along, early as it was, singing the songs of gladness that would not be pent in their hearts. Men met one another with broader and warmer smiles, and spake in more flowing and harmonious voices. It might be an illusion of the eye, or the ear, that produced this effect; but it was so pleasing an illusion that one would much rather hug it to his heart than not; nay, he would wish that it might last through the passage of the whole year.

Amy had arisen quite early on this morning, that nothing might be left undone, and that there might be no need of confusion and haste. Attired in a proper habit for travelling, she sat down to the breakfast table all ready for a start, kind Mrs. Dozy and her few other boarders

talking as fast as they could. She essayed the needless
task of answering their questions all at once, and of
swallowing hurriedly her breakfast too.

The day before had been employed in visiting her old
pupils, and in packing her clothes. It was a busy time,
indeed. Her rooms were littered with every variety of
articles, and she went down upon her knees repeatedly
to stuff something into a trunk that was plethoric already, and really needed nothing more to make its contents complete. Some things, like articles of furniture,
— and a well-used old piano among the rest, — she was
obliged to leave with her landlady; if she should ever
return again to Boston to live, she would find them all
safely kept for her; or if not, then she could either.dis-
pose of them by sale, or send for them at her new place
of residence.

"I hope you'll have a pleasant journey," said a kind
elderly lady, who formed one of Mrs. Dozy's circle of
boarders. "It's a long way for you, after all."

"Dear me," exclaimed Mrs. Dozy herself, "so 'tis;
so 'tis. I hope nothing at all will happen to you on the
way. And you'll be *so* tired, too, when you get there."

"I expect to reach the place by night," said Amy,
fixing her bonnet to put it on her head.

"You do," exclaimed one of the boarders. "Why,
how far is it?"

"About a hundred and twenty or thirty miles, I should
think."

"And do the cars carry you all the way?" asked Mrs. Dozy.

"O, no; I go in them about ninety miles, or thereabouts, and the rest of the way in the stage coach."

"Then you ride in *a stage*, do you?" eagerly returned the elderly lady who had taken so much interest in Amy's journey. "I remember something of staging myself, I guess. That's a very pleasant way to travel, I think, too; much pleasanter than the cars, for *they* don't give you a chance to see a bit of the country. And there's so much real sociability in the stage, too; there's nothing like that in the cars; if you want to say any thing in them, you have got to holler your head off, almost, before you can make yourself heard. I must say I like stage riding best. I used to go about a great deal in stage coaches, when I was younger than I am now."

And naturally enough, in being transported to those halcyon days again, the old lady let her eyes fall from the table to the floor, and there they rested for several minutes while she enjoyed the silent contemplation of the times that would never come back.

"Why, you don't eat *any thing!*" said Mrs. Dozy to Amy. "Do you think you are going to take such a long ride without any thing more than this on your stomach? Come; do try and swallow some breakfast. Let me pour you out another cup of coffee. Yes, I shall insist on your drinking another cup, whether you can or not!

5

There, now do try and eat enough to keep you from faint-
ing away."

Amy thanked her landlady over and over; she would
take all the nourishment she needed, but that would be
but little. Alas! her heart could not — *could not* in a
single moment throw off the recollections of her life in
that house, with her father's presence continually coloring and shaping that life, and his words and looks speaking through all. Nature would have its own power still;
and even when most buoyant and elastic with hope, grief
would insist on throwing down the shadow of its cloud.

Mrs. Dozy, seeing, therefore, that she ate but little at
the table, commenced putting away sweet cakes and
crackers in her travelling bag.

" You'll be faint," said she, " and I know it as well as
I want to. So I've put up a few little things for you to
bite, when you feel like it; and I charge you not to forget to do it, just as soon as you get hungry."

It was one of the most feeling hearts, that her landlady
had. She could not bear the thought of Amy's going
away unprovided for any, the smallest emergency. In
truth, — as she expressed it herself, — it made her really
heartsick that she should go at all. But as there might
be some necessity for this, she was the more willing to
part with her now.

Mrs. Dozy loved Amy, too, as she would have loved a
daughter. There were few things she would not have
exerted herself greatly to perform for her. And so did

all the rest love her. She was encircled with their affection, and grew daily deeper and deeper into their hearts. They all knew her devotion to her father, and what trials her obedience had carried her cheerfully through.   They were familiar with her kind and loving ways, with her thoughtfulness of speech for others, with her perfect freedom from pride, or envy, or malice, and with her perpetual purity of heart.   And how could they do less than receive her into the open arms of their affectionate esteem ?

All were through with breakfast, and Amy was ready to start. The trunks were packed, and her dress fairly adjusted.. Nothing remained but to bid them all farewell, and step into the carriage when it came.

And at length there was a loud ring at the door, and that was announced. " Cars will go in very few minutes! Mustn't wait a half a minute !" called out the driver. And then followed a great bustle.

" *Dear* me," cried Mrs. Dozy ; " *dear* me ! Why don't these drivers take more time when they come after any body, and not hurry so ? " And she ran hither and thither around the room, in pursuit of she knew not what, pulling at every body's arm but the one she was after, brushing away a falling tear with her checked apron, talking all the time to one and another, and telling the driver where to find the luggage, and to be very careful of the individual he was going to set agoing that morning on her journey. Poor woman ! she hardly knew what she *was* about, in the confusion and perplexity of her feelings.

But at last it came her turn to take Amy by the hand; which she did with a quivering lip and a moistened eye. Amy kissed her affectionately; and she melted then in tears. She hoped to see her soon again, and left her silent and weeping. There was not one who did not feel saddened at this parting.

"All ready!" called the driver at the foot of the stairs.

"Yes — yes; go — go!" said Mrs. Dozy, following her along and holding on by her hand.

Amy said another parting word, not omitting the servant girl in her way, and ran down the stairs. You would have thought, had you not seen her face, that she was going gayly away from the place, so lightly did she run down the stairs. But it was a forced and constrained manner, which she put on to help carry off the unpleasant impression of the moment. The driver helped her in, slammed to the door, sprang to the box, and drove off his horses at a rapid rate. Amy thought she had never turned corners faster, or rattled by the houses more swiftly. She was in a tumult of excitement, however; and this rapid motion agreed quite well with her mood. She secretly wished she might be whirled along at this rate until the mood should work itself off.

There was only a minute or two left for her after reaching the depot, which she required the whole of to purchase her ticket, pay the hackman, and give directions about her baggage. And no sooner had she been helped on the cars, than away they went in turn, carrying her off in an instant towards the green heart of the great country.

Well was it that it was so, too. Had she had time before leaving to sit and brood over the separation she had that morning undergone, it would have tinged her feelings with a deep shade of melancholy that she might not have rid herself of for the whole day. As it was, her excitement was still fed by the rattling of the train, and suffered only by degrees to subside into a state of comparative calm.

Away they went over the open country, as if they were chasing the wind. A few quick puffs from the engine, and they seemed to take wings. The wheels rolled over the rails like the sound of clattering thunder. Swiftly flew by the houses, and swiftly the fences. You saw an object a moment in the distance, and the next moment it was behind you. The trees went by like running men. Off in the distant fields cattle were racing, as if they hardly yet knew in which direction to escape the dark and rattling train that was coming with its sound of thunder.

The motion to Amy was indeed exhilarating. In her present mood of mind, it seemed just what she most needed. There was that perpetual noise and clatter, too, connected with it, that added still more to her physical excitement. It acted like a pleasant stimulant, than which perhaps not a better could have been prescribed for her. She opened the window beside her, and regaled herself with the fresh air of the morning.

5 *

In the car were many passengers, but she knew not one. She was travelling alone. No one sat on the seat with her, though several had looked at it as they passed to find one, as if it might be a very pleasant place for companionship. She sat and studied such faces as offered themselves to her eyes, or looked musingly out the window over the changing landscape.

All the while her thoughts were actively employed. There was Boston, and that dear old street, and house, and chamber; there was the memory of her life so many years with her father — that father now lost to her forever; there were her old pupils still, thinking perhaps of their parting with her, and perhaps hoping that before long she would return.

It was quite noon when she alighted at the far-off town where she was to take passage in the stage coach. Before she could well look round and ascertain if her baggage was deposited safely on the platform, the train had whizzed off again, and was already nothing but a dark streak in motion in the distance.

Then there was time to procure dinner at the quiet little hotel close by, from which the stage would start directly after. A man stepped on the platform near her, and looking at her trunks, asked if she was to go in the coach.

"Yes," she answered, "I wish to go to Valley Village."

"Ah, then you'll go in my coach," said he. "These

your trunks, ma'am? You can step right over here to
the hotel, if you like, and get dinner."

Amy thanked him, and accepted his escort to the door
of the public house. The door was open. She crossed
the spacious piazza, and went in. Her appetite, on sitting down again in the little parlor of the house, hardly
invited her, she thought, to the public table; so she took
some of Mrs. Dozy's contributions from the travelling
bag on her arm, and commenced fortifying her stomach
against the jolting ride that was still before her.

A woman came in, and asked her if she would not like
dinner; but Amy declined her offer. She wished only a
glass of water, for which she would be thankful.

Amy had some little time there, which she devoted to
a hurried review of what had recently passed, and to a
hasty sketch of the future. She leaned her head on her
hand, and looked out the window. People passed, but
she hardly saw them. Her thoughts were abstracted
about herself, her prospects, her sad past. Yet not altogether mournful were they — never despondent, however
sorrowful.

There she sat and mapped out the coming summer.
Would Heaven make it as pleasant as she had thus pic-
tured it, or was her sky to be overcast and gloomy?
Would not the song of the birds, the babble of the brooks,
the blowing rustle of the leaves, the outflowing of the free
sunshine every where over heaven, bring welcome joy to
her heart every day she dwelt among these delightful

scenes? Could grief canker even amid Nature's great
bounteousness? Would there be room for regrets to
enter in, and take forcible possession? Here, in the heart
of this serenity, would there not rather be every thing to
drive away unhappy feelings, and make the whole soul
glad?

The leisure was consumed by her in this mood, sitting
thus alone in the public room. Perhaps some day these
thoughts of hers in this very spot would hallow the place
with their almost sacred associations, and make the very
furniture of the room seem beautiful as that of a dream.

"Stage's all ready!" was the shout from without, as
she caught the rattle of wheels before the piazza. And
looking out the window, there she saw a bright yellow
coach, with four prancing horses, and her own two trunks
strapped tightly on behind.

"This is the last change," she thought, half aloud. "I
shall have no more to make at present."

At that moment the door opened, and the landlord
put in his head to announce that it was time for her to
start.

Amy bowed, and followed him out.

The landlord assisted her in, and shut the door. The
iron step fell back in its place with a slam.

"There, you get up, Henry," said a female within,
"and sit on the forward seat." •

"O, no, thank you," returned Amy, seeing that the
woman was thoughtfully making room for her beside

herself on the back seat. "I can ride just as well here."

At any rate, the woman's son — a lad perhaps of thirteen years — left his place by the side of his mother, and settled himself with his back to the horses. And Amy, seeing what had been done in spite of her protestation, stepped over and sat down in the corner by the female who had shown such thorough politeness.

The driver smacked his long whip, and away they rattled at a famous rate. He had got on the mail bags, and there was nothing more now for him to stop for. He had not another passenger to take up, either; these three were all.

"It's delightful weather," offered the lady who sat by the side of Amy.

"Delightful indeed," returned Amy.

"I didn't dare to hope for the opening of spring quite so early as this; but it seems to have come upon us like a bright smile. I declare, this weather is really enjoyable. It makes one's heart grow *warm*." And she looked round in the face of Amy with an expression of so much kindliness and sympathy, that the latter felt in an instant she had found a natural and hearty friend.

The lady seemed to be not yet forty, and had a face of an extremely sweet cast, fresh and confiding. If a countenance is ever an index of the heart, her heart must have been entirely free from the canker of unhappiness. And she went about her proffered civilities and companionships in such a delightfully frank and easy way, Amy was won over to her before she even knew what had been accomplished.

She was dressed in a suit of mourning, as was Amy likewise. It was a very plain and inexpensive habit, however, betraying perhaps a slender purse, yet a not uncultivated taste. She wore a shawl about her shoulders, which was fastened under her chin by a very neat mourning pin; and her bonnet was lined before with the whitest and finest tabs one ever sees. Amy was struck with her looks immediately; and as soon as she began to enter into conversation with her, she saw that the woman was indeed worthy of her confidence. And accordingly, in a very little time, there sprang up an intimacy between them that offered Amy a most agreeable and grateful solace for her sadness of the morning.

The coach rolled along. It took them off through open fields, winding away over the narrow country roads, that were hedged in on both sides by mossy stones and split rail fences, climbing up steep hills, whose tops were crowned with the growth of trees and shrubs, rattling down with an echoing noise through little hollows and moist-smelling dells, through which released brooks were roaring, and shooting off again over the level country with a clatter that made all merry, both inside and out.

As the stranger had told Amy, it was indeed a beautiful day; and a most delightful time was it, too, for a ride through the country in a stage coach. The air was fresh with the reviving breezes of early spring. They had let

down the coach windows, so that it could drift in and out
with every swaying motion of the vehicle. Amy felt it on
her forehead, and was grateful. It seemed in some mysterious way to revive her heart, as if a pleasant dew were
gently distilled upon it.

And riding along, they chatted easily on this thing and
that, — the weather, the past winter, riding in cars and
coaches, living in town and country, and such matters as
these, — till each seemed altogether taken up with the
other, and expressed her sympathy in every look of the
countenance and every word that was spoken. It was
such a pleasant interchange of feeling as thoroughly refreshed and delighted the orphan. She was led to forget
for the moment the old poignancy of her griefs, and to
look about and above her to the contemplation of living
objects and living thoughts. Other lights burst in upon
her soul, and opened new sources of present joy. The
old dreams and momentary visions began to show signs of
reality.

"May I ask how far you are travelling?" inquired the
stranger of Amy.

"As far as Valley Village," answered the latter.

"Is that all? Why, I am going right there myself."

The woman betrayed not a little pleasant surprise, as
Amy did also.

"I happen to *live* in Valley Village," continued the
stranger. "It has been our home for a good many years."

Amy was interested. It offered an excellent opportu-

nity for inquiring about the locality where she was going,
and of learning in advance respecting the probabilities of
success in her new vocation there.

"Have you any friends there?" asked the woman.

"Not one," answered Amy; "unless I may be allowed
to call *you* one," she added, with great candor.

They exchanged a quick glance — Amy's was one of
smiling pleasantness, and the stranger's of pure sympathy;
and that glance sealed their friendship permanently.

"I am going out there," Amy went on, rather after the
manner of a confession, "to pass the summer. It is my
wish to get together scholars enough to open a little
school. I am accustomed to teach the young, and like
the occupation. I found that I needed change of scene,
and have made this movement."

The woman glanced at Amy's mourning habit, and
seemed in a moment to comprehend her.

"What encouragement do you think I can find there?"
Amy asked, a little eager to know somewhat about her
chances.

"Very good, I should say; *very* good, just now. And
I am happy to be able to tell you so, too. There hasn't
been a summer school kept at the village for two years;
and I heard some of our people speaking of the matter
only a few weeks ago, wishing they could find the right
person to open one. How fortunate it is for you!"

"But are there many children there who go to school
in the summers?"

" Yes, quite as many as you are apt to find in places of its size. There aren't *as many*, of course, as there would be in a larger place. It's but a small and a quiet village, at the most; and those that you would get would be only such as wanted to learn to read, and sew, and do such light labor as that. It won't task your powers at all, I can tell you, except perhaps for patience. Any body wants that quality, you know, that has any thing to do with children — especially young children."

Then Amy, whose heart had been opening to this woman every moment, finally began and told her all of her individual history — acquainting her with her mode of life for several years past, and the sudden death of her father, describing her lonely feelings in that place where they had so long lived together, and the utter impossibility of remaining there any longer, and detailing the several steps by which she reached finally the resolution to go back into some quiet retreat in the country, and there labor and live calmly till duty should call her away again in another direction. The rehearsal of her story was not completed without many manifestations of emotion on the part of the youthful narrator, which in turn affected her travelling companion very visibly. The moisture was shining in her eyes when Amy got through; and she turned her face away a moment to enable her the better to master her feelings.

" You haven't any boarding place, then ? " at length she asked Amy.

6

" I haven't so much as thought of it yet. But I suppose I must begin to very soon. Is there a public house in the village ? "

" Yes, but hardly such a one as you would find it pleasant to stay at. Some of the time it's open, and some of the time there's no one about. We hardly say, in truth, that we have a public house."

Amy sat a moment, and pondered upon it.

Her new friend ventured to interrupt her train of thought : —

" If you'd as lief, I'm sure you would be welcome to stay with me until you can look about for yourself a little. I'm keeping house alone, with nobody but my son Henry here," nodding in the direction of the boy on the front seat.

" I thank you very much — very much," responded Amy, her countenance all the while expressing more gratitude than her words. " I certainly should be glad to accept your offer, and hope we may become such good friends that neither will wish a separation at all. Shall I go home with you to-night ? "

" Certainly — certainly," was the ready answer.

And at twilight the coach rattled through the street of the little village, which Amy could see was cozily dropped down in the hollow of two high hills, and all three drew up before the door of a pretty little house of a story and a half.

" This is my nest," remarked the lady, leading the way

in, after giving directions to have the trunks brought along after.

And Amy went in with a grateful heart, and on her knees that night thanked God that he had provided for her so abundantly in his loving kindness.

CHAPTER VI.

MRS. GUMMEL.

WHEN she awoke the next morning, she found herself comfortably quartered in a snug chamber, rather low, to be sure, in respect to its ceiling, with two windows, a pretty carpet stretched over the floor, and three or four chairs ranged about against the wall. There stood likewise an ample bureau beneath the looking glass, with drawers enough to hold all she wished to put in them. And a door in the farther corner opened into a convenient closet, where were pegs and nails to hang her dresses on, and a couple of shelves on which to lay away what she wished. She surveyed all these particulars of the new home she had found with a great deal of pleasure, thinking how opportunely every thing seemed to have happened.

As soon as she was dressed, she threw herself on her knees, and offered a prayer of thankfulness; and with increasing gratitude she besought a larger measure of faith, that she might resign herself more entirely into the keeping of her Maker. She prayed with her whole soul; not a thought, not a wish, not an aspiration, not the faintest desire, that did not seek God in counsel, asking for more trust, beseeching for a growth of purity and love, pleading for fresh visitations of grace, that would keep the life new and young every day, and make it abound in innocency forever.

She put aside the curtain to one of her low windows, and looked out. She could not have denied that it was almost with a fast-beating heart that she ventured upon this first look, for she anxiously hoped to find every object in harmony with her own happy thoughts. .

It was a bright morning again, fully as fair and promising as that of yesterday. She ran her eyes up and down the street as far as she could, to espy the appearance of the dwellings, and catch the rural associations generally supposed to cluster about such quiet country places. There were but few door yards, a green lawn forming a common carpet for the feet of all the passers and dwellers alike, over whose rolling surface she detected already the shooting grass, tinting it in spots with the most delicate light shades. The houses were rather small, although some of them were fully two stories in height, and painted white. Some of them offered additional attractions in the way of green blinds, and climbing vines at the doors and windows. Before them all, and seeming to run in a double row for the length of the street, were wide-spreading rock maples, whose sprays were already beginning to moisten and swell, and from which it would be but a little while

6 *

before the tender leaves would spring in all their bewildering greenness.

Amy liked the place at once. It seemed just such a
one as she had often sketched in her fruitful imagination,
where she longed to live her years out in peaceful quietude, and finally to go to her rest beloved and mourned
for by all. And while she stood there at her little window
looking out, and thinking, too, of these wishes that her
heart had cherished in silence so long, she heard a light
tap on her door, and presently saw that some one was
slowly opening it. Knowing very well who it must be,
she called to her visitor to come in.

Immediately her friend of the stage coach accosted her.
Such a happy smile! Amy asked herself, as its light
beamed over her, if such were born out of the dew and
innocence of this rural life.

"Good morning!" saluted Mrs. Gummel, — for that
was the appellation of Amy's friend; "I hope you got
a good night's rest last night. How do you feel this
morning?"

"O, never so well; as happy as I can be, and as grateful," answered Amy. And while she replied to her, she
advanced and pressed Mrs. Gummel's hand, and kissed her
affectionately.

"Well, well," said the other, "I am glad enough to
hear it. It was rather a long jaunt for you yesterday, I
confess; but there's nothing better for it than a good
night's rest. And I'm glad enough you got it."

"One must be very restless," said Amy, "if she couldn't sleep in your nice beds. I declare, as soon as I laid my head on my pillow, I sank down into utter unconsciousness; and I knew nothing more, except in my scattered dreams, until I found myself awake this morning. What a pleasant morning it is! What a sweet little street this is here! How pretty every thing looks to me! O, I know I shall be so delighted to stay! It seems to me, that if I had travelled all New England over, I could not have found such a retreat as this is."

Mrs. Gummel smiled at Amy's enthusiasm, and said she was rejoiced to find her first impressions such favorable ones. "But," she added, "you must needs take a ramble or two over the village, and go up on the hill that overlooks the whole of it, before you can get an exact idea. I hope you will like it then; and I think, too, that you will."

"If what I can see from this window is a sample of the whole," was the reply, "indeed I shall have little cause to gratify my curiosity by going farther. But I shall surely take the ramble you speak of, if only to enjoy the scenery. I am very partial to beautiful scenery; and then, too, things wear so much pleasanter an aspect in the spring, when the world begins to put on its brightest robe. O, you don't know how much enjoyment I have already promised myself here, just standing and looking out this window."

Mrs. Gummel smiled again.

"I hope, dear soul," said she, tenderly, "you won't be the least disappointed in any way."

"That is hardly possible, either," returned Amy. "For the truth is, if one does but look within for his enjoyment, it will never fail him. I try to be thankful, and always glad. I seek to color every little object that is thrown in my way with the hues of my own feelings. I try to behold God in all things; not less in my own afflictions, which I know to be for my good, than in my pleasures, and labors, and friends. And if I look inward in this way, drawing all my happiness from the living fountain that gets its supply from him, I never need fear lest true enjoyment may fail me."

Mrs. Gummel appeared deeply interested, listening with a highly intent look, and assenting continually with repeated inclinations of her head.

"I have always thought," Amy went on, "that the quiet of rural life was far more favorable to the growth of these better and deeper feelings of the soul than the jar of life in the city; for here you seem to have abundant time to possess yourself in all due patience; here are perplexities, to be sure, and interruptions, as there must be every where, yet I cannot but think, that as there is here less hurry about the provisions for mere physical wants, so there must be more calmness and room for the development of your higher nature and the culture of your purer thoughts. I think one ought to be more a philosopher in the country, more a Christian. I know that too much solitude cannot be good, but it is better so than not to enjoy any. It must be the ripest and the richest heart that grows in the silence of its own feeling."

"You speak exactly my own thoughts — what I have *known* to be true this long, long while," said her friend. "But it is so very strange I never fall in with people who talk as you do. Why don't we all use as much freedom of speech about these commonest matters? Why *don't* we, and so make more happiness than we do?"

"Sure enough. But isn't it simply because there is a lack of candor among us all? — because we are afraid to speak out our better thoughts, lest others may think us silly and weak? In other words, are we not too much afraid of one another? — slaves to the emptiest prejudices and whims that take shape in human brains? — fearers of the idle tongues that will be active because there is no present power to stop them?"

"It's so; it's verily so."

"Now, suppose we threw off these nightmares from our souls, as we escape from the dominion of our unquiet dreams with the coming up of the morning; suppose we simply say to ourselves, at the rising of every sun, 'This day I will lead a true life — true to myself and to others,' and ask God to help us in our resolution;' don't you think there would be a great deal more of deep and tender feeling interchanged between us, a great deal more real pleasure added to our lives, and a great deal more downright happiness both in our hearts and faces?"

" By all means I do."

" The truth is, all we want is simplicity. There is no
simplicity where there is no trust ; and trust is the child
of *faith*. Then what we are to seek for is *faith*. That
comes, not by setting up one's self, one's own will, or
desires, or ambition, or wish, against God ; not at all ; nor
even by asking God to help us increase through the means
of our own will and ambition ; but only by placing ourselves wholly and entirely in his hands, and praying, day
by day and hour by hour, ' Thy will be done as it is done
in heaven.' Is not that the very first condition of a truly
religious heart, Mrs. Gummel ? "

" None other can be, certainly," answered the other.
" But how often do I feel, when I think of these things,
that as much faith as may be mine now, I have still the
more need to say continually, ' Lord, increase my faith ' ! "

" Truly, truly ; and only by seeking such an increase
can you expect to possess even that which you have now.
In this thing there is no standing still ; you must either
go forward or backward. Unless there is a growth, there
is certainly a falling off."

" I think it must be so."

" And then see how easy, and flowing, and truthful life
may become under such simple conditions. Only see how
easily these abounding riches come to the heart by putting
off what is presumptuous and proud, and clothing yourself in what is lowly and simple. In this kingdom there
is no first, except that he who is last is first, and the one

who takes of himself the lowest seat is immediately called up to the highest. Envy cannot live in such an atmosphere as this, nor boastfulness, nor vanity, nor vain glorying. It is a condition of childishness and the veriest innocency. And if one can but enter in and possess this infinite kingdom, how sweetly may even the roughest life be made to pass, because there is such perfect confidence in the care of the common Father. We may know that our being is very dear to him, because he first saw fit to give it to us out of his own infinite wealth and abundance. But I do not mean to stand here at this time, and delay you from your needful occupation. I imagine that breakfast is ready, and that you came up to call me."

" I did," answered Mrs. Gummel ; " but I am so much interested in what you say, that I have not once thought of breakfast, or that it was every minute growing cold. I should love to listen to you for an hour. But I think you must need something to nourish you. So let's go down, and get breakfast."

And away they went down the short flight of stairs, landing in the snuggest box of a little entry that Amy thought she had ever seen.

Amy really did not think how much she had been saying, or that her listener was no other than a comparative stranger. It was the most unmistakable proof that her faith did so entirely possess her heart, that she was as ready at one time as another to give out the feelings in which she continually lived. While she would not for any thing have been either mawkish or affected in her utterance, she would none the less have been guilty of fear, or of any thing that looked like the timid study of policy. She would let nature speak or be silent, just as it felt inclined. Yet she was made much too happy by her own secret experiences to wish to keep all to herself; it was her chief delight to know that others tasted of the cup whose rich wine warmed her own heart with such untold emotions. So abundant is the wealth that this divine faith strews all around the path of its possessor.

Passing into the room where the breakfast table was laid, she discovered a pretty domestic scene that filled her heart with its beauty. There stood the table in the middle of the floor; before the wood fire that blazed and crackled on the hearth was an arm chair, all ready for her to sit down in for a minute, while she warmed the shivers off her shoulders; Mrs. Gummel's son Henry sat on the little chintz-covered lounge opposite, that stood against the wall; the carpet, like the pleasant fire blaze, was attractive and warm in its shades; and the happy faces of both mother and son added all that was needed to make the attractions complete and the sweet picture perfect.

Amy sat down to the table with a heart overflowing with gratefulness. Indeed, if her countenance did not that day express the happiest, and calmest, and serenest feelings, it was guilty of belying most strangely the real condition of her heart.

The coffee was nice and nourishing. The steaming

decoction of the morning had rarely tasted so refreshing to
her; and she inwardly made up her verdict, without hesitation, in favor of the skill of Mrs. Gummel in cookery.
And she ate buckwheat cakes, too, called "flapjacks"
thereabout in New England, pouring over them that most
delicious of all sirups, the maple sirup, with which the
people of Vermont are so well acquainted. The butter
was good, fresh, country butter, put on the table in a
neatly-stamped cake; and it did her city eyes good just
to look at it.

While they sat at the table, they indulged very freely
in agreeable chat, for which topics were at no moment
wanting. Amy was full of questions about the size of the
place, the character of its gathered families, the names of
the people, and the scenes there were to be got from one
part of the village and the other; and Mrs. Gummel went
into almost voluminous explanations of every object about
which her new friend inquired, eager to have her begin
her life of enjoyment at Valley Village as soon as she
could.

Henry, too, now and then offered such interesting
minutiæ of information as only boys may be supposed to
possess in any fulness, and appeared exceedingly glad to
be able to communicate all he knew so particularly. So
that between the son and the mother, with her own multiplying questions to keep one or the other almost continually engaged in answering her, and her breakfast spread
before her besides, she found herself, before she thought

7

of it, in the midst of one of the most enjoyable moods she
ever knew.

And long after the morning meal was over, and after
Mrs. Gummel had set away the dishes, too, they sat there
and talked; Amy giving rein to her fresh and free impulses till her friend really looked upon her as breathing
almost the spirit of inspiration.   So attractive and beautiful above all things seems the atmosphere of purity and
love that encircles the humble and trusting disciple.

Mrs. Gummel was more and more pleased with the yesterday's good fortune that had thrown Amy in her way.
She felt as if an angel of peace had been sent to her, and
had even now come to abide in her house.   Listening to
her pure sentiments, she saw even the commonest objects
and the humblest modes of life become hallowed.   Her
fears, diminutive as they might have been at best, slunk
out of view before the bright shining of this girl's living
and glowing faith.   She could not but ask herself continually, "Have *I* this faith?"   She saw how it filled
with courage, with joy, with innocency, with the serenest
peace ; and her heart hungered yet more and more for a
possession that so abundantly enriched and exalted those
to whom it was given of Heaven.

CHAPTER VII.

A LOOK AT THE VILLAGE.

THAT day was spent in unpacking her trunks and dis-
tributing her clothes about her room in such a manner as
would best suit her convenience. During the many and
protracted conversations of the morning and afternoon, it
was arranged between Mrs. Gummel and Amy that the
latter should stay where she was just as long as it might
prove agreeable to her, paying for her board what Amy
thought a very trifling amount, but what her new friend
insisted repeatedly was more than a full equivalent.

Amy, while alone in her little chamber, could not help
having her more cheerful moments streaked with sad
thoughts; for memory was as active as ever, and a quick
and fruitful imagination would persist in picturing old
scenes again with all their past vividness of coloring and
contrast. Her father's face *would* appear before her; and
oftentimes, while she was stepping into the closet to put
away something from her trunks, she would seem to think
that he was immediately coming out to meet her. The
morbid influences of the feelings are at all times very
powerful, but scarcely more so at any period than when

a deep and strong grief has stolen into the heart, and
usurped its jealous control.

She sang snatches of the old songs she had taught long
ago to her young music scholars, and tried all she could
to dispel the unhealthy feelings that were continually
gathering about her.   She ran up and down stairs to put
her friend as many questions as suggested themselves to
her, and speculated freely upon the kind of people she
was so soon to become acquainted with, and tried to
fashion her life here into as attractive and even poetic a
shape as was possible.   By night her room assumed the
appearance of perfect order.   One could at a glance have
seen that its youthful occupant was well qualified to take
charge of even a much more spacious establishment than
that which she was allowed to call now her own.   The
chairs were set around in the most easy way, as if they
were arranged for persons to sit in and be social.   The
little table under the glass was covered with boxes, and
baskets, and books ; and on her bureau were arranged a
few shells and trinkets which from time to time she had
been in the way of gathering.   There was also another
table, at which she was to sit and write when she felt
inclined, that stood just in the soft shadow of the
white dimity window curtain, and on which were spread
out her portfolio, her inkstand, a few books for daily
use, and some other implements pertaining to her avocation.

"There!" exclaimed she at last, regarding what she

had done with a happy countenance; "I believe now that I am quite settled."

In the latter part of the afternoon she thought she would go out for a walk. Henry was glad enough to accompany her, at his mother's suggestion, and furnished as welcome and agreeable an escort as could be found among those much older than himself.

They went on through the village street, Amy admiring it all the way, and emerged on the road that threaded its narrow path between the mountainous heights, winding finally out of sight to the far-off northward. Amy kept putting questions, that Henry had to labor hard to answer as fast as they were asked him. She would inquire who lived in this house, and who in that; what people employed themselves about who had their dwellings so far apart over the fields; who worked in the mills below, and where the proprietor's houses were; how early spring usually set in here; whether there were many wild flowers about on the hills; if people rambled much in the pleasant summer time, and whether they generally went to church on Sundays.

"There — that's the minister's house!" exclaimed Henry, when they came in sight of it.

"What is his name?" asked Amy.

"Mr. Parsons; and a real nice man he is, too. *I* like him, and so does mother, and so does every body that *I* know of."

Amy was glad to hear this much of the village minis-

7 *

ter. And she took a longer and more particular look at
his house, wondering, too, if the time would ever come
when she would be a welcome visitor across the threshold.
It was a plain, white dwelling, with a little porch over the
front door, and a woodbine at each side of the lattice. In
summer, she thought, it must be delightful there. It was
a house with what is usually termed a gambrel roof, that
made it look a dozen times more cozy and comfortable
than other houses of the same dimensions, and had a neat,
grassy door yard carefully fenced in from the street.

"This, then," said Amy, "is the parsonage. And I
like the looks of it."

"Yonder is the church," continued Henry, pointing to
the spire.

Amy had observed it from the first; but in order to get
a better view of it, she was desirous of walking by its
very doors.

It was a neat, but substantial edifice, perfectly white in
color, constructed after the simplest architectural design
consistent with the character of such a building, with a
plain spire pointing its finger heavenward, and a gilded
vane veering this way and that from its peak, as the shifting currents of the wind might direct. Amy liked the
looks of the village church fully as much as she did those
of the parsonage. She began already to esteem herself happy in the good fortune that had carried her
thither.

"Where is the little school house, now?" she asked.

"I'll show you, if you have a mind to go there with me," answered Henry.

"O, certainly; I would not fail to see that—the place where I expect to pass so many hours of the coming summer. I always want to make up my mind how such places are to look and seem to me, before I go about any thing else. But you do not go to school, I guess, in the summer —do you?"

"No, not in the summer," said he; "but that's because there's no school to go to. We've had only winter schools here for a good many years; and we haven't had the same teacher for two winters together. I haven't been now for three summers."

"Don't you like to go?"

"Yes; but mother thinks I've got too *large* to go to a woman's school." He said this with such an air of seriousness, that Amy could not help smiling as she looked down into his face. "Besides," added he, just as seriously, "mother thinks I can be a good deal of help to her at home. I like to work about home."

"Yes, that is a very good sign for a boy," said Amy. "But it is for your good, too, to go to school."

"O, I know that, Miss Lee; but then what can I do when there *isn't* any school?"

Amy smiled again at his manly earnestness.

"I don't like to be shut up in a school room any too well in the summer time," said he, seeming to follow out the train of thought into which he had fallen.

How natural that was ! What child *is* any too fond of that weary confinement, tied to the hard benches for six weary hours of the sultry day, its mind wandering here and there like the fluttering butterflies over the grass out the window, and its feelings unquiet beneath the restraint that lies so like an incubus upon every moment of the school day ? Childhood rebels, and makes it the hardest task it is compelled to perform.

Talking together after this pleasant manner, they came to an out-of-the-way spot, not exactly at the end of the street, yet so much off from its margin as to seem quite out of the village, where stood a diminutive brown building, nearly square, with a big stone chimney rising from the middle of the roof, and a padlock fastening the outer door.

" *That's* the school house," said Henry, pointing to it.

" That !" exclaimed Amy.

It was as much pleasure as it was surprise that prompted the exclamation. The view of so unique an edifice for such an ennobling purpose excited quite different feelings from what she had expected.

The house was situated in what might truly be termed a grassy square, standing away at a considerable distance from the road. On three sides were stone walls, gray with the lichens that are the fruits of time. The fourth was open to the road ; and the whole enclosure formed as roomy a play ground as the children issuing from any school house could wish to romp and gambol upon.

Amy stepped to one of the windows, and looked in. There was a row of benches all the way round the room. Also, two shorter benches stood in the middle of the floor, having high backs to them. These, she thought, must be placed for the smaller ones, whose heads needed a support by the middle of the afternoons, even if it were not necessary to stretch some of them at full length on the seat for repose.

"And I am to busy myself in this quiet room all the summer," mused Amy, turning away and surveying the thick carpet of grass that was beginning to break out a beautiful green. "I wonder if I shall do any good here ; if the children will all love me ; if I shall be sorry to break up at the last and go away. I wonder — I wonder." And in her train of thought she broke out humming a sweet and plaintive air. So perfectly seemed it to accord with the time and the place, that little Henry stopped in his walk about the house to listen, enjoying the soft and low melody with the hearty sympathy that is so easily called forth from a child's soul.

They turned at length from the place, and pursued their way homewards. The reader may be told, in order better to understand the topography of Valley Village, that the street on which the village lay ran directly north and south ; at the far northward the broad plain narrowed perceptibly between the shouldering mountains, bringing the stream that fed the reservoir below exactly across the road, where it was spanned by an ancient-looking, rustic

bridge, over whose rails you could look down dreamily
into the flowing water; at the southward, and much below
the real settlement where the dwellings were grouped, the
road and the river ran side by side for a considerable distance, when they separated finally to permit the former to
pursue its own course across the open country to the market town, some ten miles away, and allow the latter to
give a lift to the great wheels that went round and round
beneath the high factory buildings, turning dizzy spindles
almost without number.

Amy, therefore, had not yet walked entirely through the
place, but far enough quite to get a good idea of what it
might be. She had seen the church, and the parsonage,
and the school house. She knew somewhat of the scenery
formed by the bold mountain heights away to the northward. She had seen enough of the village to picture it
all out in her mind's eye again, as sleeping so peacefully
in the lap of this beautiful landscape, itself imbosomed in
a dreamy beauty.

"Shall you like to live here, do you think?" asked her
companion, after a thoughtful silence on the part of both.

As she glanced at him before giving an answer, she
found that he was looking with a highly sympathetic expression exactly in her face.

"I know I shall," said she, not a little moved by this
tender feeling of the boy. "Especially," she added, "if
I am to have you help make me happy, as you have done
this afternoon."

Now he looked perplexed to understand what she could mean. In his innocent simplicity, he could not see how *he* had been an addition to the enjoyment of one like her. The expression of sympathy was superseded by quite another.

"I promise myself a great many pleasant walks this summer up yonder," said Amy, pointing back in the northerly direction. "I want to be climbing those hills, too. And I seem to know who is going to climb them with me."

Henry blushed now.

"That is," said she again, "if you don't happen to be too much occupied about home. *Some* boys are always behindhand with their work, you know, and so they never have leisure for any thing."

"I wonder if you think *I'm* one of that kind," said he, modestly, while a smile broke out over his features.

"*Shall* I, do you think? Can I depend on you beforehand to go with me whenever I want a young companion like you?"

"I'll try to let you *see* that you can, at any rate," he answered. "I don't like to make too many promises. Mother says it's a good deal better to *do*, and not *say*, than to say, and not do."

"And your mother is right," said Amy. "Always remember what your mother tells you, and you cannot fail to be happy yourself and loved of every one else. I never knew *my* mother. She died before I can remember her."

Amy said this in such a low and tremulous voice, — not
as if she was dryly didacticizing to the boy, but as if she
had uttered what she possibly could not help uttering
aloud, — that a visible emotion took hold on his feelings,
and he walked on by her side for a long distance in
silence.   Perhaps his thoughts led him to the possibility
of some day losing his own mother.

Going back again, Amy felt confirmed in her first impressions of the village street and its houses.   It seemed
so much pleasanter, so much more quiet and charmingly
rural, that the majority of the dwellings had no door
yards before them, and the green grass grew close up to
the very thresholds.   Such a sight drove away all thoughts
of a set and selfish division of property, and gave birth to
the most delightful fancies connected with the pristine
simplicity of rustic life.   She wanted to see a country
village where a stranger could walk quietly through the
grassy street, while he could likewise look without an
effort into the open windows, and find the families sitting
about their tea tables.   This open-yard style, therefore,
suited her ; and whether the quiet villagers themselves
had ever thought of it or not, it was settled in *her* mind
that this air of free intercourse between door and door
certainly enhanced the calm beauty of the dwellings, and
set every one of them off to a much more considerable
advantage.

Chatting and musing along by the way, looking with
increasing interest at the different little dwellings they

passed, putting her thoughts continually in a frame of profound gratitude for the daily mercies that gathered around her, and suffering her heart to trip joyfully forward into the pleasant vista of the future, Amy reached at length, with her attentive young companion, the door of his mother's house; which she, on seeing them, hurried into the little entry to open, welcoming her new boarder in again with the same happy and sympathizing smile that had made her Amy's friend from the first.

"You've had a long walk, I know," said the kind Mrs. Gummel; "and now supper is all on the table, and you shall sit down and tell me all about your feelings again."

And Amy went in. And at the tea table they did sit for a long while, talking of the things that had that afternoon undergone Amy's inspection. It was gratifying to behold so pleasant an intimacy as had suddenly sprung up between Mrs. Gummel and her boarder. And it was all the more so, when one stopped to consider how accidentally it seemed to have begun, and how naturally and delightfully it was developing itself into what promised before a great while to be a rich and valuable friendship.

The wood fire blazed again on the hearth. The table at last was cleared off and set away. And Amy sat and looked thoughtfully into the coals, blessing God in every happy thought for his overflowing goodness.

8

Mrs. Gummel felt that she could not have been furnished with a better boarder, or one in whose companionship she could enjoy so much, had she been at the trouble
of hunting the six New England states all through and
through.

CHAPTER VIII.

HUNTING UP PUPILS.

AFTER breakfast was over the next morning, Amy put on her things, and started to go out to hunt up her school. It was still another pleasant morning, and every thing without doors invited her out. The signs of early spring were increasing, as it really seemed, with every hour. The grass was pricking through the soil faster; the buds were swelling; the sun grew more and more warm and genial; and the atmosphere was becoming as balmy as a soft southern gale.

"I'm sure I hope you will meet with all the success you desire," offered Mrs. Gummel, as Amy folded her shawl about her and moved towards the door. "And I think you will, too; for there's *to be* a school kept here by *somebody*, and the scholars are all ready. That much I know."

"Where shall I go first?" asked Amy. "Shall I take the houses right through the street in their order? Or shall I go over first to the minister's?"

"I think I would go and call first on Mr. Parsons. That will be the best thing you can do. He always interests himself about these matters; and if you lay your case

i (87)

frankly befqre him, and tell him exactly what you want to
do, he will assist you more than anybody else could. I
think I would go and see him first, by all means."

"Then I will," returned Amy. "I hope I shall have
good luck. Good morning, then, Mrs. Gummel! Good
morning, Henry! I shall hope to be able to bring back
my report to you by noon."

"Perhaps he will keep you with him to dinner," suggested Mrs. Gummel.

"Well, I shall see," Amy replied, laughing. "Perhaps
he will."

She went out. Mrs. Gummel's eyes followed her affectionately as far as they could along the street. That good
lady was thinking of the daughter — the only daughter —
whom she had years ago given back to Heaven, grateful
for even the brief solace that she had proved. If now
that little daughter of hers could but have grown to be as
graceful and womanly as Amy! — if she might have been
spared to a longer and a closer companionship with her
own heart! — if she could have been allowed to behold
her in the flush of youthful health and the perfection of
youthful beauty, like this dear girl that had just gone out
of her door! But was not this rebelliousness? Was it
not being dissatisfied with the ways of Him who declares
that his ways are not as our ways, nor his thoughts as our
thoughts? Was it keeping her heart trusting and humble
in the great power of Him who enriched and supported
it every day?

Reaching the gate of the parsonage, Amy opened it and went through. There was nothing by which she could alarm the inmates of the quiet house, not so much as an old-fashioned, gorgon-headed rapper; so she fell back on the first principles of social people, and employed with much vigor her knuckles.

Twice or thrice she was obliged to rap, before she succeeded in arousing any one. At length she caught the sound of an opening door in one of the apartments, and then she heard the footsteps of some one coming down the front stairs. A moment afterwards the door opened, and a gentleman dressed in his sober-colored morning gown stood before her.

" Good morning!" he saluted her, in a tone of great affability and kindness. " Will you walk in ?"

" Thank you," said Amy, and stepped across the threshold.

He waited on her into the sitting room, into which ere long came his wife, who seated herself with them, and began to take part in the conversation.

" I have called this morning, sir," Amy began, " to see what I could do about getting together pupils enough to open a summer school in the village."

" Ah, yes — yes," he immediately assented.

" And I have presumed to think that you would not be unwilling to help me about my plan," she added.

" Certainly not ; certainly not. Indeed, I have been for some time past thinking how we were to manage here

8 *

this season without one. Usually we have offers of teachers enough, and of course some of them have to go away
disappointed ; but *this* year I do not think there has been
a single person round to make inquiries whether we are
going to have a school or not. I can't seem to account
for it. You have had some experience in teaching, I
conclude ? "

"No, sir, not in ordinary *schools*. I have been engaged
chiefly with music pupils. Yet I think I could get on
very easily with such scholars as one generally finds in a
summer school."

"No doubt of it at all," he returned, glancing again at
Amy's face with an expression of satisfaction at what he
saw plainly written there.

And then ensued a short silence.

"How large a school do you think you could get along
with comfortably ? " asked the clergyman again.

"I can best answer your question, perhaps," she replied,
"by inquiring how large a school you generally have here
in the village during the summer months."

"Well, let me see," and he cast his eyes down calcu-
latingly upon the floor. "One ; four ; six ; — well, perhaps, fifteen."

"Or perhaps twenty," added his wife, who seemed to
have taken quite a secret interest in the success of the
youthful stranger's plan.

"Well, I should think there might be twenty. Do you
think you could manage with as many as that without
much difficulty ? "

"I should give myself but little anxiety on that score," answered Amy, while the countenance of the clergyman's wife beamed with a great show of sympathy for her. "The scholars are mostly young girls, I suppose."

"Yes," said Mrs. Parsons, "nearly all girls; and of them you would hardly find one above twelve years of age — perhaps the greater part of them under ten, or nine. The most that is expected in these summer schools is, to teach the little girls of the village how to read and to sew. All that one wants is patience."

"I suppose so," acquiesced Amy.

"And you would likewise find," said the clergyman, "that the introduction of *singing* into your school would be a very great attraction, as well as a relief to yourself through the day."

"I had designed to introduce it," said Amy. "I know that I can get the affection of pupils a great deal sooner by that means than by almost any other."

"And it's such a *humanizing* branch of instruction, too. Nothing, I apprehend, assists more in the culture and expansion of the heart. The human soul was created with an under current of divine harmony. Strike but the first responsive chord, and you may instantly sweep all the strings."

"Yes — yes," quickly assented his wife, whose eyes alone confessed to her belief in the sentiments he had just uttered.

"I hardly know just how to begin in this business,"

said Amy, a little embarrassed at this point. "I do not feel, sir, that coming here a perfect stranger, as I do, it can be expected by me that you should pledge me your assistance; yet I knew it was the properest step for me to take, to come first and consult with you about it."

Mr. Parsons bowed, and his wife regarded her with still a deeper interest.

Amy saw in a moment that the clergyman was quite unwilling to begin then and put her a variety of interrogatories respecting her age, her advantages, her references, if any she had, her connection, or her professions; and to relieve the moment of any further embarrassment, she at once commenced giving a narration of such portion of her past life as would lead her listeners to a more thorough judgment respecting her. When she had finished, she was gratified to see that both of them manifested a much deeper sympathy for her, and voluntarily proffered a greater degree of influence in behalf of her summer project.

"Where had I better call to get my pupils?" she asked, directing her inquiry rather to Mrs. Parsons.

"Well, I don't know," answered the latter; "had you better think of going about yourself at all?"

"Hadn't I better just mention to the people who will be likely to send children to school," interrupted the clergyman, "that there is a lady in the place who proposes to open a school, and that the school will open on such a day?"

"Yes; that *would* be better, Mr. Parsons," assented his wife.

Amy looked her thanks for his kind offer. She did not feel that she then could utter them.

"Well, then," said he again, "do you rest perfectly easy about the matter, and I will make all the needful preparations for you. I will see the parents of all the pupils you can have reason to expect, and enlist them in favor of your undertaking. I will go about it this very afternoon — this very day."

"I cannot seem to thank you as I wish to for your generous sympathy," replied Amy.

"O, never mind — never mind. Don't begin to say any thing this forenoon about *that*. We won't stop to *talk* too much before we've accomplished a little something, you know. But how soon will you begin your school, Miss Lee? · People want to know all about that, you see."

"Well," she hesitated, "as soon as may be practicable."

"Next Monday?" inquired he. "It's getting along in the season already, you know."

"Yes," said Mrs. Parsons; "I would begin as soon as that, if I conveniently could."

"There is nothing in the world to hinder me that I know of," returned Amy. "If I should consent to wait till the week following, should that delay be necessary ——"

"But I don't think it will, Miss Lee," interrupted the clergyman.

"Even if it should," continued Amy, "I shall only be waiting for the time to come round. And I think I had rather commence my school with but half the number of pupils I may expect, than to wait a whole week in comparative idleness."

"And I think so, too," added the clergyman's wife.

"You will pardon me, sir," said Amy, "for having kept you away so long from your other engagements. I really did not think I should have occasion to stay what time I have staid." And she rose to go.

"O, no, no," answered Mr. Parsons. "You are not interrupting me at all. I am really very glad you came in as you did."

"Yes, so am I," said his wife, with her old glance of sympathy.

"And I will do all I can to help you on, believe me," he added.

Amy bowed her acknowledgment of thanks.

"But you haven't been over to see your school house yet — have you?" he inquired, seeking to change the current of her thoughts.

His wife smiled.

"Well, what are *you* laughing at?" said he, turning round upon her with one of the best humored faces in the world.

"Nothing — nothing," she carelessly answered, and laughed again.

"O, yes, sir," said Amy; "I have been over there, to be sure. I was eager to see where I was to perform my summer's labor."

"It's rather a *primitive* edifice. Don't you think it is?"

"Well, rather so, sir," Amy hesitated, enjoying the genial spirit of his humor.

"Old and gray," said he; "old and gray. The chimney looks as if it might be the outwork of some heavy fortress. There is little about it that isn't quite ancient in its appearance. But did you observe our padlock?"

"I believe I did, sir," said she, exchanging a smile with the clergyman's wife.

"I call it *our* padlock because I conclude it belongs to the village — as much to me as to any body else; in other words, I claim to possess an individual interest in that particular padlock; and it's the *only* padlock, too, I believe, in which I am at all interested."

And then he threw back his head, and gave a good, hearty laugh, such as only those persons are known to enjoy whose spirits are in a state of health, and whose hearts are supposed to be always in the right place.

"However," he went on, sobering somewhat, "it's all well enough in its way, I suppose. Only we feel once in a while like making a little fun of it, as you see me doing now. No, Miss Lee; it's not in the *padlock* that the trouble lies. I tell our good people here that what we want is, not a new padlock, but a new *school house.*"

"Yes, indeed," said his wife. "I wonder, though, if they will ever have one."

"All in good time, perhaps, my dear; all in good time. It will not do to think of hurrying rational people any faster than they will go of themselves. Ten to one they'll turn round upon you, and drive you still farther back. But Miss Lee, now, must go to work, and build up a first rate reputation as a teacher, as I think from her appearance she *can* do; then the scholars will flock around her, and stay by her as long as *she* stays; next you will hear that some generous village heart has taken secret thought about a new school house, convinced that such a building is not good enough for so excellent a teacher; then the various plans and projects for another edifice will be brought forward, and discussed with all vigor in the pleasant village circles and at every happy tea table there is along the street; and finally the thing will be accomplished, will be finished; we shall have a new school house, and we will try to get along without the old iron padlock. And let us earnestly hope, my dear, that Miss Lee will be herself the happy instrument of so much progress in our little village circle."

"I hope she will, really," said Mrs. Parsons.

"I don't know about that," rejoined Amy, hesitating, and modestly embarrassed.

"Nor I either," added Mr. Parsons. "That is, I mean to say I am not so very sure it will not all come about pretty much as I have sketched it. At least, I *hope* it may."

And Amy, a stranger there in a strange place, looked into her own heart, and wished in secret that something like this might eventually happen. She longed to be doing service in the world, and she likewise possessed that common desire of humanity for the honest approval of every sincere heart near her.

After her visit at the parsonage had been still longer protracted, and after Amy had received repeated invitations, too, to run in upon them there just as often as she felt inclined, with many an expression of gratitude she took her leave, promising to do all that was in her power to carry out her designs for the summer successfully, and in her heart calling down abundant blessings upon them for their unstinted kindness.

Directly she returned home to Mrs. Gummel again, and in time to find that dinner was quite ready for her, while her friend was just as ready to hear every item of fresh intelligence that she had to communicate. She threw off her things, and sat down to dinner at once.

In the afternoon she and Mrs. Gummel enjoyed themselves famously. Amy asked as many questions as she liked, and her friend answered every one of them. Such a sociable time as they made of it! And Amy was so much pleased with her prospects! And Mrs. Gummel was so much delighted, too, with her young friend's heightening cheerfulness and vivacity!

"I do not think I could have been better suited," Amy

9

told her, "if I had come and begun my arrangements six months ago."

"Nor I," said her friend. "I am happy to find it is so — I dare say, almost as happy as you are yourself."

"Mr. Parsons is a kind man," added Amy. "Indeed, he could not have promised to do more for me, if I had been an old acquaintance."

"That's always his way. He *is* one of the very best of men, we all know. But he was probably much pleased with your appearance. He can see into a person about as soon as any man."

"And I liked his wife none the less than himself," she added. "Both of them showed me a great deal of sympathy, and took almost as much interest in my school as I could myself."

"Yes, that's just the way with both of them. I do think Mr. Parsons and his wife are the best of folks."

Before the summer was over, Amy had far better reason to think so likewise.

Well, to conclude about this matter of collecting pupils. Mr. Parsons and his wife, both of them, did go around through the village, between that day, which was Wednesday, and the following Sunday, laboring disinterestedly and with all their energies for the cause in which they had enlisted. The lukewarm they excited by urgent appeals; the indifferent they stirred into action; those who intended to send but half of their little ones they persuaded to send the whole; they secured the support of the men, the

women, and the children ; and by the time the week drew
to its close, they had succeeded even beyond their own
hopes in the object they had so much at heart.

Amy called again at the parsonage, to learn how their
efforts in her behalf were prospering ; and in turn Mrs.
Parsons came over to see her at her own lodgings.   And
when Saturday afternoon brought around the end of the
eventful week, she felt that a great deal more had been
accomplished than she could ever have hoped for in that
time, and her heart had been made lighter and happier
than for many and many a week before.

CHAPTER IX.

THE FIRST SUNDAY.

"Now, you are going to church with me all day to-day, Miss Lee," said Mrs. Gummel, as they got up from the breakfast table on Sunday morning — the first Sunday morning Amy had seen in Valley Village. "You will find, I think, that our minister is quite as good a man *in* the pulpit as he is *out* of it."

"Indeed, I do not doubt that," Amy answered. "I can readily believe all you will tell me that is good about him. But what a lovely day it's going to be! I declare I think it's too pleasant almost to stay within doors."

"Of the delicious summer days," said Mrs. Gummel, "I think that Sunday is the most heavenly of all. The air itself seems to waft happiness to you. You breathe in repose for your soul, with the atmosphere. You do not know much yet, I guess, about these pleasant Sundays in the country."

"Very little, and I am sorry to say it. But I hope my experiences of the present season may be as rich as I could desire. They certainly promise well thus far."

They were soon after ready to go, and were sitting and waiting for the next bell to ring. Master Henry was seated near one of the front windows, reading in one of the few books his mother kept lying on the table; and Amy could not help regarding him with a great deal of interest, if not affection. He wore a neat suit of black, his jacket buttoned up snugly to his chin with a row of bright metal buttons, and a plain white linen collar turned smoothly over all around his neck. His hair, which was a little inclined to curling, was combed and brushed till it shone again, and being parted so carefully from his forehead by the tasteful hand of his mother, contrasted with a most pleasing effect with the whiteness of his full temples, and lent even a lustrous expression to his dark and beaming eyes.

Presently the tongue of the last morning bell struck its alarm. The clear and melodious sound seemed to Amy to vibrate far up and down the street, shivering its harmony among the maple tree tops, floating away in its prolonged reverberations to the distant meeting of the mountains, and brooding at length like a lulling musical dream over the village that lay lapped so quietly between the hills.

Mrs. Gummel rose to go, and so did Amy. Henry opened to them the doors, and took care to secure them after him. And as they walked on slowly over the soft sward, enjoying in silence both the music of the bell and the quiet and holy thoughts of the morning, Master Henry

9 *

caught up with them after his little delay, stepping along
by the side of Amy, and appearing to enjoy his heart-full
of the influences and associations of the day.

It was truly a beautiful sight, that of all the villagers
going in procession to church. Never could that plat of
grass be made to look more inviting and delightful, nor
would the light shadows of the maple trees ever drop down
on a more attractive picture. Men and women were wend-
ing their thoughtful way along, their faces radiant with the
joy that breathed from their hearts. They discoursed with
one another about the pleasantness of the morning, and
chatted in voices of social sympathy about the more recent
affairs of their households. Now it was of the weather,
and now of the minister; at one moment of the promise
of the spring, and the next of the health of their families.
These dear, delightful pictures of rural life are nowhere in
this land to be seen in such perfection as right here among
us in New England. Nowhere in the world can the
stranger's eyes find visions that so enchant and enrich his
heart as these of the Sunday march to church, of the
gathering neighbors, of the radiant countenances, and the
Sabbath costumes.

Amy looked in every practicable direction around her,
feasting her eyes on the living scene. A sense — unde-
finable she felt it was — of profound happiness stole over
her heart, out of whose depths welled up fountains of a
refreshing joy. She thought within herself, that it would
be but a little time before she would know all these new

faces, and call each person by name, hoping, too, to call them all her friends; and her feelings led her along into the future far enough to picture for herself many and many a scene of happiness in their midst, of which at this time none of them could be thinking.

When they reached the church door, she knew they were all regarding her with a heightened interest, not to give it the less agreeable name of curiosity. Her eyes met glances from them on every side. Now she found herself gazing into the face of a young girl, and again into that of a soberer matron. There was something, too, in their glances that rather satisfied her thoughts. They looked like kind-hearted people, who had generous sentiments and open hands. So do all the people look that gather on Sunday beneath the shadows of our country churches. Even if much of it proves hollowness, or the merest falsehood, still the *general* characteristics are carried out in their first promise.

And Amy was as much struck, likewise, with the simplicity and neatness of their costumes. They seemed to express just the outward respect for the Sabbath which occurred to her as being in harmony with true and unaffected religious feelings; not at all too studied or artificial, and none too careless of the day whose worshipping hours the bell was ushering in.

Mrs. Gummel led her along up the aisle, and opened the door of her pew. But Amy insisted on Mrs. Gummel's going in first, and on taking her own place nearer the middle of the seat. And Henry entered last, and thoughtfully buttoned the door.

While the bell was yet tolling, she had some time to see the faces of those who came in. She had seen many of them, as they passed the windows of Mrs. Gummel, during the week, and now began to recognize them again. The front pew was occupied by the minister's family. They had not yet come in, but would be there directly. Behind the clergyman's seat, two or three pews backward, sat Mrs. Brown, a woman with two very pretty girls, one on each side of her, whose husband was employed as an overseer in one of the mills below the village. Mrs. Brown was a good faced woman, and kept looking over at Mrs. Gummel's pew, and finally exchanged nods with Mrs. Gummel, as much as to say that she was glad to see she had brought the new teacher out to church.

Over against the wall sat Mr. Marsh, a man who was reputed to be very well off for a farmer, and whose means were latterly said to be increasing every year. He was a considerable wool grower, and travelled a great deal at some seasons of the year to effect the most profitable sales for his products. He carried his head, which was a little bald on the top, rather statelily, and wore a pleasant smile on his countenance continually. Amy thought he had an uncommonly fatherly look, and felt her heart drawn to him as to a person of large and most humane sympathies. Three rather small children sat with him, his wife remaining at home to look after the still unfinished household duties.

And there was the honest form of the village black-smith, whose daughter Mary sat in the church choir, exactly as Longfellow has described it in his beautiful and touching ballad. Mr. Davy's face was enough of itself to invite your confidence. He had a hard hand, but it was an honest and an open one, every body said. And he had a rather low forehead, with black hair, and heavy, dark eyebrows.

Glancing still farther round her, Amy saw the face of Mrs. Moore. She was the wife of the storekeeper in the village, and was looking over towards Amy with a good deal of earnestness. Mrs. Moore wore a quite stylish bonnet, ornamented with a profusion of high-colored rib-bons. And she had four children beside her, two of whom were little boys with flaxen heads.

There sat Mr. Matson, too, supposed to be the richest man of all in the village, and wearing the name of being the greatest miser besides. He was concerned in no per-ceptible business just at that time, having as much as he wanted to do in studying the yearly management of his stocks and bonds, although he at no time objected to turning a quick penny when the opportunity offered. Mr. Matson was a married man, but he had no children. Some persons used to say, that if he had been blessed with them, his chief regret at such a dispensation would have arisen from its expensiveness. But that might be nothing but scandal.

And Mr. Blossom was there, and his family. They

jumbled into the pew as if they were in a hurry lest those
who got in last would be obliged to stand during the services. And Mr. Williams, the great fruit grower; he
raised scores of bushels of choice apples for the market
every autumn. And in one pew sat a lady whom Amy
could not but think quite different in the tone of her
manners from all the other ladies of the village. She
took her seat near the head of the pew, while the young
lady who accompanied her stationed herself nearer the
door. And as the latter glanced round the church, on
first sitting down, Amy thought that there was a face of
peculiar interest and beauty. The young lady's name
was Olive Adams; she was the niece of the lady with
whom she came in, whose name in turn was Mrs. Bucclebee. Mrs. Bucclebee was a lady of large wealth, whose
husband had removed to Valley Village several years
before for the sake of its pleasant retirement, and dying
while there, had left her a childless widow. She lived a
little distance out of the village, in a place built up by
the taste of her husband, where she yearly saw a great
many old friends from far away towns and cities, and tried
to enjoy the leisure and quiet that was to be had in her
present retirement without interruption. Olive Adams
was the daughter of a deceased sister, whom she had
voluntarily adopted as her own child, and on whose
development she looked with quite as much pride as
affection.

It would fill the book, however, to specify them all.

Besides, it would not be the very best kind of occupation for the Sunday morning hour to run through the list of village church goers, and give any sort of a description of them. And as it was, before Amy's casual observations had extended any farther, Mr. Parsons and his family came in. He assisted them into the pew, fastened the door, and proceeded up the pulpit stairs.

I will not dwell particularly on every portion of the public worship as it progressed, for my good readers will assuredly let their thoughts run far before me in such a description. Amy could not but like the singing, however. The choir was well and tastefully made up, with clear and harmonious voices. And they sang the old and time-honored tunes, than which none better, by common consent, have been composed or invented since the early days of their origin. That simple music, — it sounded as if it might indeed be heavenly. How it floated from out the church over the silent street, waking soft and worshipful harmonies every where! What a sweet and singular power lay in those few notes, enough to enrapture a heart already inclined to devotion, and fill it with all the countless melodies of lovely thoughts and exalted aspirations! How it brooded over the feelings of that simple-minded congregation, even as soft and golden mists brood over the laps of pleasant valleys!

The clergyman's discourses, both morning and afternoon, entirely made good Amy's first prepossessions in his favor. The morning sermon was on the subject of the

opening season; and all its beautiful thoughts and ador-
ing expressions fanned the feelings of Amy's heart into
glowing flames. He took for his text that oft-quoted
passage in Scripture, " He hath made every thing beautiful in its time."

After a general and a rather poetic exordium, he went
on with a minute and lively description of the opening
spring and summer. He entered at once into the subject
with his whole heart. He spoke of the earliest and most
welcome signs of spring, such as the whistle of the frogs
at the marsh, and the first notes of the returned robin,
and described the new joys even those faint and trifling
sounds awoke in the human breast, that was always prepared to greet them. Then he entered, with the expansion of his subject, upon a view of the world after the
influences of the summer had really begun to reign; how
the sun was pleasant to the bodily feelings, and did not
fail even to warm the genial soil of the heart; how the
frequent showers opened the warmed earth, fertilizing the
furrows from the very clouds that thus literally dropped
fatness; how the grass grew dark and thick, and began to
wave in the rolling billows of the wind, ready for the
glittering scythe of the mower; how the cattle straggled
every where over the green pasture lands, and the hill
sides were white with the heavy fleeces of sheep; how the
flowers climbed about the doors and windows of one's
dwelling, and gemmed the meadows like stars in a vast
heaven, and fringed the flowing courses of the living water

brooks; how the trees were full of singing birds, that
mingled their songs with the ravishing fragrance of the
blossoms, and heightened their bright and indescribable
beauty with the many colors of their own brilliant plu-
mage; and how both heaven above and earth beneath
answered each to the other in unfolding and illustrating
the vast love of God for his whole creation.

Thence he passed on in glowing language to descant
upon the need there was that we should all have gratitude; that love should continually abound within us, and
increase towards God and towards man forevermore; that
we should become more and more childlike, and truthful,
and humble, never setting up our own desires against the
higher and better laws of the God who rules over us and
in us; and, finally, that we should seek and pray for
nothing so much as faith — that faith which taught us
to lie low and obedient in the Lord's vast power, ascribing evermore to him the glory, because by every means
he has thus clearly revealed to us his blessed purposes
and grace.

The appeal with which his discourse closed was so feeling and eloquent as to send a thrill of glad emotion to
many a bosom in that little country church, and make
them desire a closer walk all their days with God, and a
calmer, more peaceful, more thoroughly religious frame of
mind. Not that Mr. Parsons was a man who prided himself on the possession of so rare a gift as eloquence, or
scarcely was conscious of even possessing that quality; for

10

had such a pride stepped into his heart, that moment the
true gift would have departed; it does not dwell with
presumption, and will never consent to take up its abode
with vanity. But he was so simple, and earnest, and
childlike in his feelings, his sympathies were always so
acute and active both with outward and inward nature, he
let his thoughts run the round of all the better and profounder emotions of the human heart so easily, that his
eloquence was no more than the simplest report, made
with all joyfulness, of his insight into what other men are
still willing to call mysteries, and still willing not to know
except from the moving lips of those who now and then
address them.

The evening seemed to Amy a calm and holy time
indeed. All labor had ceased for so long; the street was
so quiet and calm; the twilight had come down with
such a sense of sweet joy and peace; the hands of care
seemed folded so resignedly in the lap of labor; there
were so many silent influences stealing from the landscape, from the air, from the stillness itself in which the
thoughts half slept, — that Amy felt that if this was
one of the blessed enjoyments of the country life, it was
truly worth quite all the pleasures of the uneasy town
together.

And she laid her head that night on her pillow, glad
beyond her ability to express it that her lines had at last
fallen to her in such pleasant places. Her soul was filled
with gratefulness and love; and these would perpetually

overflow their boundaries, and make green and new the influences that would go unseen out of her heart during all the days, and weeks, and months of her abode in this quiet and happy place.

CHAPTER X.

OPENING SCHOOL.

MONDAY morning came; and with key in hand, — the key to that same padlock Mr. Parsons was inclined to make so much fun about, — Amy walked with a pleasant countenance over to the school house, and opened the door that was to let her in to her summer labors.

As soon as she stepped across the threshold, she seemed to breathe the mixed atmosphere of all the winter and summer schools that had been kept there before she had even heard of such a nook as Valley Village. The room was close and musty. She bustled round immediately, and opened every window; and as the door still stood wide open in the entry, she felt certain of securing a freshening draught of air. The benches she proceeded to arrange over again, so as to answer more conveniently the designs of her government economy. And, finally, after all things had been fixed to her mind, she passed a little time in pacing up and down the floor, looking now at the ceiling and cobwebs, and now out the windows over the fields and distant gardens.

In the course of that short and solitary walk, she

reviewed the way of her life and fortunes since the death of her father with much thoughtfulness and care. From the point to which her mind would continually revert with such persistence, she went forward slowly through the armies of fears and anxieties that afterwards beleaguered her soul, sweeping the many chords of feeling that had vibrated sadly and sorrowfully since that dark day, rehearsing the little histories of her plans, and hopes, and designs, and desires, coming along on her journey again to this same Valley Village, where she now found herself waiting to begin her first day of usefulness, and at last devoutly thanking her kind heavenly Father that he had still provided for her, and had never ceased to remember her as one of his own created children.

The tears stole into her eyes, through whose dim veil she still regarded the promising landscape. "O, if I can but do the whole of my duty!" said she within herself. "If I do not come short in the very least of my promises! If I can but go on in perfect trust and peace from day to day, pursuing my humble occupation in the spirit of love, looking for my only reward in the good itself that will flow from my faith and obedience."

And her heart offered a silent, but fervent supplication, praying God, her Father, to bestow on her the spirit whose fruit was nothing but goodness, and gentleness, and love. This was, in truth, the opening prayer of her little school —a silent prayer, offered in solitude, while her feet walked slowly the floor of that quiet school house.

10 *

Presently she saw a shadow fall across the threshold; then two; then three; and then a whole nest and knot of shadows. She stepped towards the door, and a snarl of happy faces saluted her with looks of joy.

"Good morning! good morning, dears!" Amy called to them, extending both hands with gladness. "Come; won't you come in and stay with me this forenoon, and see what we can learn all together? Come!" And the little ones, who happened to be every one girls, glanced round smiling on each other, and then stepped, half timidly, half roguishly, in.

"Now we'll have a nice time of it — won't we?" said Amy, her own beautiful face attracting them to her even more than her words. "Come; let's take off our things, — you see I've got mine off, — and then we will all sit down and tell who we are, and what we have come to school for, and if we are going to love each other all summer long, and where we live, and every thing about it. Come, little girls, let me take off your hoods and shawls."

She began the work by disrobing the one next her; but no sooner did they see what was to be done, than the rest performed each one the task for herself, smiling the while at one another, as if in a long time they had enjoyed nothing better.

"Now we will sit down," Amy directed, pointing to the vacant benches. "There; that is very pleasant and very pretty. I think we shall have a nice time of it yet."

And again the little ones looked at each other and laughed.

While she stood before them all, talking to them in the kindest and sweetest tones, telling them what they had come there for, and what she was going to do, too, and successfully interesting them beyond what she had at first dared to hope for, others entered the room, boys and girls together, the former standing foremost in the little groups, while the latter were modestly leaning against the benches or the wall. And these she welcomed as fast as they came, assisting them to take off their caps and bonnets, and laying her hands gently on their heads, and by her looks and words trying to impress them with the love she felt for them all. It is needless to say that those who came last were as well received and as much delighted as those who had got there before them. So agreeable did Amy try to make every thing seem in their eyes, they hardly felt that they were in that usually forbidding place called a school room, but rather that they had got together there to have a good time of it, and very likely — as matters at first looked — to wind up with broken crockery housekeeping, and a general tea drink off of bits of glistening china.

Amy had as fine tact as feeling. She knew how important it was to enlist the *affections* of her little school, first of all. If she could rely upon their love, she was certain that the most difficult part of her work was already done.

Among those present, she found the children of many
of the parents whom she had seen at church the day
before ; indeed, she recognized the faces of many of the
children themselves.   There were those of Mr. Brown, the
overseer in the mills; and all three of Mr. Marsh, the
farmer; and two of the blacksmith, Mr. Davy, whose
anvil was undoubtedly ringing at that moment with the
hearty strokes of his hammer; and all four of the storekeeper, Mr. Moore ; and the only little girl of Dr. Sillby ; and —— Well, not to enumerate them one by one,
Amy found that she could count sixteen ; and sixteen
was a highly promising number, too, she thought, to make
a beginning with.   Her heart rejoiced, on looking round
upon her little flock ; and she knew how many kind and
generous words the good clergyman and his wife had
spoken for her through the village.

The forenoon slipped away before she was aware of it.
Those three hours of the morning, that sometimes drag so
slowly for many and many an instructor, for Amy were
crowded with real delight.   She thought she should ex-
aggerate in no wise, nor affect in the least a happiness
that she did not possess, if she confessed that those three
first hours of her school-keeping life were the pleasantest
she had known in a long, long time.

When the village bell rung for noon, she found a row
of eager eyes glistening all round the room in expectation of release; and she dismissed them with a pleasant
word, bidding them come early to school again in the

afternoon, and wishing them a happy play time during the intermission. And Amy went home herself to dinner, scarcely conscious whether she walked or ran all the way.

"How do you come on?" Mrs. Gummel asked her, with a face expressive of the deepest interest in her undertaking.

"O, so famously! You ought to drop in and see for yourself what a perfect queen I am there among my little subjects."

"Well, well, if I ain't glad enough for it! But how many of them did you get together this morning?" she pursued. "What number do you count, to begin with?"

"Sixteen," answered Amy, her eyes dilating with pleasure. "Only think of it, Mrs. Gummel."

So Mrs. Gummel did stand a moment, and did think of it. At length she seemed to comprehend the whole of the matter, and exclaimed to Amy, extending her left hand towards her as she spoke, —

"That's a good beginning, Miss Lee. That's really better than I dared to hope for."

And with a few additional words of a congratulatory character, she begged her to sit down with herself and Henry to dinner, for it was quite ready.

Not long after dinner, — for Amy felt as if she could not stay at home quietly while she was so deeply interested in her new charge, — she threw on her shawl and bonnet again, and hurried away to her occupation. As

she drew near the old school house, she saw her little
flock at play about the building — the girls, some of
them, at mimic housekeeping under one of the brown
stone walls, and the boys at more active games on the
turf. Their faces were glowing with health and happiness. As soon as they caught sight of her, they involuntarily ceased from their more boisterous sport, and stood
around seemingly in doubt whether to be more pleased
or afraid at her approach. They did not yet fully understand her nature.

Amy was quick to perceive their hesitancy, and not less
quick to set their feelings in motion again in the right
direction. So she went round among the various groups,
asking them what they were playing at, putting her hand
beneath some few of their dimpled chins to get a better
view of their bright faces, telling them that some day she
meant to come out herself and romp with them a little
while, and offering such remarks as would naturally be
most pleasing and conciliatory to them.

And after she had gone into her school room, even, she
was obliged by the beautiful attractiveness of the sight to
pause before a window, and regard them at their enjoyment. She thought of her own childhood, lost in the past
forever; that glowing season of life, when there is nothing
but a warm and bursting imagination to sketch the world
with so attractively; that time of pomps and shows, evermore marching in stately and bewildering procession forward — forward — we know not and think not whither.

Many were the lights, and many, too, the shadows, that
sailed like straggling clouds at that moment over the
heaven of her soul. She could easily go back — O, so
easily! But to come forward, to hurry on, to leave the
beautiful and romantic past behind, and to realize that it
was all — all gone, and she at this very moment standing in the midst of hearts as young as hers had been, —
standing among them, not to romp and play in the gentle
spring winds, as they were playing, but to teach them to
regard her as their instructor, as gifted with a wisdom and
an experience that did not belong at all to them, — this
was a something to call up her deepest feelings from their
wonted hiding-places, and almost extort a sigh that these
blessed days had departed forever.

Presently, to break the web of these sadly delicious
feelings, she stepped to the door and called them in.
There was not one, she observed with pleasure, who hesitated or delayed as soon as the call was given. They
came trooping in through the little door, fairly surround-
ing her. Their eyes were glistening; their faces were
ruddy and glowing; they were smiling and laughing with
one another; and the best of humor seemed to prevail
among them all.

Soon after seating them, and when they had managed
to get rested a little from the fatigue of their playground
sports, Amy stepped to the front of them, and gave notice
that she was going to teach them to sing. This intelligence was received immediately with marked evidences

of delight. She saw she had struck the right chord, and
knew that harmony would come out of it. And in the
course of the afternoon, she began that series of primary
lessons in vocal music, which eventuated in so much good
to her youthful pupils, and such increased happiness to
herself.

At nearly the close of the afternoon exercises, the minister came in. He told Amy he had merely called to see
what success she started with, and to help her on in her
undertaking with a pleasant word or two. She thanked
him many times for the kind interest he had taken in her
welfare, adding that it was her intention to stop at the
parsonage on her way home at night, and inform him of
the exact state of things. Both agreed that so good a
beginning was sufficient cause for self-congratulation, and
highly encouraging for continued effort.

Then Mr. Parsons — whose appearance among them the
children all seemed to welcome with unaffected pleasure —
proceeded to talk with them while they were sitting on
the benches, and to tell them the reason why their mothers
and fathers sent them to school, and to explain why they
ought to love their teacher and each other.

And he went on in that agreeable strain to them, illustrating his remarks by pleasant stories and most apt anec-
dotes, showing what the worth of knowledge was to every
one; and how little it was worth, too, without a kind
temper, a sweet and gentle disposition, and a pure and
noble heart. " Unless your *heart* is educated," he said to

them, " all the education you can give your head will but serve at length to make you more wretched and miserable." Mr. Parsons was one of the clear-sighted men in this world who understand how much greater the soul is than the mere intellect, and how like a disease the culture only of the latter in time grows to be.

At the close of the school hours, therefore, he offered a brief and feeling prayer before the pupils, and they received their dismissal. There was many a one who said aloud, on getting out into the open air again, " I shall come all the time Miss Lee keeps." And many a one reported in an excited manner to his or her parents that night of the delight they experienced in that first day's schooling under the new teacher.

Amy and the clergyman walked slowly homewards, conversing upon the promises and prospects. Not a single proper opportunity did she suffer to pass unimproved, that allowed her to express in any way her gratefulness to him for his sympathy and counsel. Already, as they walked on, she felt as if she had known him for years. It suggested itself to her thoughts that she had found a valuable friend where she had least been looking for one. While she was oppressed in secret with the haunting fears of loneliness and friendlessness, she made the discovery that the best of friends had suddenly been raised up for her on every side. And in deep thankfulness her heart lifted itself to God, ascribing to him the welcome, welcome whole.

11

Leaving Mr. Parsons at his own gate, she tripped along over the grassy street with a light foot and a much lighter heart. She felt as if joy was all around and within her. She loved every one whom she in that tumultuous moment could think of. She would have embraced all her friends, all the world, and called them each one "dear brother" and "dear sister." As her eyes chased the colors that streamed in such delicate tints along the sky, or lost their glances in amazing bewilderment among the green sprays of the trees that lined the village street, or looked down to admire the soft carpet of grass that Nature had spread so carefully for her feet, she wished for nothing but to clasp her hands together in ecstatic delight, and pray that all the world might be as happy as she.

Mrs. Gummel and Henry both received her narratives respecting this auspicious day's labor with a great deal of interest; the former — good woman! — continually interrupting Amy with such rapid and fervent exclamations of joy as came first to her tongue. She said she could not really have believed that Amy was to have such good luck at the very beginning of it; and yet she always *knew* that the people of Valley Village were not a kind that would let such a needful enterprise as this go a-begging.

And between congratulations and plans, sketching outlines of what was to come, and dwelling thankfully upon what had already occurred, the evening soon passed away.

Amy's prayers that night came from a heart filled with a joy that was unspeakable; for she felt as for a long time the weakness of our poor humanity would not let her feel — that God had indeed drawn very nigh her with his all-providing, all-protecting hand.

CHAPTER XI.

LEAVES FROM A JOURNAL.

For some little time past Amy had kept a journal; over which she sat down at her table, and from day to day indulged in the pleasure of a free and untrammelled intercourse with herself; making for her own eye alone such confessions as her heart daily had to give up, and mingling wish with experience, prayer with regrets, and speculation with fresh narrative so intricately, that in order to get at the one it was necessary to read it page by page, keeping swift company with her changing thoughts and feelings.

I shall assume the liberty of believing that occasional extracts from this journal will be welcome to the readers of this narrative of her experiences; much more so, indeed, than the mere history which my own pen has attempted to delineate, inasmuch as the former are brought away directly from her innermost life and from the depths of her being.

Such extracts as the following are presented to the reader in this place : —

"*Sunday night.* This is my first Sunday in this little village. If I only *liked* it before, I must confess I am *in love* with it now.

" Went to church all day, and enjoyed exceedingly the devotional exercises. The discourses from the clergyman — Mr. Parsons — were most excellent. The one in the forenoon took hold upon my feelings in particular. He gave us such beautifully flowing descriptions of God's unmeasured goodness, as discoverable in the world about us, I almost wished he would go on in that strain till nightfall. His burning words moved and melted me. When I brought home to my own heart so many proofs of its thankless feelings, of its forgetfulness of Him who sustains me from hour to hour and day to day, of its disposition to rise up and desire for itself a good that is at war with his most fatherly designs, I saw too plainly in what a slough of despondency I should always lie, unable to help myself in the least out of its treacherous depths, unless I corrected my former thought at once, and acknowledged only him to be my Lord and Father.

" O the power and the beauty with which the outer world testifies to the benevolence of God! If we would but behold and read the pages that are written thickly with lessons for us on every hand! If we would put off this vanity, this selfishness, this feeling that we are something of ourselves, and become learners like little children; live only the life that a deep and holy faith directs; cease to be proud of our own external possessions, or our inter-

11 *

nal attainments, feeling that we can be nothing and do nothing except the Father shines through us; learn, first of all, faith, and then love, and then patience, — how much more spiritual indeed would the world become, producing works that would more and more abound to its own glory and the glory of the Father!

"I am sitting alone to-night in my little chamber, with nothing to interrupt the course of my thoughts. They will take me back and away to the other times, and the other scenes, but the sorrow does not darken; it only shades. I repose so joyfully at this hour in the arms of my kind Father, no earthly dispensation can make my heart rebellious against Him by whose ordering it is. I feel that what is for my good will surely come to me; and none the less shall I greet it because I do not follow my own short-seeing desires in its pursuit. God knows, and God orders. I am assured that 'he doeth all things well.'

"This sweet little village I trust I may find a nursery for my better thoughts. The silence that perpetually reigns about the place, broken only by the occasional shouts of glad children, is very sweet indeed to me. I am glad to be rid of the stunning rattle of carts, and the cry of strange voices. This brooding stillness is like a balm; and I know it will heal a spirit that has already been wounded as mine has. I always had a desire to taste the pleasures of a rural life, and at last I am gratified. But in no one thing have I yet been able to see such a marked difference between the city and the country as in

the observance of this day that has drawn to its close.
Here Sunday is truly a blessed and a beautiful time. It
forms a festival day indeed for the soul. I have had such
feelings stirred within me by what I have seen and been
surrounded with to-day, as I never thought belonged to
my being. The stillness seems so holy. The very atmosphere encircles you with a spirit of praise and prayer.

" *Monday night.* It is quiet every where. I do not
hear so much as a sound all over the street. When I put
aside my curtains to look out the window, I can see three
or four lights on the opposite side, half concealed by the
thickening foliage of the trees ; and I think of those who
are sitting by them, either reading, or chatting, or sewing.
These are pleasant sights to eyes that delight to look into
human hearts. They draw me more than crowds, or art-
ful pictures, or tumultuous enjoyments. About many a
table, I know, are gathered the loving inmates of these
households, whose thoughts are knit closely in bands of
affection. They are talking with one another at this very
hour of what has been done through the day, what is
purposed for the morrow, and of how deep is their simple
devotion each to the other. I always thought I should
love this calm way of life ; but I was not prepared to find
such abundant resources of enjoyment in it. I am taught
how little and false is much of what we deem happiness
in the world, when it is looked for in outward shows and
external circumstances. How deep, how vast, how rich,
and how exhaustless are the resources of the inner life, I

cannot tell ; I am made glad beyond utterance in being
allowed to catch only a glimpse of them. I long, I love,
I hope, I aspire, in the light of these entrancing gleams
from heaven, and pray with all my heart that it may all
— all become real and earnest in my daily life and conversation.

"This is the first day of my little school. I have now
begun a project that is to occupy my attention for the
entire summer ; if circumstances favor, I may even be
induced to keep this present retirement for a much longer
time. I have had more pupils than I at first thought I
should get, and try to be accordingly grateful. Good Mr.
Parsons and his wife have done a great deal more for me
than I asked, and more than I shall ever repay. They
have gone about themselves with my proposal to open a
school in the village, and laid it before all the families
where there were any children to send. And the result
is what I have seen to-day. How happy this kindness
has made me ! It opens to my sight visions of dear,
delightful friendships such as I have not before in my
whole short life experienced. And Mr. Parsons further
showed the interest he took in my new enterprise, by
walking over to the school house this afternoon, and dropping a few words of kindness both for my pupils and
myself.

"This school keeping is going to be a delightful task
to me, I know. I love so much the society of fresh and
innocent children. They make my thoughts sweet and

clean, and my heart pure. From their childish talk I
learn simplicity; and truth seems a possession that enters
not into the soul without this first condition of simplicity.

"Yet there is some sort of a sadness connected with
this occupation, or at least with my earliest experience in
it, that will not wholly take its shadow off my feelings.
How can I forget for a single moment? How can I ever
allow myself to pass over the days that are gone? How
can I cease to remember, when memory is always so
active, and sketches its pictures so vividly?

"I cannot look in the faces of these dear children of
mine — for I must begin now to call them *mine* — without feeling a strange sensation that my own childhood is
gone. It is difficult exactly to realize that such is the
truth. And yet it is not because of my dissatisfaction
with the new positions into which each new day seems to
lead me; I am calm, and contented, and, I trust for myself, entirely happy. I entertain no fears for the future,
for I am well assured that He who has created me and
brought me thus far in safety will provide; if I do but
work and live, work and live in this faith, what is there
that I *should* have reason to fear?

"But these dancing pictures of childhood will work a
mysterious influence. Even while they steal over my
thought with their strange sadness, they likewise fascinate
beyond description. I love to stand by the window, as I
did this day, and watch the little ones at play on the grass
about the school house door. I love to listen to their

merry voices, so clear, so free from deceit and distrust, so
full of a whole-hearted innocence! I love to look into
their guileless faces, and study youth, and simplicity, and
truth. They seem like good angels about my path; and
in their company I feel that I may be perpetually young.
These days are golden days to them, as they are once in
life to every one. They drop richness on the youthful
heart from sun to sun. They are filled full with joys that
linger, like the recollection of old flavors on the palate,
to the last hour of life upon the enchanted memory. I
would keep myself always young.' Not all the petty cares
and anxieties of this present life should have power to
make a single wrinkle on my face, or draw a single sigh
from my heart."

"*Wednesday.* I have taken occasion to make several
calls around the village, on the mothers of my pupils;
and they have received me, without a single exception,
with open cordiality. I felt rejoiced to find so much good
feeling around me. I can go on with a great deal better
spirit about my daily duties, and know that I am not
laboring alone. It is so pleasant to be assured of the
sympathy and coöperation of others.

"Mrs. Davy, the wife of the village blacksmith, seems
one of the best women in the world. And I am much
pleased, too, with the appearance of her daughter Mary.
She tells me she is a member of the village choir, which
makes me think a little more tenderly of her, I must confess; for music is such a refinement for the feelings, and

makes one more bond of friendship and love. I have invited Mary to come into my school whenever she would, and help us at our singing exercise in the afternoon. How much I could enjoy any thing like that!"

" *Thursday.* Such beautiful weather as we are having is beyond the expectations of all. People say it is an uncommonly forward season; and, little as I am able to judge of the fact from my acquaintance with rural affairs, I should think that such was the case.

" It delights me to go out to my little school in the morning, feeling the freshness of this balmy air. The dandelions already are thick in the turf all along the village street, and the buttercups are beginning to blossom, too. It makes the grass look as if it concealed beds of gold, of which only these small and bright flecks show themselves through the dark green covering. As I walk along to school, I am as happy as the children whom I see trudging on at a distance before me. I feel as if I could start off and chase the dancing butterflies, too, and clap down my bonnet over them with quite as boisterous a joy as they.

" These maple trees are dense with their spreading and thickening shadows. I could not have believed, without seeing it for myself, what a magical change this shade has wrought for the entire street; the tender leaves, still so delicate in their deepening hues, make such a pleasant covering for the boughs, I almost wish I were myself a bird, to build my home somewhere in their airy chambers,

where I could catch the earliest glimpse of the red dawn,
or sit and watch in calmness the stars that burn in such
mysterious clusters all over the heavens at night.

" It is really a picture of repose, and none the less
attractive on that account, the men going in the early
morning to their labor in the far-off fields, driving away
cart loads of ploughs, and harrows, and chains. There is
a look of independence about them, too, that seems to be
wanting in those whom I have been accustomed to see in
the town streets. I must say I like the sign, for it con-
fesses plainly enough to freer hearts and a smaller burden
of mere worldly vanity.

" To-day I have written a letter to Mrs. Dozy, giving
her a brief account of my journey here, of what so fortu-
nately befell me on the way, and how I am getting on. I
think the good woman will rejoice for me with her whole
heart; for I took my leave of her in such a confused state
of feeling, that she could not discover the resignation and
courage I tried all the while to exhibit — but, alas! exhibited so poorly at the best. I hope Mrs. Dozy, when
she receives this letter, will be somewhat comforted. I
have told her where I find the strength that sustains me
through all that comes, and how freely it flows into my
heart for the earnest asking. There need be nothing in
this world to fear; if we put the foolish croakings and
warnings of those who have no faith behind us altogether,
we may be strong, and courageous, and filled with comfort to the end of our days."

CHAPTER XII.

SATURDAY AFTERNOON.

THREE weeks had gone already. It was now the very last of May. And so rapidly had the season advanced, that the earth was teeming with the beauties that had burst from its soil, and Nature seemed to go reeling under her load of blossoms and flowers.

Amy had become acquainted personally with the parents of every one of her pupils, visiting them as soon after opening her school as she could find time. The impressions she had at first entertained respecting them were daily confirmed and extended. They promised her all the assistance she could desire in her work. They offered her such pleasant counsel as would make her feel most easy among them. They spoke words of encouragement, and affection, and deep sympathy.

The school itself thrived steadily. There were now twenty-two pupils, and she did not desire to have any more if she could. The children all learned at an early day to love her, feeling a trust in her affection such as childhood every where desires to repose in its elders and superiors. She paced the floor of her miniature domain

12

with a light step; for her heart was in her work, and sho
was happy. It is to be questioned if even the young
scholars themselves were at any time of gayer spirits
than she.

As she stood day after day and talked so affectionately
to them all, or sat in that old-fashioned chair with a flag
seat and heard them severally read, or spell, or recite the
wonderful discoveries they had made among the two dozen
and more letters of the alphabet, she looked indeed a
picture of perfect happiness and contentment. Amy Lee
possessed a talent for that which would much outshine
her present humble employment, and she very well knew
it. But she had thoroughly searched her heart; she had
studied with close attentiveness all the habits of her
mind; she had considered the insidiousness with which
a particular sorrow is often apt to make its way into the
inner recesses of the nature; and this was the simple, but
highly useful occupation she had chosen, by whose quiet
pursuit she knew she could best promote her happiness.
To-day she was glad to teach an infant school; to-morrow
she would be as glad to perform any other duty that
offered, even were it less in the estimation of the vain
world than this. Amy tried not to live to opinions, but
to herself. In this way alone could she get at the life
that has the real truth in its heart. Thus she dwelt at
the very centre of her being, and not at the circumference;
and the central heart would be more sure now to radiate
to the surface, and thence to the lives of those around her
in all possible directions.

These Saturday afternoons, in her own school days, were the blank half pages in the little book of the week. Then she used to look forward to them, she remembered, with a dancing heart. That was the time when she played with the other children in silent garrets, if it happened to rain, or in delightful gardens and back yards, if it was pleasant. The recollections of the house-playing scenes, when pies were made from mud and baked on pieces of shivered plates and saucers, and when they all used to sit down round a large rock and drink as many cups of tea as they supposed themselves capable of holding; of the rides she used to take with her playmates in a highly imaginary way, crossing the country, water not excepted, at a rate that would almost put the style of telegraph travel out of conceit with itself; and of the dear old garrets under whose eaves she had repeatedly crawled, listening with a fast-beating heart to the mystery of the rain, — all such endeared recollections swarmed about her at times like these, and she almost felt as if she must call out for the companions that had since departed and died.

Amy was fond of living over her enjoyments yet a second time, and a third. She held that a pleasure repeated was as good as a new pleasure. And she also held with that, that of all our pleasures none were capable of yielding so rich a store of delight as those which in themselves were the very simplest.

So she bethought herself, it being the last Saturday

afternoon in May, to take a stroll over the village northward, and up among the slopes of the higher lands, and by
herself to live over again the old and happy times of her
childish days. She got along as far as the school house,
however, and could not go by; it seemed really impera-
tive that she should just cast a look in at the window,
and see how still the place appeared.

While she was standing and indulging her fancies in
their idle waywardness, the sound of footsteps fell on her
ear, and turning about, she discovered one of her own
pupils coming round the corner of the building. It was
little Susy Moore. The child did not at first see her,
but was walking forward with her hands behind her, and
her eyes to the ground. She seemed in a highly contemplative mood.

"Why, Susy!" exclaimed Amy, in surprise.

The child stopped suddenly and looked up. There was
such an expression of mixed surprise and delight in her
countenance, Amy could hardly restrain herself from rush-
ing forward and catching her up in her arms.

"Dear little one," said she, "what are you doing here
all alone?"

"Looking for Charlie," answered the girl. "Have you
seen Charlie, Miss Lee?"

"No, I haven't. Has he been here with you this
afternoon?"

"We came over to the school house to play," said
Susy. "All the other girls were coming, too. And

brother Charlie came with me when I came. Haven't you
seen Charlie, *truly*, Miss Lee ? "

"Indeed I haven't," answered Amy a second time.
" But I will help you hunt for him, though. Where do
you suppose he went ? "

"I don't know. He's run away ; and mother said, if
he didn't stay with me, I must come home."

"I'm afraid you will have to go home, then. Poor
little Susy ! Your brother shouldn't leave you in this
way — should he ? We'll find him if we can, at any
rate."

So Amy took her by the hand, and hunted about in
every direction for the roguish delinquent. First they
went to the opposite wall, and Amy looked over it up and
down its length as far as she could see. Then they approached the street, and gazed one way and the other.
Then Amy searched in all directions about the school
house. But to no purpose. Nothing whatever was to be
discovered of the runaway.

"How strange this is !" said Amy, as if talking to
herself; and immediately they turned the back corner of
the building.

A little, dark, doubled-up object presented itself to
their sight just as they got round the other side, and Amy
half started with surprise.

As she hesitated a moment · to learn what it could be,
whom should her eyes fall on but the roguish little brother

12 *

of Susy, his head bent considerably downwards, and his
jacket pulled completely over it !

The instant Susy recognized him, she let go of Amy's
hand, and ran up to him, pulling his head out of its
hiding-place, and commencing playfully to upbraid him
for his faithlessness.   When he looked up and saw who
was with his sister, he hung his head for shame.   He did
not know what to say, or where to begin.

"You shouldn't hide away from your little sister —
should you ?" Amy asked him, scarcely able herself to
keep her soberness at seeing the ludicrous situation in
which he had placed himself.

He half smiled, rubbed his shoulder against the side
of the house, worked his fingers busily together, and
looked down steadily at the ground.

"You wasn't a-goin' to run away from me — was you,
Charley ?" said Susy, throwing her arms about him as far
as they would go.

"I only wanted to *scare* her," he replied, looking a
trifle more up towards Amy's face.

"Then I'm sure I wouldn't try to scare my little sister,"
said the latter, stooping down and joining their hands.
"Play with her, but don't ever run away from her."

And thus cautioning and advising the children, Amy
amused herself with them till the other expected ones came
up.   There they straggled along, mostly girls, intent on a
good Saturday afternoon's play around the old school house.
Amy regarded them with real delight.   She knew how

much enjoyment was in all this, and again those indefinable longings for a returned childhood revisited her heart.

Perhaps she lingered and amused herself with them for half an hour. She marked out new territories for their little households; she sat and piled up cobble stones under the wall till there were no more left for her to put her hand on; and she initiated them into many novel playground mysteries they had never before heard of. And when she finally withdrew from their midst, and prepared to continue her afternoon walk wherever her eyes might entice and her feet carry her, they all formed in one silent group as she was leaving, and stood gazing affectionately after her till she was out of sight.

"O, blessed memory of childhood!" exclaimed Amy aloud, getting on a little over the grassy road. "How sweet it is to the human soul! How sweet it is!"

Her course conducted her a long distance to the northward of the village, and to the point where the mountains began to come down and meet in the road. She came to the old bridge, made so roughly of heavy logs and timbers, and stopped in the middle of it, leaning on the rail. It was a still hour, and a still scene. The water below flowed tranquilly and silent. She could scarcely catch the sound of a gush or a gurgle from either shore. The green boughs were some of them dipping in the limpid current, and lifting themselves slowly and with a graceful motion. So still was the hour, so quiet the scene, so tranquil every association that feeling or memory flung about her, she

felt that she could remain there till the evening shadows
trooped down the mountains, and live many and many a
rich experience in the time that would pass so swiftly.
She leaned her arm on the rude rail of the bridge, and
her head on her hand.

"It is like human life — like my own life," her lips
involuntarily murmured, while she looked down into the
stream. "So swift, so smooth, so noiseless." And with
tears in her eyes at length she turned away.

Striking into a wild-looking meadow, or pasture land,
from the road, she climbed among rocks and brambles,
ascending greenly carpeted slopes and toiling up ascent
after ascent till her breath grew quite short and difficult ;
when she finally sat down upon a natural cushion of moss
that tufted a rock close at hand, and in the shadow of a
young walnut tree gazed off over the village. She found
she had attained to quite a height, even a greater one
than she had expected that afternoon to reach.

There lay Valley Village almost at her feet. It was a
beautiful cluster of plain and unpretending houses, whose
roofs were darkened by the shade of the street maples.
Only a nest of little dwellings lay hidden among those
trees, right in the lap of the quiet valley. It seemed as
if she could hold it all in the hollow of her hand.

Her delighted eyes caught the shining thread of the river
at a point just below the bridge she had so lately crossed,
and followed it onward in its winding courses, — onward
and onward still, — now half secreted by an interposing

knoll of grassy earth, now plunging itself into the sleepy shadows of entangling bush, and brake, and brier, till it swept along by the village in its bright career, and debouched into the basin far down, where the great water wheels of the mills were daily fed with its dashing power.

Behind her still rose the greater heights of the mountain, afar off at their summits clothed with a dense forest. She could behold many a pile of craggy rocks beetling up in the most grand and surprising configurations, and longed already to climb them to their very peaks, and there to look abroad over the face of the extended landscape, and feel that she never, never was so free.

All around her was grass and leaves, fresh and green. Above spread the boundless blue sky, with hardly a feather of a cloud sailing across its dreamy sea. Below stretched out a broad landscape of astonishing variety, and freshness, and suggestive beauty. Not an object did her eyes alight upon that did not answer as a symbol for some corresponding emotion in her soul. She sat there entranced. Words would poorly have answered the end of conveying the varying feelings that drifted across her heart. There was but one thought within her, but one affection, but one desire; and that was of and for God.

And for one whole most enriching hour did she there silently gaze, and dream, and pray, and aspire.

CHAPTER XIII.

DOLLY TATTERAGS.

ONE of her pupils remained with her a while, after school was out one afternoon in early June, and seemed waiting to communicate something. The child was the daughter of a farmer at the northern part of the village, and Amy called her Ann Rackett.

"Are you waiting for me, Ann?" asked Amy, turning round in surprise to find she had staid so long after all the others had gone.

The little one hesitated, and began to pull at her apron by way of working off some of her embarrassment.

Amy stepped nearer, and took hold of her hand to encourage her.

"What does Ann want with me to-night?" she asked again, in a kind voice. "Does she want to say any thing to me?"

"If you please, ma'am — if you please ——"

And there the young thing stopped.

"Well, then," encouraged Amy, "*what* if I do please? Don't be at all afraid to tell me what you wish to, Ann. Come, let us sit down together on this bench here, and then you shall tell me all about it. Now, what was it you wanted me to do, if I pleased ? "

With an effort the child got it finally all out.

" *Dolly* wants to come to school," said she. " I told her so much about you, she wants to come, too."

" But who is Dolly ? That is somebody I have not yet seen ; Dolly who ? "

" Dolly Tatterags," she answered, looking up into her teacher's face as with surprise that she did not understand what " Dolly " meant.

" Well, but who is Dolly Tatterags ? Can't you tell me ? Where does she live ? "

" 'Way up over the hill," answered the child, pointing in that direction with an outstretched arm.

" Has she got a mother, then, and a father ? " asked Amy.

" O, yes ; and a good many brothers and sisters, too."

" Well, but why doesn't she *come* to school, then ? Are you sure she wants to ? "

" O, I know she does," said the child, gathering confidence. " She told me so herself. I *know* she wants to come."

" Do you live near where she does ? "

" It's a good way further over to her house ; but she comes to our house sometimes, and then she and I play together."

" Well, will you tell her, the next time you see her, that she is welcome to come to school, and that I shall be

glad to have her come ?   Will you tell her that, and that
I say so ? "

"Yes, ma'am ; but — but ———— "

And then a silence.

"But *what*, child ?   Don't you want to tell her what
I say ? "

"O, yes ; but — but her father's so poor."

It all flashed over Amy, and a sweet fountain sent its
living waters gushing out from her heart.

"Dear child ! " she softly and tenderly exclaimed.   "Is
that the reason why she doesn't come?   Is *that* the only
reason — because her father is *poor* ? "

"She says she wants to come dreadfully, and learn
something, like the other girls ; but her mother told her
they couldn't afford to send her, and so she says she tries
to stay at home.   But she *wants* to come, and she told me
so ; and I didn't know what to do."

"Did she ask you to say any thing to me about it ? "
inquired Amy.

"O, no ; she only said that she would like to come so
much.   I'm sorry her father is so poor ; I love Dolly
Tatterags very much."

Amy instinctively drew the child nearer to her heart.

"Then she didn't tell you to say any thing to me about
coming to school ? "

"O, no, ma'am ; no, ma'am."

"And you thought of it all yourself, did you, dear
Ann ? "

The little one hung her head, not certain but she had done something entirely wrong.

"You are a *good* girl, Annie," said Amy; "and you shall go and tell her that she may come to school if her father *is* poor. She needn't stay away for that. Now, will you bring her with you by next Monday? Will you .promise not to come without her?"

Little Ann looked too delighted to speak. Her eyes were glowing with pleasure.

"Tell her Miss Lee says she may read and spell with all the other children, and learn to sew and sing, too. She needn't pay any thing for it, either. She may come just as much as if her father wasn't poor. Now, do you think you can tell her that? Do you think you shan't forget any of it?"

"I guess I can," quickly answered the delighted girl. "O, I know Dolly'll be *so* glad to go to school. I know she will."

And without further ceremony, forgetful where she was or with whom she was talking, little Ann Rackett skipped out of the school room, and skipped like a young cricket off home.

It was one of Amy's ways to produce as much happiness with her limited facilities as possible. The instant the child left her again to herself, she resolved to go over and see the Tatterag family between then and Monday morning herself. Ann might first have the boundless satisfaction of communicating such unexpected intelligence

13

to little Dolly and her mother; but she likewise would herself enjoy the delight of making them happy. This was one little instance of Amy's kind considerateness.

The first thing to be done, therefore, on reaching home, was to ask Mrs. Gummel all about the history and situation of the Tatterags. She had her feelings suddenly enlisted in their behalf. The very name of their child pleased her in a manner that it would be impossible to explain. She knew there was a something about them that drew her sympathies. And then she told Mrs. Gummel, too, about the way in which their names had been first brought to her notice.

"Well," began her friend, eager to impart such information as was needed most, "Ann Rackett has told you truly enough that they are *poor*. Mr. Tatterags himself is a woodchopper. He goes out into the forests in winter, and works for the farmers, chopping the logs they carry to market the next winter. It's a hard way of getting a living, I do suppose," added Mrs. Gummel; "but it seems to be what he's best fitted for. And people all say he's a good hand at woodchopping. I've had him cut up many a wood pile for me."

"He can get work enough, then?" asked Amy.

"Why," said Mrs. Gummel, "I suppose so; but he's intolerably *lazy* — not dissolute, that I ever heard of, but indolent, without any sort of calculation, and indisposed to do any more work than barely enough to help him along. And his wife, too, isn't thought to be any different. She's what we call a 'complaining woman.' Nothing ever goes right with her. She is always finding fault with her husband and with whatever happens; forever brooding over the worst side of things, and making a bugbear for herself out of nothing at all. I do not say this to slander her, for that is certainly not my wish; but every body knows just how it is, and you have asked to know only what is so generally understood."

" But how many children have they ? " pursued Amy, growing more thoughtful.

" There are more than half a dozen of them, I know; but how many more, is really more than I can tell you. You'll find the number usual for very poor people, I think, however."

" I'll go over and see them myself Saturday afternoon," said Amy, "and learn if I can do any thing for them.. This little Dolly shall certainly come to school, if she will, money or no money; that's the last thing for *me* to think of."

The time between then and Saturday went off rapidly and quietly. The next opportunity she had she asked Ann what Dolly said to the message she carried her.

" She said she didn't believe her mother'd let her come now," answered the child.

" Not let her come! But why not? Doesn't her mother want Dolly to learn all she can ? "

" But Dolly's afraid you won't like her, after she's got here ; and she told me so herself."

" Don't *you* like her ? "

" I guess I do," she answered smilingly.

" Then don't you think *I* shall ? "

" I told her you would, and how you wanted to see her
at school 'long with the other girls; but she's afraid; she
says she don't know; and she don't dare to ask her
mother any thing about it, for she feels so sure her
mother'll make her stay at home with the rest of 'em."

" Well, never mind," said Amy; "I think we will
manage to get her here in *some* way."

Early on Saturday afternoon, therefore, she left her
room to walk over to the residence of the Tatterags. Mrs.
Gummel had directed her with all possible particularity,
so that there was little danger of her missing her way.
The route lay not far from the walk Amy took before, as
described in the last chapter, only that she would be
obliged to climb the opposite hill from the one she then
climbed.

The afternoon was delicious and inspiring. The air
was not at all too hot, but occasional draughts fanned her
temples and face, and kept her continually refreshed. If
she walked a little too fast at any time, as soon as she
felt fatigued she sat down upon a rock or a stone until
she was rested again.

She crossed the bridge, but not without stopping as
before to lean on its rail, and gaze for a few minutes
thoughtfully into the stream that swam below. In that
place, and in that position, the same sweet and holy

feelings flowed like that clear current through her heart. She caught glimpses of the same beautiful dreams dancing in the water, and saw heaven in the same blue and almost cloudless sky that threw its deep concave far, far beneath the bed of the stream.

As she passed on, she found the narrow road that Mrs. Gummel had been so careful to describe conducting her up the high lands on her left. She turned in at once, and went on resolutely. At one time she was pacing a level of quite considerable breadth and extent; then she came to a steep acclivity, where mossy rocks and trunks of old trees were confusedly piled together, but through which the narrow cart path carried her with due precision and regularity. She toiled along with wonderful courage, and felt that the task was good for her. The odors from the pines that in spots were sprinkled around invigorated her lungs. She feasted on the fragrance of the wild flowers that were hidden by thousands among the trees and rocks. She felt a sense of new physical power, as the draughts of air came whirling down from the old mountain top, and saluting her eyes, her cheeks, her forehead, and her lips. Her thoughts danced in perfect harmony, and her pulses tripped to a perfect tune, as she sat down from time to time during the ascent, and gazed in mute rapture over the living landscape of June.

Walking and stopping, toiling and resting, thinking now of one thing and now of another, she finally reached a broad steppe, over which the road still conducted her, and

13 *

afterwards wound with a sudden turn around the sharp
shoulder of the mountain. The view from this natural
terrace was of all others most enchanting; it was more to
Amy's soul — it was sublime. She sought a convenient
resting-place after so much persevering travel, and sat
down a few moments to enjoy the sight that so filled her
eyes and her heart.

  " O that there were some dear one here, to share all
this beauty with me !" exclaimed she aloud. " To have
it only to myself, to be alone in a place like this, — who
would wish it ? I would tell something of my rapture to
the heart of another, that is enchanted just like mine."

  While she still sat there, viewing the magnificent scene
around her, she was startled by hearing what she thought
the cry of a child. It sounded very faint, and not very
near. She erected her form and listened attentively.

  Again she heard it ; and again. And now she was certain from what direction it came. Still intent to catch
every variety of the cry, and perceiving that it continually
came nearer and nearer, she turned to look towards the
spot where the path turned the sharp angle of the mountain, and in a very short time discovered the cause of her
alarm.

  There was a little girl coming round the corner at a
slow pace, with one hand to her eyes, crying bitterly.

  Amy continued gazing at her ; for she was not only
interested to know what could be the matter, but she was
equally certain that this little thing was one of the Tat-

terag family. And she kept her seat quietly, waiting for the young stranger's nearer approach.

Along she came, but now her wail seemed to lose somewhat of its strength and volume. As she proceeded, she dropped her hand from her eyes, and began to look down over the lovely valley. It seemed as if she well knew she had got to the place where the most beauty was to be seen, and there ceased from her grief to enjoy what was always ready for her eyes.

Amy could not but be struck with the attitude and features of the child. At once she made her mind up it was Dolly Tatterags.

There she stood, keeping the posture her little figure had just assumed. She looked as if the view of such a wonderful glory had dried her tears, stopped the sobbings of her sorrow, and called upon her to admire and wonder in silence.

Her head was bare; and brown locks, curled and tangled all together, showered over her naked shoulders. She wore an exceedingly short frock of faded calico, not over-clean pantalets, and went barefooted. The sleeves, too, of her frock were short, revealing fat and pretty arms, though considerably browned by the spring winds and the summer suns.

For a minute or two she gazed in earnest thoughtfulness over the valley below. Then slowly she looked away, and turned to regard the familiar objects around her.

The very first one her eyes fell on was Amy. The latter

was looking at her as well, and saw that this sudden discovery caused her a great deal of surprise, and perhaps
fear.   So she called out to her at once, still keeping the
seat she had chosen, —

"What is the matter, my little girl?   What are you
crying so about?"

The other immediately dropped her eyes to the ground,
and commenced working her feet and toes busily.   Amy
saw that she was somewhat in fear of her, as well as
embarrassed; and she got up and went to her.

"Won't you tell me what your name is?" she asked,
taking her by the hand.

"It's Dolly," was the answer, though the child still
kept her eyes upon the ground.

"Dolly, is it?   Well, I thought it was," said Amy.
"And Dolly is a very nice name, too, for a little girl;
don't you think it is?"

Now the child took courage to look up timidly, though
not yet into Amy's face, and smile as faintly as her small
courage would suffer her.

"What is the rest of your name?   Can't you tell me?"
Amy pursued, putting one hand under her brown chin.
"Dolly what?"

"Dolly Tatterags."   It came out round and full.

"Well, I thought it might be you, after all.   I have
heard of you before, I guess; and you have heard of me,
too.   Don't you know little Annie Rackett?"

In reply to this, the eyes of Dolly met those of her

interrogator with a most expressive sparkle and glow.
The child's eyes were a beautiful dark blue; and Amy
saw how radiant they were at the first glance.

"Aren't you the little girl who wanted to come to my
school?" asked Amy, now holding her hand in both her
own, while she stooped down that she might the better
watch the working of her features.

"Yes, ma'am," she answered timidly.

"And you're coming, aren't you? I told Annie to
tell you to be sure and come Monday, if you didn't before.
Did she tell you what I said about it?"

Dolly assured her faintly that she did.

"Well, then, wasn't you coming?"

The tears again stole into the child's eyes, and Amy
thought she had never seen such a picture of returning
sorrow.

"Why, what is the matter? What *is* the matter?
And what was it you was crying about just now, when
you came round the corner?"

The little stranger's bosom now began to heave, her lip
to quiver again, and in spite of herself she soon sobbed
aloud. The tears ran down her cheeks, and dropped in
the grass at her feet.

"Why, won't you tell me what it is that troubles you
so much?" Amy insisted, caressing her affectionately.
"You mustn't cry so, for it won't do you any good.
Come, tell me all about your trouble, and let me see if I
can't do something now to make you feel better. Come;

what is it? Why do you cry so? Won't you tell me, now?"

A moment the child hesitated. Then she told the whole in a single sob of a breath.

"Mother says I shan't go to school with the other girls."

And she began to cry as hard as she could cry.

Amy drew her to her arms, and continued for a long time trying by every method to soothe and pacify her. She told her that she would go home with her, and see her mother, and ask her to let her go. She promised to do all she could to induce her parents to accede to her proposal, and had no doubt they would listen to what she would have to say about it.

And so after a time she stopped crying, while Amy wiped away the tears with her own handkerchief. But her little bosom still heaved with the quick-drawn sobs, and the cloud still rested on her face, shading it with a look of sorrow.

CHAPTER XIV.

THE TATTERAG FAMILY.

WHEN Dolly had become entirely calm, Amy rose and walked with her guidance in the direction of the home of her parents.

After coming to this angle, or shoulder, of the mountain's side, she could see that the road conducted in a still more devious course, leading them rather down than up the slope, and into a small copse of live oaks, walnuts, and chestnuts. As soon as they had passed through that, she discovered that a broad extent of open field spread out before her, swelling gently with risings of verdure-covered land, on which there were few or no trees, and the whole picture of which in her eye was a smoothly-rounded and evenly-sloping bit of landscape. Its appearance was wonderfully soft and inviting.

Round the inner edge of this tract the road skirted, which they persistently pursued, talking pleasantly all the way. At length, as they came to a particular spot where more stones than usual seemed to be scattered about the ground, Dolly suddenly interrupted her companion's talk, by exclaiming, —

"There! We must turn in here."

Scattered trees grew on that side the path, and they at
once turned into the track that made its dark, broad line
through them. Their way was still downwards, till they
came out from the midst of the trees all at once on a little
clearing that bore marks of human occupancy. Amy
looked with all her eyes; and straight before her stood
a little, story-and-a-half brown house, neither shingled on
the roof nor clapboarded at its sides, with a stone chimney
rising from the middle of it, and the low door, which was
exactly the dividing line of the dwelling's front, standing
wide open.

There was an apology for a fence around the front yard,
that had been made by separate contributions of rail,
stones, brushwood, and old boards, on the inner side of
which, and to the right and left hand of the house, lay
what might charitably be admitted a garden. There were
a few hills of scraggy beans in this enclosure, trying the
best they could to clamber without assistance up the
jagged, ragged, unseemly, and irregular little platoon
of freshly-cut birch bean poles; also, some hills of
squashes, that thrust their big golden blossoms through
the insufficient fence, offering half their eventual products
to any stragglers who might chance to be going that way
when their full ripeness had overtaken them. And Amy
could see hills of corn, and of potatoes, and a little
patch here and there of some other esculent, known thereabouts as so many different specimens of "garden sarse."

It was all very well indeed, but it lacked the essential look of tidiness. A pig was running around at his pleasure outside the fence; and the one-sided gate was fastened as far as it could be with a curled-up leather strap, hitching over a rusty nail in the post.

Dolly let go Amy's hand, and ran forward to open the gate. As they passed up to the door, their feet fell on hard-worn ground, smooth as the paths in an old ropewalk. Chickens were running around the yard, and in and out the door. Dolly kept considerably ahead, and began to run about and cry, "Shoo! shoo!" to them, waving her arms and hands.

They went through the door, and Amy stood next in a little square entry, the boards beneath her feet yielding to every pressure occasioned by her moving. The little girl went into a room at the right, and Amy could hear her say in a rather low voice, —

"Mother! mother! there's somebody here; there's somebody to the door, mother!"

"Good land! *who's* to the door, child? What does he want? Tell him Israel ain't to home."

Amy, seeing that the woman did not understand what was meant, was on the point of stepping forward into the room, when she caught the words of Dolly again, and hesitated.

"It ain't a *man*, mother," said she; "it's a *lady*."

Immediately she could hear the movements of the child's parent to make preparations for a visitor.

14

" Why didn't you come and tell me of it before, child?
Land! how every thing looks here!" And then she
began to step in the direction of the door.

As she came in full view of Amy, who had till this
moment purposely secreted herself around the door post,
she stopped short in her sudden surprise, gazed vacantly
in her face, and began to smooth down her hair with the
palm of each hand.

" Good afternoon," said Amy, smiling pleasantly.

" Afternoon," answered the woman in a half whisper,
still staring at Amy, and laboring now to smooth out the
folds of her frock.

Amy thought she would wait and let her invite her in ;
but as she showed no symptoms of doing so, there was
nothing left but to begin an explanation of her errand.

" You may perhaps think it is strange that I have come
in on you in this way ; but I found your little girl over
on the mountain, and became so much interested in her
that I wanted to come and see her mother. She was crying so bitterly, I took pity on her."

" What was you crying about, Doll ? " asked her
mother, turning to where she was then standing right
behind her.

The child hung her head.

" I will tell you," said Amy, pleasantly. " In fact, I
will begin and tell the whole story."

And as Amy at this announcement made a feigned
movement as if she would like to go in and sit down, the

woman stepped back from the door which she had been blockading, and remarked with all the civility that she seemed to understand, —

"Perhaps you'll come in and take a chair."

"Thank you," offered Amy in reply. "I think I should like to; for I am very tired, climbing this mountain."

As soon, therefore, as she had occupied the chair that Dolly's mother dusted out so hastily for her, Amy cast her eyes around the apartment to get a more thorough impression of their condition, and continued, —

"Your little girl was crying so hard," said she, "I went to her to learn what was the matter. She wouldn't tell me at first; but afterwards she said it was because her mother wouldn't let her go to school with the other children."

"*That's* pretty, now — ain't it, Dolly?" said the mother, giving little Dolly a very sharp and cutting look, that made her hang her head.

"O, don't blame her at all, I beg of you, ma'am," pleaded Amy in her behalf. "I'm sure she wouldn't have told me any thing about it except for my persisting to know. She didn't want to tell me at all; but I kept begging to find out. So that *I* am in fault about it, if any one is. I certainly hope I've done no harm, for I didn't intend any such thing."

"O, no; nothing of that," the woman assured her, falling in with the agreeable tone and temper that Amy displayed. " But she needn't tell all she knows, if 'tis true."

" No, that she needn't ; but to confess the whole to you, ma'am, I had heard of little Dolly here through one of my scholars."

" Then you're the schoolmistress," interrupted the woman in great surprise. " Well, I thought you must be, the minute I set eyes on you in the door. Why, who'd ha' thought of this ? " And she looked confusedly around the cluttered apartment, as if she would give almost any thing if her visitor would step out a few minutes, and let her put the room more " to rights." Amy instantly detected her sudden embarrassment, and availed herself of the opportunity to turn her attention another way.

" I only walked over," she continued, " to beg of you, as a particular favor, — a favor to myself, — to let little Dolly come to school to me. I've heard of her, and I want to do as much for her as I can for any of the rest of my pupils. Besides, she really seems to me to *deserve* all the instruction she needs. I think she is a very promising child," she added in a lower voice.

The mother was instantly mollified.

" But we couldn't *think* of paying a quarter's schooling for a single child we've got," said she. " I don't know as you know it, but we're nothing but *poor folks* up here, and there don't seem to be much *use* in tryin'. So we give it up entirely, and are as contented as we know how to be, to say nothin' about it."

" Well, but I have come to ask if you will not allow
me to *give* her the schooling. I do not wish you to pay
me any thing. I do not need it."

" O," answered the mother, " I'm glad to see *one* person
that ain't as poor as we are. But I don't know; it's hard
gettin' along in *this* way."

" As for that matter," Amy went on, " *I* am not better
off than *you* are. I suppose *you* have to work to secure a
living, and so do *I.* So what is the great difference
between us, after all ? "

" Yes, but — but *your* work *pays* you somethin'. Now,
we're glad enough, if, with all our children, we can only
get along. We're thankful, I say, even for *that* much."

" Well," answered Amy musingly, and doubting either
the propriety or profit of pursuing that point any further
at this time, " I don't know. But why won't you just
allow Dolly to come into school with all the rest of the
children ? She may learn to read, and to sew, and to sing,
and to do whatever the others learn to do ; and you shall
be welcome to her schooling, I'm sure."

" Indeed, you're very kind, ma'am — *very* kind. But
I don't know what her father'd say to it. *Perhaps* he'd
agree to it, but I can't say."

" I rather think he would have no objections," said
Amy ; " at least, I hope not."

" The child's got no clothes," added her mother, much
softened by Amy's generous and kindly manner.

" O, yes, I have, mother," interrupted Dolly herself.

14 *

" Can't I wear my pink frock, you know? And I've got a nice sun bonnet, too."

Her mother faintly smiled, as if she was not much used to it.

" But you haven't got any *shoes*," said she, looking at the little toes that were at work on the bare floor.

" I will give her a new pair," offered Amy.

" O, you're very kind, ma'am, I'm sure."

" And I will see that she wants for nothing that will make her look tidy and comfortable. Now will you say she may come? "

" Aha ! " the mother half laughed out; " you're *very* kind, I know. I wish that half the folks hereabout were as good as you."

" Perhaps they are ; I don't know. At any rate, let *us* do right, you know, whether other people do or not. Isn't that the way? "

Her only answer was an affirmative nod of the head.

" I think you have got a delightful spot up here to live in," Amy continued, changing the course of her remarks a little. " What a fine view you get of all the village below ! "

" It ain't quite so pleasant in *winter*, I guess you'd think," the mother replied.

" That may be ; but will you tell me where any landscape view *is* pleasant in winter? I admit that you can find a great many *sublime* scenes, but none, to my mind, that are quite as enticing as those of summer. The only really delightful spot in winter, is, *I* think, one's own *home*."

The woman silently assented.

"If you let Dolly go to school this summer, I think you will find me a frequent visitor up this way. I have been so charmed with what I have seen this afternoon, that I do not really want to go down again into the valley. But I shall go with a much lighter heart, I can tell you, if you consent to my proposal. Don't you want to go to school, Dolly?"

"Yes, ma'am," the child promptly answered. And then her mother's face again broke out in one of her sickly smiles.

"I'll think about it, at any rate," said the latter, "as you've taken so much more interest in her than any body else ever did, and seein' you've been so kind as to come clear up here jest for that. I'll see what her father has to say."

Just then an infant's cry broke forth from the pine cradle in the farther corner of the room, and the mother hastened to take it up into her arms. When she had fairly got hold of it, she began to try to hush it with such family phrases and voices as had sufficed for the training of the whole line of its predecessors. Amy looked at the child's face to see if it interested her as much as Dolly did. It was very doubtful. Its eyes were as yet but half open; its hair was sticking out as if all the rest of the children had taken turns in having a good pull at it; its

dress was terribly soiled and much too short for an infant's
style of drapery ; and its face showed signs of a terrible
scarcity of water in that neighborhood.   For all this, it
was its mother's own child, and a mother's heart beat as
warmly to its little heart as if it were the child of a prin-
cess in royal arms.

Amy now beckoned Dolly to her, and suffered her to
lean against her, while she threw her own arm over the
little girl's shoulders.

" Dolly ! " sharply called out her mother, as soon as
she saw her position.   " What do you lay up on the lady
so for ? "

" O, I drew her up to me," Amy explained.   " I wanted
to talk with her a little about what she was going to do
when you let her come to school.   I am very fond of children, you see."

Dolly's mother said nothing more, affecting to be perfectly pacified ; and, in truth, there was something very
influential for her in the tones of Amy's voice.   She had
at last found one person whom she acknowledged to be
capable of persuading and dissuading her.   Perhaps it
was because Amy had set out with nothing but the simple power of love, which others may have been more chary
in exhibiting in her presence.

While this little scene was enacting, in rushed the whole
tribe, from the least unto the greatest.   Such a snarl of
them !   Such heads ! such faces ! such eyes !   How they
stopped !   How short they breathed !   How eagerly they
stared !

" Are these all yours ? " asked Amy, not a little affected with the ludicrousness of the sight.

" Yes'm," she answered ; " and a *wuss* set o' children I guess you never *did* see. Jackson ! why don't ye wipe your nose there ? " she called out to one of the boys. " Hain't ye got no handkerchief? *E*-lizabeth Tatterags ! don't you see there's a lady here ? An' do you *dare* to cut up any o' your shines now ? These children " — as if speaking to herself now — " *will* be the death of me some day, I know. Can't make 'em mind, more'n so many mules."

They stood grouped in the farther corner, staring at their sister thus leaning on Amy, and now and then ex-changing smiles and knowing looks with her. Amy could not help thinking she had never seen such a hard-looking little horde before. Of the many sights of human pov-erty she had witnessed, this stood ready to bear off the palm.

" You've a good house full, haven't you ? " she said to the mother encouragingly. " I haven't seen as many children together in one family in a long time."

The woman said, " Well, she didn't know," and smiled, and turned over the baby in her arms on its other side. Then she took another searching look over her brood, shaking her head at one, gazing with a very severe intent-ness at another, making a wry face at a third, stamping her foot at a fourth, then bestowing a. quick glance at Dolly, who still stood at Amy's side, and finally concen-

trating all her observational powers on the infant in her
arms.

"I don't see for the life of me," said she, turning full
on Amy, "how it is you manage with children. I'm sure
I shouldn't think you'd be goin' round tryin' to git *more*.
You must have your hands full all the time. How *do*
you manage with 'em, pray?"

Amy smiled.

"O, well," she returned, "I try and make them all *love*
me. I don't think there is any better way than that."

The woman seemed incredulously astonished at so simple a rule as this.

"But what if they *won't* love ye? What if they can't
be *made* to love ye?"

Her earnestness raised another smile on the countenance of Amy.

"What" — she persisted — "if there's no such thing
as love *in* 'em? All that, I think myself, is a very pretty
matter to *talk* about; but to go to work where there's
nothing to work *on*, — that's quite another affair. E-liza-
beth Tatterags! *be* still!"

This last emphatic charge was caused by the discovery
that the girl so named was busily engaged in pulling the
hair of an elder brother in the little squad, and then dodging back behind one of the others for concealment.

"I'm sure," said Mrs. Tatterags, stepping to the low
window, and stooping down to look out, "I don't see's
Isril *is* a-comin'. I don't know 'xacly *where* he is. He

may be here in a very few minutes, and he may not be home till dark; or he *may* be here in a few minutes. I shouldn't wonder if he was; and I shouldn't wonder if he warn't, too. Children, don't ye know where'bouts your father is?"

They all sounded up in a snarl of voices, —

"He's gone a-fishin', for I seen him."

"No, he hain't, nuther; for I seen him go down into the medder, with a hoe on his shoulder."

"He said how't he was a-goin' over to Mr. Rackett's, to help him grind some scythes."

The mother was confused. Amy was still more so. It was impossible to unravel a meaning from the heart of such an entangled jumble.

Some time passed, during which Amy exerted herself to reach their better feelings. She held some further conversation with the mother, urging her all the while to consent that little Dolly should be sent to school, and explaining to her in various ways how she would be the gainer by it. And seeing that there was little prospect of the father's coming home before it would be too late for her to think of descending the mountain, she rose to take her leave.

"Well," said she, at parting, "I will expect to see Dolly, then, on Monday — shall I not?"

"O, la sakes! I'm *sure* I don't know. I don't know what *to* say about it. But I'll see, when her father comes home."

"Yes, mother," pleaded the child, pulling at her gown; "*do* let me go."

Amy looked to see if her mother *would* say "yes."

"We'll see; we'll see, ma'am," added the woman. "You're very good, at any rate; and I'm not one that ever means to *forgit* such things. I wish you good day, ma'am. Good day."

In a few minutes Amy had doubled the spur of the mountain, and stood on the broad plateau, gazing at the western sky. It was beautiful indeed. The clouds were piled masses of purple and gold. They formed pavilions of matchless grandeur and glory. In the soul of the worshipful girl they awoke grand aspirations, and stirred inexpressible longings after the beauty that is hidden within the veil.

Dolly *did* come to school on Monday; and Amy expressed her pleasure by presenting her, after school hours were over, with a nice pair of new shoes, bidding her assist her mother all she could at home, and try and be as good a little girl as she knew how.

CHAPTER XV.

OLIVE ADAMS.

AMY had been home but a short time one afternoon, after having dismissed her school, when Mrs. Gummel tapped on her door, and informed her that there was a visitor below, who wished to see her.

"Mr. Parsons, I conclude," said Amy, rising, and putting away her portfolio.

"No, it's Olive Adams; Mrs. Bucclebee's niece, you know."

"Ah! I'll be right down, Mrs. Gummel! I *must* smooth out my hair a little, for I look like a fright."

Mrs. Gummel left her, and in a few minutes she was in the room with her visitor, talking away with her at a famous rate. One would think they had both been acquainted for months.

"I have been promising myself the pleasure of a call on you this long time," said Olive. "I have thought a great deal of you, and felt that you must want for society here; you have probably been accustomed to a great deal more than one would be apt to find in a place like this."

"O, no," answered Amy; "I have been very little in

15   (169)

society. I have been compelled, from my earliest days, to look chiefly for enjoyment within myself. I had the misfortune to lose my mother when I was quite young."

Olive seemed much moved by this unexpected confession.

" I am without a mother myself," said she, in a lower and a touching tone.

Immediately a strong and silent pledge of friendship had passed between them. Both motherless — both hungering and thirsting for such love as none but a mother's heart knows how to give — both abiding in the shadow of the same ceaseless sorrow — it was wholly natural that they should give each to the other her deepest sympathies without hesitation.

There was a short pause. Amy broke the silence herself.

" I suppose you have lived in Valley Village a long time," said she. " Do you not think it a charming place ? "

" O, only three years," answered Olive. " It *is* a pretty spot, as every one says who comes this way. I have become very much attached to it too. I walk a great deal, and so I think I can form a pretty candid judgment. Do you like walking ? "

" Very much ; I usually ramble away every pleasant Saturday afternoon, and at night after school I very frequently take a little stroll. My *favorite* walk is over in the direction of the bridge, at the north. I like to climb up that mountain."

" That *is* a fine walk. I have often taken it myself. But as we live more to the westward, on what one might

call a by-road, I am more in the habit of rambling across
the meadows and pastures in that neighborhood. I can
enjoy quite a pleasant view of our little village from over
there, and of the river where it runs below nearer the
mills. Then we have woods not a great way from us, and
I go into them at times, and gather wild flowers of all
sorts. I have got to be quite a botanist, I find, merely
from picking such blossoms as I fall in with in the woods."

"I should be glad to go on your little excursions with
you," said Amy. "I like nothing better in the world."

"Should you? should you? Well, if there could be
any thing more to my mind! I'm sure I should be delighted to have you. And I've been about so much alone
too, aunt begins to think I must have seen all there is
worth seeing. Sometimes she calls me a great romp."

"I shall certainly take the first opportunity," returned
Amy, "to call on you for one of these exercises. I think
you will find, too, that *I* am somewhat accustomed to it.
You'll not tire, I hope."

Her friend laughed. "Never do you fear for that,"
said she. "In fact, I do not doubt we both shall get all
the exercise that will be good for us."

"My time is not as much at my own disposal as yours
probably is," continued Amy. "But what I do have I
mean to make the most of. And there's nothing I like
more, in pleasant weather, than to ramble in the fields and
woods. I am very glad you have consented to my becoming your companion."

" I think *I* shall have more reason to be pleased with it
than *you* will," returned her companion.   " But how large
a school have you now ? "

" I count twenty-three," said Amy.

" Well done !   That's a very noisy little nest of them
— isn't it ? "

" A very *pleasant* little nest," replied Amy, smiling.
" I don't find any fault with their being *noisy*.   I rather
like it, if any thing."

" Do you, indeed ?   Well done !   But it does me good
to hear one make such candid confessions.   Now, if I like
a thing, I am always ready to say so ; and I'm none the
less backward about telling of it if I *don't* like it.   I must
say I have a partiality for candid people."

" So have I," assented Amy.   " Nothing is gained by
deceit, I verily believe.   It works its own destruction,
always."

" I wonder if *I* would make a good school teacher,"
said Olive, looking down musingly upon the carpet.
" What do you think, Miss Lee ?   It seems to me sometimes as if I wasn't doing any thing for any body.   My
idle way of life reproaches me."

" Well, I don't know.   I am not yet enough acquainted
with your feelings to tell you.   In truth, I hardly know
yet whether I am going to become a passable teacher or
not myself."

" You don't hear what people say of you then, I suppose."

Amy smiled.   It was the first praise she had received

in her new field of labor; and few can understand how sweet it was.

" Have you much patience with children? " she inquired of Olive, turning the subject. " I could tell better how good a teacher you might make after I find out that."

" Patience? Yes — no — *yes*; I declare," — and she bowed her head as she laughed aloud, — " I can't tell whether I've got any patience or not. But at any rate, when you get better acquainted with me, and with my ways, you shall find out the exact truth; and you shall tell me too. Will you promise that? "

Amy felt a little inclined to hesitate; but the manner of Olive was exceedingly affectionate and unconstrained, and they had both suffered from the same grief.

" Then you're not *always* inclined to be candid? " interrupted Olive, seeing her hesitation.

Amy's face broke out in a highly genial smile; so genial that her companion felt her heart drawn to her even more strongly than before.

" Yes, I *mean* to be candid," answered Amy. " But you must teach me one lesson in it that I've not yet learned. I hardly know how to answer you as I should."

And Olive laughed again, and the boundaries of reserve were faster and faster melting away.

Mrs. Gummel came in at this juncture, and helped along the pleasant understanding that had so naturally sprung up.

Olive was young yet, perhaps about the same age with Amy. She had received excellent training, and enjoyed

15 *

the advantages of the best schools. Her father had been
at great pains with her during his lifetime, none of which
had been relaxed by her mother. And now her aunt carried forward the work, though it must be confessed she
was hardly the same woman that Olive's mother was. She
took different views of the world; had a greater pride;
stood more on empty formularies; and made as much as
possible of social state and position. Yet withal was she
regarded as a generous woman, an excellent neighbor, and
bestowing charities with an open and ready hand.

Her niece was a sprightly and vivacious girl, a child yet
in all her feelings. If she took a sudden fancy to romp
across the fields, walls and fences stood not a whit in her
way. She was warm-hearted, frank to the last degree,
and full of the most generous impulses. What she thought
she was very apt to say without any reserve. She seemed
to keep nothing back, and best liked those who were
equally ingenuous and candid with herself.

In person, Amy saw at a single glance that her new
friend was much to be admired. With a perfectly sym-
metrical figure, she possessed a face that was full of freshness, and an eye that expressed a language never wholly
written. People would very likely have said she was
handsome; and so they could not help saying of Amy:
but the types of their personal beauty were strikingly
distinct. And this, in turn, quickened still more the
already excited sympathies on both sides, making them
first admire, and then love one another. A beautiful face

has a wonderful power. Never is it *so* powerful over the heart, as when it expresses the serenity, and the sweetness, and the love, that lie at the centre of the being. Olive had such a face, in a large degree; but Amy had it still more strikingly. It was enough, however, that they were captivated at the very first with one another. That alone promised a long and close friendship.

"I was talking with Miss Lee," said Olive, addressing Mrs. Gummel, "about what sort of a teacher I should make. What do *you* think of it ? "

" Well," answered that lady, rather evasively, " I don't know why you wouldn't make a *good* one."

" There, now! Just hear that! Now, I beg you to take Mrs. Gummel's word for it, after this, and set me down at once for a proficient in that line."

" I am very willing to, I am sure," answered Amy. " Mrs. Gummel's judgment is probably a great deal better than mine."

" Are you fond of young children ? " Mrs. Gummel further asked her.

" O, very; *very*, I assure you. Where's Henry now? Bring in Henry, and just see for yourself! " And she went off again in a merry peal of laughter.

" I think I'll offer to come over to the school house some day, Miss Lee, and assist you. How should you like a little help of that sort ? "

" O, I should be very glad to have you come in at any time," answered Amy. " If you would but like the work

as much as *I* do, there would be room for us to enter into
partnership."

"What a capital idea that would be, though! Mrs.
Gummel, how do you think the firm would sound to the
world — Lee and Adams? What do you think of it now?"

"I don't think you could get a better one," said Mrs.
Gummel. "Why don't you, seriously, try it? Wouldn't
there be scholars enough to support such a project?"

"O, don't say any thing about the *support* of the thing!
That would just spoil the whole of it. Miss Lee should
of course pocket all the profits, for hers was the enterprise.
I should be perfectly content with the office and the responsibility. Come, Miss Lee, what do you say? Let
me teach the alphabet, for instance, as I feel somewhat *at
home* in that department, and you may take care of the
balance! What do you say to it?"

"I will fall into the arrangement quite as soon as *you*
will," replied Amy, laughing with the others.

All this warm-hearted talk, offered for the very purpose
of doing away with petty reserve, and thrown off in the
glee of good spirits and the perfect abandonment of innocent delight, gave Amy at once a strong prepossession in
favor of her new acquaintance. As time passed on, they
would greatly aid one another in their feelings and aspirations. They would read the same books, view the same
landscape together, and enjoy the same rich and deep
emotions. Olive had heard much of Amy since her arrival
at Valley Village, and she thought she should find in her

the friend she wanted. And, on coming nearer, it was a source of undiminished delight that, in her first hopes, she had not been obliged to suffer any disappointment.

Olive took her leave; but not until she had extorted a promise from Amy to come over to their house on the first pleasant afternoon. "For," added she, as frank as ever, "I want aunt to know you. She will like you; and that will be good news enough for me. Will you certainly come?"

Amy promised to go after school, at no distant day.

"And it's strawberry time now," said her friend. "You love strawberries, I suppose, like all the rest of the folks. Well, only come soon, and I'll see that you get as many as you think you can eat. *Now,* will you come?" And she still held Amy's hand.

"I am fond enough of strawberries," answered the latter; "but I should need no such additional temptation, I think."

Olive blushed, smiled gratefully for so delicate a compliment, and with a friendly pressure of the hand, bade her good afternoon.

And Amy went to her room, and in her journal jotted down some of those fresh and flowing feelings that formed her new experience, with a glow at her heart that she had that day found another such a friend.

CHAPTER XVI.

IVY LODGE.

AFTER her duties for the day were concluded, early in the succeeding week, Amy locked the door of the school house, and, without going home at all, bent her steps in the direction of Mrs. Bucclebee's. As Olive had described it, and as Amy well knew, too, the house was situated on what might be termed a by-road, to the west of the main street of the village, and conducting travellers to the town that lay some seven miles away in that course. The walk was a perfectly quiet one, leading her into the most silent and solitary places. On either side, the old road was bounded by stone walls, whose tops were spotted and streaked with mosses. Broad strips of grass were growing on both sides of the wheel tracks, and the softest and greenest turf furnished a delightful carpet for the feet of the traveller.

It was a calm and almost a holy hour, as it always is in summer, at the close of the afternoon, in such still country places. Amy threw off her bonnet, swinging it carelessly in her hand. Her eyes were roving every where. They sought now the deeps of the blue heaven above her, and

now they delighted themselves with the sights of animal
life that were presented all around her. She saw gay little
squirrels leaping and frisking along on the walls, and
young cattle romping in the far-off pastures, and birds
fluttering among the leafy branches of the trees. She
caught the sound of the lowing of the kine, of the singing
of the birds, and now and then of the babbling and rip-
pling of the brooks. The fragrant air was so grateful to
her forehead, after escaping from the confinement of the
school room. She was refreshed by the odors from so
many flowers, blossoming every where in the thick, green
turf. The colors of the western sky kindled indescribable
feelings in her soul. Her spirits grew innocently gay and
sprightly. She felt a sense of gratitude continually stealing over her, that so much enjoyment was freely her own.
She would have skipped like a child, in her joy. She
would have sung, trying to imitate the outgushing chorals
of the happy birds. She longed for wings, to soar into
the blue depths that stretched away, and far away, above
her forever.

Occupied with a swift succession of such thoughts and
feelings as these, she soon found herself in the vicinity
of the place to which her feet were directed. The first
signs of it discoverable were a neat garden fence, winding
about a beautiful curve in the road. Beyond was a thick
nest of foliage ; and out from the trees she saw a couple
of chimneys. Then, as she turned the curve, she came in
full view of the house.

It was a low cottage house, built after a very tasteful
and somewhat quaint design, and inwalled with dense and
dark shrubbery. Countless evergreens had been with great
care transplanted from the woods, and were now growing
vigorously all over the yard. A neat gravel walk wound
about a circular plat of turf up to the piazza ; and as the
gate stood open, Amy without further hesitation went
through.

The nearer she went to the house, the better pleased
she was. It offered to her eyes a picture of serene contentment and calm ease. The little piazza, with the front
windows of the house reaching down to its floor, invited
her very sensibly to repose. The flower pots on the stand
look inviting and tasteful, carrying a sweet touch of nature right into the dwelling itself. The vines that twined
with so much affection about the posts robed the whole
with a grace and a beauty that were irresistible.

While she was slowly walking onward, her thoughts
intent on the many delights that offered themselves to her
senses, suddenly she observed a movement of some white
object in the bushes ; and before she was able fully to
collect herself, out bounded the lithe figure of Olive, hurrying forward with extended hand to greet her. Her face
was a perpetual smile. Her lips were rosy; and she
showed a pair of sparkling eyes that gave character to the
place itself immediately.

" O, I *thought* you'd come out to Ivy Lodge," exclaimed she. " I'm *very* glad to see you. Come — come

in at once." And she still kept hold of Amy's hand, and sought to lead her along.

"How beautiful! how beautiful!" the latter was forced to reply, before she could answer particularly to Olive's remarks. "It's like a little earthly paradise. This is poetry; this is enchantment itself."

"O, no," answered Olive, pleased with her friend's gratification; "it's nothing but a plain bit of nature, you see. We've put forth no pretensions at all. It's only what may be accomplished with a very little taste almost any where. But come in; I'll introduce you to aunt at once."

So up the short flight of wooden steps they climbed, crossed the piazza, and went in through the door around the corner. Amy was filled with secret admiration all the way. They reached a pleasant sitting room in the back part of the house, where a lady was to be seen engaged in sewing.

"Aunt!" called out Olive; "aunt!" And the lady turned her head.

Amy saw the face of a woman of middle age, fair and expressive, abounding with determination, yet full of social kindliness and grace.

"This is Miss Lee, aunt," said Olive, presenting her new friend. "I tell her I'm glad enough she's come out here, for I have none too much society in so quiet a place as this."

Mrs. Bucclebee rose and received Amy with a cordial,

16

though a somewhat stately grace, and asked her to be
seated. She spoke of the delicious summer weather, and
its influence on herself. She asked Amy how she was
pleased with her new life in Valley Village, and if she
was altogether satisfied with her little school. She had
much to say to her about the new and perhaps strange
associations that surrounded her in this calm country life,
and inquired to know if they were quite congenial to her
feelings.

Amy spoke in such an easy, candid, and unaffected
manner, in answering her questions, that Mrs. Bucclebee
could not fail to be favorably impressed with her from the
first. She rendered glowing and almost romantic accounts
of every thing around her. It would be very difficult to
say that she disliked any thing at all. She was satisfied
with her school, and more than satisfied. It even outran
her largest expectations. She had never found more delightful scenery, and nowhere rambled among so many
enticing landscapes. The river was a picture of beauty,
fresh and living. The mountains lifted magnificent crowns
to the skies; and she spent worshipful hours on their
sides, in the serene society of these hoary old companions.

And thus she went on. Mrs. Bucclebee herself was
warmed with what she heard; but Olive would fain have
embraced her friend over and over again on the spot.

It took not long to bring about quite a thorough acquaintance. They all three seemed to understand one

another at once. And presently the conversation was as
free and hearty as either one could have desired. Mrs.
Bucclebee betrayed to Amy much sympathy with her in
her relations to the town, and expressed the hope in all
sincerity that she might attain perfect success in her
undertakings. Of course Olive was nowise behindhand,
with *her* quick sympathies, wishing her every possible
degree of happiness.

Mrs. Bucclebee was a woman who always wore a look
of decision in her face, and betrayed it quite as plainly
in her manner. She was rather tall in figure, just enough
so to furnish her the air of stateliness that best agreed
with her countenance; given somewhat to the employment of high-sounding phrases and sentences; easily
touched in her pride, and abounding with confidence in
herself. These were some of her more prominent points,
such as a stranger of any acuteness of perception would
be likely to remark.

The apartment she was in was a rather spacious one,
considering the only comfortable dimensions of the house,
quite tastefully furnished, with its back windows shaded
by the ivy vines that trailed along their sides and over
their tops. Amy saw every sign of both comfort and
refinement there; yet nothing more than might be done
in every country home, if people would but decorate
their hearths as they do their pride. These delicate and
touching evidences of refinement were just what Amy in
that place most longed to find; and now that her eyes

had in such a variety of ways been gratified, she did not
see why this country life did not contain within itself all
the necessary elements of happiness and expansion. This
quiet mode of existence was the best to give wide scope
to the thoughts. It helped the mind to introvert its eye
upon its own secret operations. It drove away the frequent temptations to pride, envy, frivolity, and falsehood.
O, this was as *sweet* a life, as *whole* and *perfect* a life, as
on earth could be devised. Why — why did not all men
flee from the cities and the towns out into the calm re-
treats of the country? Why would they shut the light
of heaven out of their living rooms, and the smile of God
out of their hearts, by erecting such barriers of ceremony
and conventionalism before, and behind, and all around
them, when so short a step would open them to the reception of all good influences, and enrich them with all deep
and flowing experiences?

   " Come," said Olive, after they had sat and chatted a
while, " don't let's forget our strawberries. You shan't
have it to say that I invited you here to eat strawberries,
and then, after getting you here, had forgotten the feast.
No such thing as that."

   Her aunt asked if any had been picked that afternoon.

   " I don't know any thing about that, aunt," she answered. " We were going to have the fun of soiling our
own fingers over them."

   She smiled, as if that were not altogether the best mode
of entertaining her company ; and Amy took occasion to

assure her that she would much prefer a walk in the garden, which would in some degree help her to an appetite when the fruit came to be served.

"If you have not got one already," added Mrs. Bucclebee, "I think the walk out here is *something*, certainly. But you are at perfect liberty to do as you like, however."

"Yes, aunt," broke in Olive, now pulling her friend gently along; "she wants to go out and see the garden, I know. The air out of doors is a great deal pleasanter than it is here, too. Come; let's go a-strawberrying."

And with these playful expressions, affection and delight beaming brightly in her eyes, she conducted Amy along to the beds where the ripe fruit was blushing beneath the leaves, and reddening the ground for yards and yards.

Amy could hardly contain her surprise at what her eyes beheld. Such luscious berries she certainly had never seen before. How temptingly they nestled and tried to hide themselves in the leaves! How juicy they looked, making the beholder's mouth water with the most hasty glance! How boldly and boastingly some of the plumper ones thrust up their glowing heads through the insufficient leaves, showing to such dainty advantage by force of the contrast of the two colors! What a mass of richness they presented to the eye, packing the fancy with pleasant thoughts of smiling plenty, gushing ripeness, bewildering redness, and a heaping bounty piled up without end!

16 *

For a moment Amy stood and in silence enjoyed her
astonishment.

" Come," called Olive ; " you'll not get your share, I'm
afraid. Fall to, or I shall get them all away from you.
See there ! " and she held up her already deeply stained
fingers ; " that's the way to begin about it. Do you think
you could pick a quart in fifteen minutes ? "

" It seems to me," said Amy, as she went down to her
enticing work, " that one could pick a bushel here in that
time. I never saw berries so large and thick. What a
perfect luxury this must be to you ! "

" Yes, at first it was ; but I've got a little more used
to it now. I'd rather see my friends eat them than to
eat them myself."

Olive had brought a large bowl out with her, which at
first she refused to allow Amy to pick in at all. She was
going to insist on her eating what she gathered, and after
that, on her returning to the house and feasting herself
again on berries with cream. But Amy preferred to work
with Olive ; and in a very short time the bowl was heaping full — a mass of ripe, rich, scarlet fruit.

They made a short turn around the garden walks before
going into the house, which afforded Amy just the opportunity she desired for looking at the various plants, shrubs,
and flowers. The latter were both profuse and beautiful.
A gardener was regularly kept on the place, whose special
care it was to attend to these matters, and who apparently
performed his work with thoroughness and taste.

When they reached the room again where Mrs. Bucclebee was sitting, still engaged with her sewing, the latter
looked to learn their success, and complimented them for
their nimbleness. Olive then disappeared for a few minutes; but when she returned, it was with a salver covered
with dishes of the fruit, over which was poured rich and
clotted cream. It was a tempting sight enough. One's
mouth would water all the sooner now. The berries were
fairly smothered in the cream. And their red stains began to shed themselves over the surface of the liquid, like
faint clouds of ruby wine.

It may not be questioned that Amy did ample justice
to her part of the feast. She declared again and again
that she never remembered to have eaten any thing one
half as nice and tempting. It did Olive a great deal of
good to see her enjoy them so highly; and the pleasure
that spoke in Amy's countenance every moment gave
utterance to the enjoyment of her heart within. Such
another garden entertainment she had not had, she knew
not the time when.

It began at length to show signs of nightfall. The sun
had set, and twilight would soon be on. Amy feared lest
Mrs. Gummel might feel uneasy about her, inasmuch as
she had said nothing of this walk to Ivy Lodge beforehand, and so bethought herself of the necessity of a speedy
return. But she expressed herself many times grateful
for the friendly attentions shown her, and promised to do
what was in her power to carry forward so agreeable a
friendship.

She took her leave, Mrs. Bucclebee saying she should
be glad to see her there again, and always glad to see her
there, and Olive wishing she would come out and stay
with her all the time, but insisting, at all events, that she
should be a frequent visitor.

As Amy walked homeward over the grassy road, she
felt that she could spend her days in such a calm retreat
as Ivy Lodge, and thought she had suddenly discovered
new and strange ties to hold her heart to this pleasant
little village.

From this day forward she and Olive were close friends.

CHAPTER XVII.

LEAVES FROM A JOURNAL.

"*Saturday night.* This has been one of my happiest weeks here. My little school becomes all the time more and more interesting. It enlists my feelings almost entirely. How I love those little children no one can tell. I take as great delight in teaching them their letters, and even more delight, than if I were engaged in what the world might think 'bigger business.' For me, there is a mysterious charm, colored, too, with the thought of responsibility, in opening to infant minds the outer doors of knowledge, and truth, and expansion. My thoughts follow my present daily labor along, till I can see those same little ones who now stand at my knee, passed out into the wider fields of life's action, or entered on the experiences of another and a better world. I cannot but remember that what I now teach will be making itself felt on the character then; and in all humility I pray God to enlighten me, that I may lead them into no other than the true paths.

"On Saturday nights I am in the habit of looking back over the week just gone, and reviewing my work; if I

think I can find that I have been faithful, not only help-
ing others to progress, but making progress likewise myself, dispensing around me true, and graceful, and beautiful
influences, teaching by my daily and hourly example only
love, and simplicity, and faith — then I am, above all pos-
sibilities, happy. But this thought of duty performed I
cannot at all times enjoy. Now I am lax, and weary, and
faint; now I grow forgetful, and lose sight of the spirit
that ought to hold out its clear and steady illumination
within. I can only keep my heart in all humility. I can
only burn for more faith, more love, more strength to
resist and to rise.

" To-morrow is Sunday again. There is nothing that I
like the approach of more than these quiet Sundays. I
know not if they be as pleasant in winter, but I have
never experienced such calm enjoyments as they hold out
to me in summer. The people will all go silently along
to church again, — fathers, and mothers, and children, —
tramping over the soft turf in the village street. The
familiar faces will show themselves in the accustomed
pews; there will be the same sweet music from the village
choir; I shall hear again the welcome voice of our good
minister, whom I have learned to love so much; all my
little pupils will be gathered about me over the church;
the air from out of doors will draw through the opened
windows; my spirit will be calm, serene, worshipful; and
I shall be indeed happy! These Sabbaths are my dear
delight. They offer me the true rest. I take such sweet

repose, for which my soul is continually longing. Earth
seems then to have become holy. Its landscapes are
bathed in a beautiful atmosphere, that seems almost
spiritual. O, if the people in the cities knew how much
sweetness there is in this simplicity! How much added
and enlarging trust comes by putting off what is proud,
and worldly, and frivolous! How the heart best expands
in this atmosphere of purity, living on the bracing airs
that blow straight from heaven!"

"*Wednesday night.* Over at Ivy Lodge again this
afternoon, Olive having come to the school house to meet
me as soon as I had dismissed my little ones. I am more
and more delighted with that place, and with my acquaintance there. Olive seems to be to me a friend indeed.
Her feelings are very ardent and impulsive, and her sympathies are all exceedingly acute. She is so very frank,
too, I cannot believe that falsehood can dwell in her presence. We have had strawberry feasts, till the berries are
all gone; and now we turn more particular attention to
the flowers, studying their habits and peculiarities. Olive
is a good botanist, and I have learned much from hearing
her talk of her favorites in the garden. I think I must
study botany myself. It will furnish me the pleasantest
companionship when I roam the woods and fields. It
amazes me every day to see how the volume of nature is
continually opening. I knew there was a vast and unexplored world over our heads, but there are few who think
what worlds there are beneath our very feet.

" Mrs. Bucclebee is devoted to Olive; yet it is not the
devotion one would find in a *mother*. No person can ever
hope to supply to a child the place of a lost mother. Olive
loves her aunt, I feel satisfied; and her aunt thinks that
the affection is abundantly returned, no doubt; but I
should hardly wish any friend to teach me all the time the
precepts of a worldly *pride*, that I might not, by any mis-
take, fail in due time to make a flattering appearance and
sensation. Olive has a singularly sweet and amiable
nature, and a kind hand ought rather to pull out such
hurtful weeds, than to be at pains to plant them over and
over again. It is plain that the niece and the aunt are
none too closely related in *spirit*, however close the visible
connection. Mrs. B. is a very dignified woman, and never
seems to *forget herself*: she is always self-possessed. I
sometimes wish, when I am sitting in their company, that
she would by some accident once lose her balance, and
show herself nothing but a *woman!* She gazes at me so
strangely with her piercing dark eyes, too, as if she was
not quite sure yet that she understood and had read me
thoroughly. Olive is so different! I cannot seem to explain it to my entire satisfaction.

" But she is a good girl, and has won my deepest love
already. I spend many an hour with her, that I should
otherwise spend alone. We walk much together, across
the pastures and through the woods. Already we have
climbed the mountains, both of them, and I have listened
in silent delight to her admiration of the grand scene at

our feet. She is as enthusiastic as I am myself in her admiration of landscape; and I am very sure she is much more impulsive in betraying it.

"Once we went together to see my little friend Dolly — the only time Olive had been in sight of the house. She expressed her astonishment at what she saw, and commended me for seeking out such people to do them good. Ah, if I were sure that I *could* but do them any good! Yet let me be faithful to the little I have undertaken, and hopeful likewise. It is we who must labor, but it is the Father alone who gives the increase. So let me trust. Nothing is of me. I am but a grateful borrower. I shine only by the light that is placed within me. It must be my care that that light is not hidden away from others."

"*Monday night.* What a pleasant surprise I have had to-day! First, there came a letter from one of my old music scholars in Boston, offering me all sorts of affectionate wishes, and hoping I should be willing to go back to town again next winter. I don't know about that yet. I find I like the country so much that if it is at all practicable, I should be glad to see if a winter's experience might not be quite as pleasant and profitable. Perhaps I should prefer the winter here to the summer. Who can tell?

"Second, little Dolly came to school this morning, clad in a new and tasteful dress, and looking the picture of prettiness and grace. And when, after school was over, I asked her in a whisper who made the clothes for her, and who had shown her how to wear them so tastefully, my

17

heart was thrilled with unspeakable delight to hear it was
all the work of my dear friend Olive! O, what money
could purchase such happiness! She has carried the feeling into more hearts than one, and by so simple and delicate an act as this. Who would *not* be charitable, and
generous, and kind, when the reward is so boundless and
enriching?

" Of course I went over to Ivy Lodge after school at
night, on purpose to thank my dear friend for so acceptable a service; for it is no less a cause of gratitude to me
than to the little child whom her gift more immediately
serves. She knew the interest I took in Dolly, and it
must have been that she was first led to this kindness by
her regard for me. I did not have to go all the way to
Ivy Lodge, for I met her on the road, coming over to the
school house. It was a pleasant surprise for me. When
I told Olive how grateful I felt — ' O, pray don't think
that was any thing,' said she in her engaging way; ' I
only thought I would encourage your little friend a trifle,
and am glad enough if I have done the least good.'

" She knew not *how much* good she had done. For me
to see that the work was all of her own hand was enough
to increase my love for her beyond its former limits. I
tried to thank her again and again; but she would hear
nothing of the kind, and playfully stopped her ears with
the palms of her hands.

" Dear Olive! I sincerely hope your gift has done your
own heart the good it has done mine."

"*Wednesday night.* . It is midnight now. I am alone
in my chamber. I can hear only the beating of my own
heart. The wind is not to be heard without, and not even
a leaf on the trees is ruffled or shaken. I have pushed
aside the curtain for a few moments, and sat at the window
looking out. O, such beauty, such beauty — that surpasses
description ! It can be enjoyed only in silence.

" The moon is full, and it is shining now with its clear
white light all over the street. Every household is at rest.
I cannot see the faintest glimmer of a light any where in
the little village. All are sleeping, and I sit here awake.
I can have all this happiness to myself. Not an echo
breaks the soft wave of silence that flows over the town.
I do not catch the sound even of the humming beetles
among the trees, and about my windows. My thoughts
dwell much on the past to-night, and my dear father's
face is before me. I see him as he used to be to me, un-
changed by misfortunes. I hear his voice again, and it is
full of affection. O my father ! if you could have lived
to show your only child the way among men ! If you
could but have seen this day, and beheld me laboring here
with such cheerfulness to make myself and others happy,
would you not have changed many of your opinions of the
world's coldness and insensibility to kindness ?

" I cannot sleep. My thoughts will not suffer me. It
is too bright a night, and the influences are too active for
the heart's repose. Earth, too, seems so lovely, I would
even be out in this cool air, and let it flow upon my face

and temples. Are there such scenes as these in the cities?
Is the summer night as sweet there — as fragrant with
delicious associations — as free from all vicious exhalations
— as open to the influences of Heaven on all sides? Is
the moon shining there as brightly now? And does it
look down on no scenes of crime, and terror, and wretchedness, that are not to be witnessed here in the retirements
of nature?

    " The summer is going fast — so fast that I can scarcely
realize it at all. My occupation takes up so much of my
time, and my friendships are so pleasant, that my heart is
kept full continually. This little place has become of
itself a great world to me. I pray I may slight no duty,
and forget no relation. Happiness alone is my aim; it is
to be got here as well as elsewhere ; more and more certain
am I that it comes not from without, but only and altogether from within. Once find the centre of your existence
where it really is — in the good Father — and the prob-
lems and perplexities of the world are like the trifling
puzzles of children, and as easily unravelled."

CHAPTER XVIII.

PROGRESS.

AMY's life at Valley Village was continually affording
her the best advantages for self-culture, and opening to
her heart the richest experiences. She was in a humble
vocation, but none too humble for so faithful a disciple.
It must have been an extraordinary trial now that could
warp her feelings from the line of perfect obedience she
had chosen. She saw the path that conducted her to
peace, and her feet were to be found perseveringly within it.

Her school went on with all the promise of its beginning. She had but two dozen scholars, but they were
enough. Their tuition brought her in an ample support,
and left her something in her purse besides to do good
with. Day after day she sat patiently through the dreamy
summer weather in her buzzing school room, teaching one
tender one to spell, another to read, a third to sew, a
fourth its letters, and all of them the beauty and the harmony of singing. This last was the exercise of the day
to which all looked forward with delight. If a visitor
had at any time looked in on her during those calm

17 *   (197)

afternoons, she would have found many a weary one
stretched out in slumber on the bare wooden benches,
with her little arm laid carefully across her breast. Or
she might have heard the pleasant hum of youthful voices
going in concert all over the room, as the little brood
conned their lessons half aloud.

The mothers of the children not unfrequently dropped
into school of a quiet afternoon, at Amy's own request;
she showed them how engaged she was herself in their
offspring's welfare, and so incited them to increased interest in the purpose she had set out to accomplish. If she
could receive their coöperation, what more was there to
be asked for?

And parents and children, therefore, learned to feel very
much at home in that old school room together, and even
looked forward with as much pleasant satisfaction to their
reunions there as if they were all scholars and all youthful. Amy was visibly encouraged by it. Her heart was
made inexpressibly glad; Olive knew how glad, for she
was the recipient of all her confidences; and Mrs. Gummel, too, understood something of it, for with so good a
friend as she Amy was frank and confiding in the extreme.
The signs multiplied on every hand that promised to keep
Amy in Valley Village even after the summer was gone.
She read them herself in the praise of others; in their
wondering why they never could have such a school before; in the marked favor with which she was met by the
entire population, male and female, men, women, and

children; in the love of her pupils themselves, some of
them telling her in an exceedingly affectionate way that
they hoped she never would go away, and that she would
keep school just as long as they went.

Amy passed much of her spare time, too, with Mr. and
Mrs. Parsons. There were no better people thereabout
than the good clergyman and his wife. In their society
Amy was neighbor to all noble and exalting influences.
She was very fond of running in as she passed along
home from school, and chatting a few minutes with Mrs.
Parsons, who certainly enjoyed it as much as herself. In
the course of these unceremonious little visits, Amy caught
many new thoughts about the aims, and enjoyments, and
satisfactions of life, and drank in fresh inspirations of love
and truth. By so many more bonds was she held to the
clergyman's family. It would be a lasting loss to her to
be obliged to go away from the sphere of their lovely
influence. Whenever she had been talking with them for
a half hour, she would go home to her chamber, wondering what secret power it was that gave the world such a
new aspect and atmosphere. She left care, and anxiety,
and all thoughts of a troublesome future behind her, and
came out into the glorious air of trust, and hope, and perfect love, expanding her soul with the deep draughts of
the new element in which it was bathed.

Mr. Parsons, too, never forgot to call on her in her
school, when the opportunity offered, or even if he chanced
to be walking by; and the affection he showed for all of

them helped the growth of the school wonderfully. There
is no more vigorous nutriment for any plant than love.
First it engages ; then it surrounds and enriches; and
lastly it gives strength and power. So the little school
felt its energies increase gradually with its affection.
Amy had intentionally struck this chord at the beginning;
and now she was enjoying to the utmost the satisfactions
that flow always from the heart rather than the head.

Her way of life at the pleasant cottage of Mrs. Gummel
was exceedingly enjoyable. That lady had shown her so
much friendliness and sympathy from the first, that although Amy might at any moment have been joyfully
received into the bosom of Mr. Parsons's family, she felt
an attachment for her which would not suffer her to think
of leaving the little roof she was under. Mrs. Gummel
loved the character of her new boarder more and more. She
became exceedingly fond of her society. Evenings, after
the cares of the day were put by, they used to sit in the
little parlor at the open windows, and chat by the hour of
the thoughts and feelings that made the mingled web of
their separate experiences. Frequently they would revert
to the day when they first met in the stage coach, and
each would repeat her gratitude for the occurrence of so
happy a circumstance in their lives.

Much attention, too, was Amy in the habit of bestowing upon Henry. He was an amiable boy, devoted to
his mother, always to be found about home, and disposed
in every way to make improvement. Whatever, therefore,

his mother or Amy told him he was eager to heed and remember. Parents all over the village were in the habit of pointing their children to Henry as a most exemplary boy, and one whose many good qualities would furnish them with excellent patterns.

During the summer he busied himself about home with his mother, hoeing and spading in the garden, running of errands, assisting in whatever little matters assistance was desirable, and making himself no less useful than happy. He had a disposition like the sunshine. Every thing went smoothly with him; or if it did not, no one was the wiser for his complaints. Such a thing as fretfulness was with him quite out of the question. In his leisure he was in the habit of reading such books as he could procure, sometimes running over to Mrs. Parsons to see if she was not in the receipt of something he had not yet seen. Amy loved to lend him all the books she had brought with her, and would sit and hear him read them aloud at night or early in the morning, engaged herself the while with her needle. She felt that it was a source both of delight to herself and of improvement to him.

The village people proved good friends to Amy, all of them; though there was quite as great a diversity as might be looked for generally among so many characters, and the motives that influenced them were as various as the individuals themselves. There was Dr. Sillby, the only physician there was in the village, who had a very bluff way with him, and was as apt to make his jokes as

uncomfortably practical as any body's, — he was, after all,
a stanch friend to the little village school, and never hesitated to lend it the support that might be expected from
a man in his social position. Amy was but triflingly
acquainted with his family, however; for, save the one
girl he sent to her for instruction, there was little else to
draw her into his house. His wife was a feeble woman,
never quite well, and always quite gloomy. He never
came home but she had a call for him — some new complaint whose diagnosis was a mystery no less to him than
to the entire medical faculty. She rarely wanted any
society, unless it might be the society of those who were
willing to listen in resigned silence to her complainings,
and such were few indeed through the length and breadth
of the village. Yet Dr. Sillby himself, as if to fulfil the
law of compensation in this matter, was a remarkably jolly
man, and hardly ever opened his mouth to speak unless
he laughed first. So opposite were their tastes and ten-
dencies in these things, people used to wonder what it
was that ever brought them together in marriage; and
people were still expressing their wonder about it as freely
as ever when Amy went to Valley Village to gain her
summer's short experience.

Of all her pupils, perhaps Amy became the most ob-
servably attached to little Dolly Tatterags. As the child
went on with her daily instructions at school, her progress
was rapid and perceptible. Her manners improved, too,
and she became graceful and attractive. Amy labored

with patience to help her unlearn the many uncouth and
not altogether proper expressions she had been taught at
home, and supplied her with prettier and more lovely
phrases, that better became the person and the heart of a
young creature so fair.

She continued to be a very frequent visitor, likewise, at
the Tatterag domicile, and when there always offered the
mother some new token of her kind sympathy. The latter
very soon came to change her views of the world entirely;
and Amy had been the unconscious instrument of the
same. Wheras Mrs. Tatterags had heretofore soured her
thoughts with a continual apprehension of injury and
hatred from those more agreeably situated in life than
herself, and had always looked upon the slightest proffer
of friendship or assistance with a suspicion that made her
at times perfectly miserable, now she was fast opening her
eyes to an altogether pleasanter truth, and had already,
before the summer was gone, come into the better belief
that there *was* such a thing in this world even as *love*, and
that it would work far mightier results than all the powers
of hatred, and suspicion, and jealousy combined.

The words of Amy, ever gentle and full of tender sympathy, lodged in the good soil of her heart. They fructi-
fied and sprang up like seed that had been sown, and
promised in time to perform an acceptable office. There
was now more room for the sunlight; and as fast as that
entered in, of course, the darkness fled away. In no one
thing was the change in the woman so perceptible as in

her habit of querulousness and complaint. Now she really
began to see something to live for. Her many children
were no longer a burden ; they furnished her with sources
of comfort and happiness. She treated them more like a
mother, devoted to the welfare, rather than the successful
riddance, of her offspring. It was not as easy to move
her husband, and Amy saw but little of him. He was off
the most of the time, now straggling in the neighborhood,
and now picking up such easy jobs as he felt willing to
perform. But there *was* a chance left to set him right —
it would be through his favorite little daughter. He began
to be *proud* of her already.

And so Amy worked, and worked on. She suffered her
spirit to relax none of its energies, and sought of Heaven
continually the needed strength to carry forward her labors. She was hopeful, and patient, and full of faith. In
good time she would see the fruits of her doings.

CHAPTER XIX.

DOLLY IN A NEW PLACE.

AMY had planned a pleasant surprise for her young pupil, one Saturday afternoon; so on the Friday night before, when she went home from school, she bade her dress herself as tidily as she could on the next day, for she was to go home at noon with her; and after dinner she promised Dolly they would go visiting together.

Of course Dolly's mother, now that her feelings had undergone such modification, was exceedingly pleased with the idea. Her vanity might have been touched as well as her heart; for mothers *will* continue to be proud of their children, especially if they think there is any ground for it, till the last day allowed them. Mr. Tatterags heard what was to be done, for his little daughter herself told him; but he merely turned his head away, uttered a lazy "pooh," and went on fondling her. Yet he was secretly touched with this new proof of Amy's regard for his child, only he lacked the manliness and the truth to admit it. There are thousands more in the world very much like him.

It gave Amy the sincerest pleasure to see, the next

18   (205)

morning, when the children began to assemble in the
school room, that Dolly had been decked out by the hand
of her mother in the very best attire that belonged to her,
and to look into a face so bright and happy as hers was
for thinking of the happiness that day was to bring. The
child's heart danced with delight; and it was evident she
could scarcely restrain her feet from a good hop-skip-and-
a-jump across the floor. A smile rested on Amy's face,
which she exerted herself to conceal, when she saw some
of the trifling subterfuges to which the mother was driven
in dressing her, and some of the odd combinations of taste
and fancy that were here and there so readily discoverable
about her.

Little Dolly got up from her seat, and for a moment
hesitated. The other children kept coming in. Now she
threw a timid glance at Amy, and now at the door. Her
face wore very changeful expressions. Amy was narrowly
watching her, and was much interested to understand the
mystery of her behavior.

Finally the child thrust out a foot into the floor, and
started for her teacher's chair with all speed.

"Please, ma'am," said she, the instant she reached
Amy's side, while she held down her hands beside her and
drew short and quick breaths, — "please, ma'am, mother
wants to know if I look *fit*."

This simple message, brought in so earnest and sudden a manner, made Amy smile now in spite of herself.

"Do you look *fit*?" she repeated, trying to draw her
face down to soberness; "what do you mean?"

"My clothes," the child answered, looking quickly down over them.

"Why, certainly," said Amy, putting her hand gently on her shoulder. "You look very nicely, I am sure. Who brushed your hair so good for you?"

This she asked in a low voice, lest some of the rest might overhear.

"My mother."

"Well, you must tell your mother, when you go home to-night, that she has fixed you up quite prettily. Will you?"

Of course no child like Dolly would forget a message like that. So after a few more words she returned to her seat, and the usual exercises of the morning began in their order.

Perhaps Dolly's thoughts were nowhere but within the school room that forenoon, however many times her eyes may have wandered out the open window. She best knew about that herself. At any rate, Amy very frequently observed that she would hold her eyes dreamily fixed on the floor at times, or on the trees, or on the sky, as if she were already trying to realize some of the visions of the afternoon's pleasure, that floated like beautiful pictures across her brain.

The moment school was done at noon, and the rest of the children had cleared the room, Dolly walked quietly to her teacher's side, and stood waiting there, without a word, for her to start for home.

Amy turned from what she happened at the instant to
be doing, and saw her.

" Your mother was perfectly willing you should go
home with me to-day — wasn't she ? " asked she.

" O, yes ; and she said she hoped I'd be a good girl,
too, and not do any thing you wouldn't want me to."

" Well, I certainly trust you will not. I guess you
mean to be a pretty good girl — don't you ? But come ;
let us go now and get some dinner, and then we will talk
about something else."

So Amy took her by the hand, after locking the door on
the labors of another week, and led her along over the
grass to Mrs. Gummel's. She had not told the latter of
her intention to bring Dolly home with her, and the surprise was a very agreeable one. Amy took her up into
her room while dinner was being prepared, and proceeded
to show her all the little objects likely to interest her.
She opened her books to the places where engravings
were to be found, and saw the child's eyes dilate with
pleasure. She showed her such pretty needlework as she
happened to have completed, samples of embroidery and
the like, asking her how long she thought it would be
before *she* should learn to use the needle, and produce
tasteful articles like these.

At dinner Dolly was lost. She sat by Amy's side, and
hardly knew what to do with herself. Amy helped her to
what was on the table, Mrs. Gummel finding there was no
room for *her* services at all. They did not say much to

her, however, during the meal, lest she might become too much embarrassed to enjoy it. But the conversation, nevertheless, was kept up briskly, and the child had an opportunity to see that happiness alone was at the board.

By two o'clock, or thereabouts, Amy took her little friend by the hand, and proceeded to Ivy Lodge. It had been arranged between her and Olive that she should bring Dolly over there, in order to open her heart to the loving influence of flowers, and the beautiful sights to be seen in the garden. These were what she rarely came in contact with; and Amy wished to carry on the work of cultivation which she had begun in the most varied way possible. Above all, situated as the child was, too, she would instruct her to take delight in nature, and learn in that always open book to worship the good Father whose work it all is. Besides, Olive had already betrayed interest enough in Dolly to wish to watch her improvement for herself from time to time, and was now quite as eager to see her at Ivy Lodge as Amy could be.

The moment they reached the gate, the little girl began to exclaim, —

" Isn't it *pretty* here, Miss Lee ? "

" Very beautiful, I think myself," answered Amy.

When they got through the gate, therefore, Amy began to point out to her such objects as would be likely to furnish her the most delight. She talked to her, walking very slowly towards the house, about the fir trees, whose green feathery boughs looked so gracefully, thus pencilled

18 *

against the sky; and the flower beds across the garden,
offering such brilliant colors to the eye; and the borders
to the walks, looking so freshly and green; and the cool
piazza, whose posts were circled with climbing vines; and
the house roof, almost buried under the mass of ivy leaves
that clambered over it every where.

"Shouldn't you like to *live* here?" she asked Dolly,
whose eyes were opened as wide as they ever would be.

"O, yes," she answered immediately; "but I should
want mother to live here too."

Olive had been waiting for her new visitors, and took
an occasional lookout for their approach from the piazza;
and the moment she saw them coming up the walk, she
ran down the steps to meet them.

"I began to think you weren't coming," said she, first
kissing her friend Amy, and then stooping down and performing the same office for the child. "What kept you
so late, pray? But I am glad you're here at last, surely.
How do you do to-day? How do *you* do, little one?
Come; come up on the piazza, and let's sit down a minute on the bench. Aunt is lying down a little while,
as she usually does after dinner; so we'll not go in
just yet."

Amy thought it was much pleasanter on the piazza;
and no doubt Dolly was abundantly satisfied with the
arrangement, too, especially if one were to judge from
the delighted expression of her face.

They lifted her up on the seat between them, and

smiled at one another to see her little feet hang off,
swinging to and fro.   Olive took a look at her shoes, at
her bonnet, and at her little white dress, with the pink
bows secured to each shoulder just at the place where the
apron bands went over.   And Amy, as she silently returned the glances of her friend, certainly *looked* the
grateful feelings she could not speak.

"Who dressed you so nicely?" asked Olive.

"My mother," said the child, looking so happily up in
her face.

Amy was thankful for her asking the question; for
Dolly would be sure to report it faithfully to her mother
on reaching home, and the woman would secretly take
encouragement.   O, there are *so many* ways, some of them
so delicate and trifling, too, in which help may be extended to the suspicious and shivering nature!   Only a
little generous feeling, only a single little word spoken
in love, only a look or a smile even, and mountains in a
swift moment are removed, and all that is pure, and noble,
and true is let in.

"Well," said Olive in a very kind voice, "your mother
is a very good mother, I am sure, to dress you up so well.
Don't you think she is?   Don't you love your mother
very much?"

"O, yes, ma'am," Dolly answered, her large eyes mois-
tening; and immediately she dropped her gaze to the
floor, and seemed lost in thought.   The two girls exchanged glances of affection over her head.   They could

that moment have embraced one another or cried together
for joy.

After they had sat and chatted a while, Olive asked
Amy if she would not take a little stroll down the garden
walks before they went in. The latter readily assented;
and they all three set out, Amy leading her little friend by
the hand. Olive continually went before them, and called
the child's attention to such objects as were rare and beautiful. She gave her short and pleasant histories of the
habits of some of the flowers, telling her how they closed
when the sun went down, and opened again at its rising;
showing her some that turned whithersoever the sun
went, worshipping it like a god; pointing out others that
were so very sensitive, that the instant you touched them
they shrivelled and shrank as if they were afraid of you;
and explaining all the secrets and mysteries of the various
colors, showing her how to mix them with taste in little
bunches and bouquets, and inquiring to know which of
them all pleased her fancy the most, and why she had a
preference for them.

If Dolly was delighted with what she heard and saw,
Olive was hardly less so. The perfect innocence and
ingenuousness of the child took her heart captive in spite
of herself. Her frank and ready answers charmed her.
The dancing expressions of delight that were from one
moment to another visible on her countenance made her
heart feel fresh, and sweet, and whole. It was like the
influence of a beautiful picture to her; and much more,
for this was the picture of a living child.

They walked around till they came up to the house again, when Olive proposed that they should all go in. When they entered the cool little parlors, whose doors had been thrown wide open, the thick vines affording such grateful shadows about the windows, they found Mrs. Bucclebee sitting in an easy chair, apparently recovering from the effects of her short slumber. Amy went directly towards her, and offered her hand, hoping she was quite well.

" Yes, thank you," said she, rather chillingly, and without rising. " Sit down. Who've you got there, Olive, with those high pink bows on her shoulders? I *should* think — well, I won't *say*."

Amy could not help feeling hurt at Mrs. B.'s manner, and thought she might have been a little more prudent, if not more kindly. Olive's face showed her perplexity, but she betrayed the feeling in no other way.

" This is *Amy's* little friend, aunt," she explained, leading her forward a trifle. " Dolly Tatterags."

" Ah!" exclaimed her aunt, with a very faint and somewhat sarcastic smile on her face. " I didn't know who you might have got there."

For a moment there was nothing said. Olive felt cut, and Amy was none too much elated with the reception. Nevertheless, as she caught the sympathetic and almost melting glance of Olive's eye, she drove back her embarrassment in an instant, and spoke in just the free and independent strain of her spirit.

"I have interested myself a good deal in the child, ma'am," said she, firmly but touchingly, "and hope to do a great deal more for her. To-day I proposed to bring her over to Ivy Lodge, and show her your beautiful garden and the flowers."

"Yes; very kind in *you*, I've no doubt," said Mrs. Bucclebee.

"Her parents are very destitute, and have a large family of small children dependent on them," added Amy, in a voice that the child could not hear. "I took so much pity on her, poor thing! and saw that there was a good prospect of making her a very different child from what she otherwise might be. I have been greatly encouraged, thus far. Don't you think she has an extremely pretty face, Mrs. Bucclebee? and a pretty figure, too?"

"Well, I don't know; she —— "

"But I have found that she has a *nature* far more beautiful than either," interrupted Amy, with some enthusiasm.

"Yes," half soliloquized Mrs. B., patronizingly.

"And that was all *I* wanted to know," continued Amy.

As if to break the force of her aunt's iciness, and to restore to Amy perfect equanimity of feeling again, Olive led their little friend around the rooms, showing her the books, the pictures, and the pretty sea shells, talking about this and about that as fast as she could, in order to take up her entire attention. And after this was over, they came round again to Amy, not to resume their seats, but to start her out into the garden with them once more.

Oilve was impatient to breathe the out-door air. She wished to break away from the strange feeling of restraint that held her as in a mesh there in the presence of her aunt.

Once more they traversed the grounds, exerting themselves in every ingenious manner to take up Dolly's attention. They went to the summer house at last, and there passed the remainder of the afternoon. And to Dolly — *such* an afternoon !

It passed away, however, very speedily, as all pleasures do. But its memories would not be apt to fade so soon. Amy knew that they must at *some* time go through the gate homewards ; and she was careful to start seasonably, for her little charge had a good walk to take yet.

Dolly held a pretty bouquet when she took her leave. of Olive, and said she was going to give it to her mother. With those beautiful flowers in her hand, she looked not like the crying little Dolly Tatterags Amy first saw, but like another — a bright and happy being.

Amy went with her some way homewards, lest she might want company. She kissed her affectionately at parting, and told her to be good to her brothers and sisters, and teach them how to love one another and to love her. And as they separated on that silent old country road, tears might have been seen gathering like films in their eyes, testifying to the new joy with which their hearts had that day been baptized.

CHAPTER XX.

THE SCHOOL EXAMINATION.

" Now," said Mr. Parsons, talking to the collected children in that affectionate way that made him so much
beloved by them, — " now we are going to see who have
tried to do well this summer, and how much they have
learned, and if they are all worthy of the praise of their
friends."

The little flock looked round wisely at one another, and
then exchanged glances with their teacher. Her look
meant only encouragement.

The school room was packed full. The mothers,
especially, were all there, watching their children anxiously. Some of the fathers had come in too, but not many :
their vocation just at this season of the year called them
off in other and very necessary directions. They were
perfectly willing to confide in the judgment of their wives,
and the latter were out in full force accordingly.

It was quite a warm afternoon, at the very last of summer. The windows and doors were wide open, and the
old oak floor of the school room had been plashed with
water to cool the air. Many a little one tried to sit up

(216)

straight on the benches, and gave it up as a present impossibility. They were obliged to lean a little on one another, looking close into each other's faces and smiling.

There they all were, Amy's whole school. Some of them looked bright and peculiarly happy, and others tired and peculiarly sleepy. Some had bits of red, pink, and blue ribbons tied to the ends of their braided hair, flowing down their backs or sticking out at their temples. Some wore their very whitest little dresses, and slippers laced prettily over the instep and about the ankles. You could see that every head had been particularly well cared for that day, in some instances not even a loose lock straying outward from the general plaster and platitude. There were little heads, too, of all shapes, sizes, and colors. But the variety of faces produced the greatest interest, even to those who very well knew each face by itself. It is that chiefly which always attracts to such pleasant places.

Amy brought them forward, class after class. First came the little abecedarians. They were funny little creatures, and made a great deal of laughter by some of their ludicrous mistakes in calling off the letters. And whenever they found the visitors laughing, what did they do but gaze about and laugh too, as if they were enjoying themselves to the very top of their desires! These were the lambs of the flock; the tenderest ones of all. They showed happy faces, and their mothers knew that they really loved their teacher. That was a great deal. Any mother is shrewd enough to know that the first need in a

19

child's heart, even before "the letters" are indelibly im-
printed in her brain, is love. That is the broader, the
deeper, and the better foundation.

Then followed classes in reading, exhibiting their powers to the assembled visitors to the very best advantage.
They had certainly made progress in these exercises, and
on behalf of the rest, Mr. Parsons took occasion to express his decided commendation. Amy's heart was full,
for she could read the deep, deep satisfaction in the faces
of the parents.

Between the various exercises, and at convenient intervals, Amy introduced their singing. Every one was gratified with this. The faces of all were lighted up with still
greater pleasure. They betrayed their appreciative sympathy in every possible way. It was easy to see that this
was an exercise that did not affect the children alone.
The parents, too, felt the harmony that was begotten of it.

Now their united voices sounded loud and clear, so that
they could be heard far away from the school house. Now
they sang softly and low, in sweet and touching strains,
keeping a perfect and delightful chord. The place seemed
all at once a little heaven. Here the best, the purest, the
tenderest, the most aspiring emotions of the heart were
suddenly awakened ; and this little volume of harmony,
this delightful accord of the voices of innocent and lovely
children, was all that had produced a change so sudden
and wonderful. O, blessed is song! Blessed are the
pleasant voices of happy children ! Blessed are the clear

and heartfelt strains that pass across one's consciousness, and throw down into the mysterious deeps of the soul such thrilling, such all-searching echoes, waking it to a life that nothing in this world can ever hope to satisfy!

It is enough to say that these little songs and hymns, that Amy had taught her scholars with so much patience, were well received from beginning to end. Whenever the singing was announced, the room was instantly hushed, and every whisper died away. The interest was general, and the attention undivided. The parents wore the pleasantest smiles on their faces, as they watched the happy enthusiasm of their little ones, and seemed to feel as if they could break in and sing with them, with a good relish of enjoyment indeed.

Then the samples of needlework were placed on exhibition. Some were specimens of plain sewing, and all very neatly done. Some were pieces of fine stitching, that looked as if young eyes, however sharp, could never find the way along with the thread. There were also some old-fashioned "samplers," in red, and green, and yellow cloth, with the letters of the alphabet and the names of the owners worked plainly and prettily on their ground. These were handed about with a great deal of satisfaction among the visitors, and the children to whom they belonged watched each the progress of her own "sampler" from one hand to another, with anxious and eager eyes.

And Amy had the pleasure, too, of submitting a very few specimens of embroidery; nothing very extravagant

in point either of workmanship or design, as she well
knew, but yet affording cheering evidence of the growing
taste and skill of those in her charge. One of these
specimens was an attempt to work a face upon the cloth ;
and though for a mere *attempt* it was all no doubt well
enough, for a *face* it was something quite out of the limits
of description. And besides this there were roses, and
tulips, and vines; the former looking for all the world as
if they really grew and blossomed out of the cloth, and
the latter as if they were bent on creeping off of it! Still
they were good, by way of exhibitions ; and the commend-
atory remarks they drew from the visitors were evidence
sufficient of the esteem in which the patient laborers were
held.

Amy made them read aloud in unison, to practise them
in harmony of intonation and a quicker ear to detect dis-
cord. And they recited the tables of the arithmetics
together, as is the custom in almost all New England
schools of that character. And still "toeing the mark"
in the old oaken floor, and with faces turned to their
teacher, they exhibited to the visitors the sense of order
and precision they had been taught to respect, in all the
other exercises that were brought forward.

Then they were allowed an intermission, after a while,
during which interval Amy went about among the parents,
chatting easily of one and another pupil, answering the
various questions put her with perfect frankness and grace,
and in every method possible testifying to the pleasure she

received from their countenance and commendation that day. All were not of the same degree of culture with herself — that she well knew; but it was this very same culture that led her to make herself perfectly easy with them, to meet them with warm sympathy on their own grounds, and to exhibit to them in the properest way, and with the greatest prospect of advantage, the sweet nature of her disposition and character.

Again came on the classes, and finally a parting hymn. Then Mr. Parsons rose and addressed the school, offering them the best advice he had to give, complimenting them very highly for their marked proficiency, speaking with much satisfaction of their affection for their teacher, hoping that they might not lose her yet, but prevail on her to remain with them longer, and closing by wishing them every one a happy vacation.

And after a prayer, Amy thanked the parents present for their attendance, and dismissed the school.

It was truly delightful to see the sorry eagerness with which the little ones crowded around their teacher to wish her "good by," and to get one more kind word from her lips before they separated; and Mr. Parsons lingered a little to enjoy the sight. Some of them were a little more timid about it than the others, but Amy stooped down and kissed them all, and bade them always be good children, whether they came to school to her again or not. And when they had taken their leave, scholars and parents, she stood in the middle of the deserted school room, looked

19 *

around her thoughtfully, and for a moment felt that she was
alone. In that single moment it seemed to her again that
there was nothing between herself and the world. She
had this afternoon finished her summer school, her pupils
had every one taken their leave, the busy old school room
was silent, the benches were all empty, and now *a future*
once more burst upon her vision. Hitherto, at least since
her arrival in Valley Village, she had been living only in
the immediate and busy *present.* Up to this time the
feeling had strictly been "sufficient unto the day." But
now there occurred a gap. There was an opening in her
prospects. She had room to discuss probabilities and pos-
sibilities. She questioned, and queried, and weighed, and
wondered. And with all this her heart could hardly be
said to know the freedom from doubt and anxiety it had
enjoyed through the summer. Still there was no such
feeling as fear, and no such disposition as that of complaint.
Girl though she was, and in one sad sense solitary and
alone in the world, Amy never allowed herself for a moment to doubt the power of the good Father to provide
for her, and would have repined at no lot to which she
might have been directed. With her the wealth was not
from without, but entirely from within. Such a trifle as
circumstance, or position, or personal comfort, never
troubled her thoughts. Where *she* was, where her *soul*
exhibited itself at work and at its enjoyment, *there* was
her life. She existed at the centre, rather than at the
circumference.

For two weeks — the last weeks of August — she remained in the village, making calls around on her patrons, collecting her school bills, rambling about wherever the fancy led her, and enjoying herself with her more intimate friends. She made a visit of a few days at Olive's house, and felt while there as if she never wanted to come away again. She did not forget the Tatterag family, either, but went to see them often in their perch on the mountain, encouraging the faint-hearted mother, and trying to open to her thoughts larger sources of enjoyment than had yet entered her mind. Dolly used to come to see her, too, at Mrs. Gummel's, and went on with her lessons while there, reading and spelling to Amy in her chamber. She grew in beauty every day. Amy's conversation with her was a means of refinement, and from it she gathered many and many a sweet and spiritual lesson.

And so the time passed. Amy was always up early in the morning, and as soon as the sunrise bell rang in the church belfry, she issued forth on her usual walk towards her favorite old bridge. She wrote much in her journal, and filled its pages with her happy experiences. And she went frequently to Mr. Parsons's house, and with her good friends there she discussed her prospects for the immediate future.

CHAPTER XXI.

DEATH AT THE DOOR.

AFTER much consideration of the subject, the leading persons of the village concluded, principally at Mr. Parsons's personal instigation, to offer employment to Amy as a teacher until the ensuing spring. They admitted that she had taught an excellent school during the past season; and the glowing reports of her little examination were every where acceptably received. Accordingly, she was one day waited on by the proper committee, all in regular form and with not a little ceremony, who made her the necessary proposals. Mr. Parsons was one of the committee, and of course its spokesman. He offered Amy a guaranty of a certain amount of money, provided she would consent to stay till the spring, and as full and pleasant a school as could be collected for her. As it happened, too, — and all the more pleasantly for Amy, no doubt, — there were none but quite small scholars in the village to be sent; and this fact might have helped influence her favorably towards the proposal.

At all events, she thought over the matter a few days, and finally sent word to the committee that she was ready

to accept their offer. Mr. Parsons interested himself
enough more to see that the school room was made as
comfortable as possible for the winter; the gaping cracks
about the floor, the door, and the windows were all properly closed, and an abundant wood pile was stored where
it could be got at without either exposure or difficulty.
The bargain was fully concluded, and Amy set about her
few preparations accordingly.

Early in September, therefore, she commenced her fall
term. She was gratified to find all her old scholars back
again, and a few new ones besides. Among the latter was
young Henry Gummel. The girls laughed a little at him
and with one another when they saw him come in, for he
was the largest and oldest boy that Amy had; he knew
enough, however, to let them laugh on as long as they
enjoyed it, for there was no question but they would be
glad of his company before the term was over.

Before the term was over! Alas! before it was yet
half gone, he was laid on a sick bed, and forbidden to
enter into the little circle that loved him so well.

· About the first of October he was taken down by fever.
The attack was insidious, as such attacks always are, and
excited little alarm till it had gained an entrance into
life's citadel.

Mrs. Gummel's heart was truly afflicted. This child
was her all, and her only stay. For him she seemed to
live, to labor, to hope. In his little life, just now beginning to open itself in such beautiful proportions, she saw
the entire unfolding of her fondest desires.

For several days his disease kept working its way silently — silently, there in the mysterious stillness and shadow of that sick chamber, pursuing its course unchecked by the skill of medical help, rioting by itself in the freshness and vigor of his youthful blood, and burning its path onward to his brain. Day by day its hold on his system grew stronger and stronger. It went down beneath the surface, and held its revels at the very portal of his heart's life. It scorched its way along his veins, burning him up as with torturing fires.

Now he was flushed and heated, the colors mounting to his cheeks and temples, and his skin feeling fearfully hot to the hand. Now he was cold, and without apparent life, seeming scarcely to breathe at all. He was no longer in possession of his senses, but his eyes would wander idly and inexpressibly all the day long. He took hardly any nourishment, and that was such as was administered in the most trifling quantities, that would not seem indeed to be of any service.

The little school was sad enough when it first heard of Henry's sickness; and the scholars gathered in groups, talking about it in hushed voices and in whispers of childish fear. From the place of delight the school room had till that day been, it became suddenly the most gloomy spot to which the children looked forward in their thoughts. Every morning they would gather around Amy with looks of the deepest anxiety, and inquire how Henry was, and if he was any better, and if she thought he was going to get well; and one little girl, after the rest had got through with their questions, stepped quietly to the lap of Amy, and asked, with tears standing in her eyes, "Will he *die*, Miss Lee?" Amy drew the child to her bosom, and whispered affectionately to her as she leaned forward, "My child, God knows what is best; we must not complain even if he takes little Henry away."

Dr. Sillby was attentive, and exerted himself to the extent of his skill. He felt more than a merely professional interest in this case; for, like the rest, he really loved the boy, and esteemed him for his many virtues. He went constantly to the house; and whenever he met Amy either going to or returning from school, he stopped to ask about his very latest symptoms. Yet Dr. Sillby could not do more than any other mere man. He could not work miracles, although his heart might secretly wish that such a gift were in this present case his. He might tax his skill to the utmost, and his heart might bleed for the agonies of others; but there the human work was obliged to stop. The rest must be left without a murmur, or even an inquiry, to God.

The neighbors throughout the village were exceedingly kind, as they always are in such cases of serious sickness. They sent in continually to be advised of the slightest change. They offered their sympathies at every turn. They came in every day, bringing of their own provisions to Mrs. Gummel, that she might have every needed moment with Henry. And then they were all so ready to

watch with him during the night, or during the day to
assist his mother about her accumulating labors.   She
had but to utter a wish ; and if it was within the power
of her neighbors and friends, it was gratified.   " How different," thought Amy, " from the customs of the city,
where the sick seem rather to take care of themselves, or,
if they have a physician, have scarcely any one else ! "
This certainly was the better way, for it bespoke human
sympathy, and recognized the most precious feelings of
the human heart.

And every night, till at least midnight, did Amy herself sit and watch by that bedside. She counted the quick
breathings of the sick boy almost as closely as if she had
been his sister or his mother.   She knew all the names
of the many mixtures that were crowded so thickly on
the little stand, and could tell exactly when the proper
time came for the administration of each.   So long had
she been with him, and so patiently had she sat out the
lengthening hours, that she was as familiar with the para-
phernalia of the apartment as the boy's own mother.

Often she sat alone with him for half the night, and
after that gave up the responsibility to some one else.   In
those silent night watches of the autumn, with the hoarse
cry of the katydids in the maple trees along the village
street, and the fading rim of the old moon going out of
sight behind the leaves, her thoughts led her back to those
other days when she had a dear charge of her own to
keep, and felt that a single breath might at any moment

blow her happiness all away. She listened sadly to the
ticking of the little clock on the mantel, wondering if its
turning hands would bring life or death. She could hear
the beating of her own heart in the midnight silence. She
caught the breathing of the sick boy. And all three
sounds, each in its own mysterious way, kept telling her,
as no other voices could have done, " Passing away! passing away ! " And then would immediately follow her own
bounding thought, " If life goes so soon, there is no time
to be lost in complaint or morbid fear; what we do, we
must do quickly ; the few advantages we have are to be
improved now; life is only one continual NOW; there is
no future, for we know nothing but a perpetual present;
therefore ought this present to be enlarged to the very
heavens with our prayers, our efforts, and our aspirations.

After supper one afternoon, Mrs. Gummel, who had
been extremely silent and sad for the past day or two,
began to talk with Amy quite seriously about the issue
that now threatened.

" I'm afraid — I'm afraid," said she, slowly shaking her
head, and pulling at a corner of the table cloth. " Dr.
Sillby doesn't seem to hold out any hope. What shall I
do ? How *can* I bear it ? "

" Mrs. Gummel," calmly returned Amy, " you ought not
to allow yourself to feel at all anxious or unquiet. I know
you love Henry as none but a mother can love a child."
Here Mrs. Gummel wept. " But even if what we call the
worst comes, are you not ready from your heart to think it

20

is the *best?*   Cannot you look up to Heaven, and say in all the humility of a true faith, ' Thy will be done on earth as it is done in heaven ' ? "

"O, but a mother's own child! my only, darling boy! the hope of my age — the delight of my life every day! O, it is *too* hard — *too* hard." And she continued weeping profusely.

"But is not your faith greater than this, my dear Mrs. Gummel?   Look up, — O, look up, — and see the face of the Lord smiling on you forever!   Has he not *given?* And will you think of murmuring because in his fatherly wisdom he sees fit to *take away?*   O, I know myself too well — indeed, I know much too well — how these separations tear asunder the tenderest ties of the heart, and threaten almost to crush the very life itself; but nothing comes, dear Mrs. Gummel, but for good.   Think of that, and never forget to think of it.   Keep it always in mind that God is the Father.   We cannot help ourselves at all; and shall we refuse to trust him?   Is not that just what he calls on us to do, every time he takes away one of our earthly idols — to trust more completely in him, be one with him, love only him, live to him?   Is not that the meaning of all these trials, dear Mrs. Gummel? "

"O, I know that what you say is all true, Miss Lee, — all true.   But my child — my dear child!   Must he die? Can I give him up?   Must I go through life alone? "

"Think," answered Amy, in a voice of love and tenderness that was peace itself to the heart of the afflicted mother, — "think what God has done for you already, Mrs. Gummel. He has enriched your life by giving you this dear child. It was he who gave; and if he now takes away, have you not the true trust of a child to say, 'Blessed be the name of the Lord'? O, do but be calm. Do not look only at this earthly, this narrow condition. This is not the whole of life. Can you not feel that there is a glorious life beyond, in that exalted resurrection state where we shall have spiritual bodies, and be free forever from the dead and dreary weights of these earthly bodies? Do not forget for one moment, my dear Mrs. Gummel, that God is entirely good. We could not love him unless we believed that. He it is who cares for us every moment; who surrounds each one of us with the circumstances that make our life and call out our souls' faculties; who keeps us by day and by night in the hollow of his hand. You have trusted him so far, and that trust has been the only source of your happiness; can you not trust him to the end? Is he not as good now as he ever has been? Has he ever failed you when your soul went out to him in humility and love? And do you think, dear Mrs. Gummel, that because he calls away your boy to a better land, he has turned his face from you entirely, and loves you no longer? If this is to be your chastening, do you not believe that 'he loveth whom he chasteneth'?"

The woman was dumb. Her tears ceased to flow. Her breast no longer was convulsed with sobbing. She sat calmly and reflected. It was even as Amy had told her;

there was no room for dodging, or fleeing, or deceit ; if
God chose at this time to take the boy, it certainly was
because he loved both the child and his mother.   Look at
it as she would, it could be no otherwise.

And Amy was the reconciler, the immediate comforter.
She was the human means of leading back this unquiet
and almost rebellious heart to the love of its God.   Could
Mrs. Gummel have thought that so it was to be when she
first saw Amy, a stranger, getting into the stage coach,
and when she moved to make room for her at her side !
Ah ! so very strange are human events — so mysteriously
arranged — yet ever so perfectly developed among the
maze of circumstances, and the blessed meaning of their
lessons so surely brought at last to the open light.

Mrs. Gummel's heart was more at rest.   There was but
one place where she could hope to find peace, and that
was in God.   To him, therefore, she went, and implored
him, as a good Father, not to save the life of her boy, not
to give her any temporal comforts, any mere physical ben-
efits, but to fill her soul to overflowing with faith, that
under any circumstance, and all circumstances, she might
rely in peace on the promises that are everlasting.

The very next afternoon Amy dismissed her school
somewhat earlier than was customary, and hastened home
to Mrs. Gummel again.   She felt a little anxious, not yet
fully confident of the poor woman's strength of spirit.
The children all went home in different ways, careful to
make no noise along the street; for she had told them

how low Henry was, and begged them to do nothing going home that would disturb him.

As she walked homewards she was sensible of the silence that reigned every where. There was no air stirring among the gayly-attired trees, no singing of birds, no chirp of the insects. The doors of all the dwellings were shut, and the yards as still as if the indwellers had left the town. So quiet a picture half startled her.

She reached the door of Mrs. Gummel's house, and found it ajar. As she cautiously pushed it farther back, she saw that the rooms were filled with persons, and that all were in tears. She caught also stifled and half-suppressed sobs, as of mothers trying to choke down their grief, or of young girls whose sympathies were too deep for control.

At once laying aside her things, she passed by them all, and hurried to the sick chamber. The door was shut; but she caught the low sound of prayer within. She softly opened it, and entered.

There lay little Henry on the bed, motionless and still. His happy spirit on that pleasant afternoon had departed. Both his mother and Mr. Parsons were kneeling at the bedside, and the latter was offering prayer. Amy immediately dropped on her knees by the side of the bereaved mother, and, winding her arm affectionately about her waist, joined them in their strain of supplication at the throne.

"O thou great and good Father! May thy kingdom

20 *

come, and thy will be done on earth as it is done in heaven. Draw us closer and closer to thee, and give us the faith of truly innocent and trustful children. Lift us up continually, that on earth we may daily behold thee. Give us pure hearts, that we may see thee always. O, thine be the kingdom, and the power, and the glory, forever and ever. Amen."

Amy looked in Mrs. Gummel's face as they rose again, and kissed her. That moment their hearts were knit indissolubly. The mother stood and looked at the passionless face of her child, placed her palm upon his marble forehead, toyed with his thin hair, and now and then drew deep, deep sighs, that spoke of the anguish through which she had been called to pass. But all the time she remained calm ; she uttered not a complaint or a murmur ; she felt it was God's doing, and he knew what was best.

On Sunday came the burial. The ceremonies were observed at the church, calling many people together. The funeral discourse was an exceedingly appropriate and happy production, and abounded with the comforting thoughts that bring such sweet peace and such placid joy. There were few present who were not affected with the exercises of that quiet afternoon.

All the scholars followed the little coffin to the grave with sad faces and eyes full of tears. This was a great sorrow for them ; but from these crushed blossoms would be distilled a rich and abounding fragrance. Even children have need of this sad discipline ; and never, never should it be suffered to lodge itself in their souls, except with such other feelings as those of faith, and love, and humility. Far off be the unhealthy influence that brings to the young heart nothing but quaking and trembling fear !

So Mrs. Gummel was alone in the world. But no ; she was now many times more surrounded with friends than before. Every hour her thoughts dwelt with those who had gone before, and day and night they blessed her spirit with their angel presence.

And thus this great grief became an exalted and a measureless joy.

CHAPTER XXII.

AMY AT THE PARSONAGE.

Mrs. Parsons and she were alone in the room, each sitting at a corner of the hearth. The fire was blazing brightly, for it was a chilly autumn day, and quite late in the season. Looking out the window, Amy saw that the leaves were gone, and the trees were standing stripped and bare, and looking as if ready to shiver in the blasts that threatened.

" Do you think Mrs. Gummel is entirely reconciled to her loss?" asked the minister's wife, rocking gently to and fro in her chair, and changing her knitting needle.

" Yes," said Amy, drawing out her thread and looking contemplatively into the fire, " I think she is. Such cheerfulness as hers is can certainly come only from a heart that is altogether at peace."

" It was a great affliction, at least as people usually regard such things," added Mrs. Parsons. " Many could not have kept up under it. They would have complained to Heaven, that it was really more than they could bear. But I do not think it is so with Mrs. Gummel. She seems to me to be resigned."

(236)

" Yes, she *is* resigned.   I think she would be resigned now to any thing."

" That is the happiest state of the heart," said Mrs. Parsons, looking expressively over at Amy.   " Can you conceive any condition more blessed ? "

" O, no ; especially if it is the *true* resignation.   That will always bring more abundant peace than it can ever take away."

" Then you think there is more than *one* kind of resignation ? "

" But one *true* and *real* resignation," answered Amy, " and that is to be perfectly at one with God ; no less in one thing than another ; in great as well as small."

" Yet how can you conceive of a state in which the spirit that is resigned is really *less* so than in this you have described ? "

" Literally I cannot ; yet some persons, you know, suffer their feelings merely to relapse into a morbid and sullen condition, as if God might be a tyrant as well as a Father, and say they are willing that he should do exactly as he chooses ; not simply because, like little children, they *love* him, but because they think they are quite in his *power*, and so feel the folly of making complaint."

" There are such persons," said Mrs. Parsons, with some emphasis.   " There is certainly just such a sort of resignation as this in the world."

" But it is a falsehood, the whole of it !   Do you not think so, Mrs. Parsons ? "

" I do; I certainly do."

" The obedience that comes by *fear* I cannot conceive to be obedience," added Amy, her soul catching a glow from her subject. " The true obedience, and that which brings this resigned state of feeling under all circumstances and on all occasions, in life or in death, in sunshine or cloud, among friends or among fearful perils, in riches or in poverty, with kind hearts all about us or in the midst of malicious and designing enemies — *that* kind of obedience can come only by *faith* —— "

" Yes, yes, Amy; that is true enough."

" By a faith that keeps itself alive by feeding on the very substance hoped for, yet now in one sense unseen; not a faith that drives one to the ends of the created universe with *fear*, but that draws continually nearer and nearer by the strong cords of *love* — the perfect love that *casteth out* fear — the love that swells in our hearts because we know that He first loved *us !* Such is the faith that seems to me to work obedience, and works besides all its manifold and blessed fruits. It grows greater by the steady contemplation of the God who has given it to us to enjoy. It takes in all conditions, all classes, all circumstances. It enfolds the soul in a garment of its own, so that it walks through the world spotless and holy. It makes us children, and full of humility; and at the same time it enlarges us, expands us, and prompts us all the time to aspire, till we see that *only* by obedience, and *only* by perfect and willing resignation, can we find the true centre of our being."

" How true it all is, Amy! I declare, I long for an experience such as yours is!"

"*Mine*, Mrs. Parsons? It is not much, yet it makes me grateful. I am grateful for every thing. I mean to consider *nothing as sorrow*; there are no sorrows; they exist only in the diseased imaginations of men, and spring out of their selfishness, and impatience, and puny ambition, and perpetual querulousness. If we would but cast behind us this *ambition*, Mrs. Parsons — put it entirely beneath our feet, mock at it, despise it as not at all worthy to associate with our lofty capacities — if we would but do *this*, and let our ambition become a noble and a spiritual *aspiration*, how different the result to all of us!"

" But men *will* trust themselves, before they trust any one else," said Mrs. Parsons. " They are so choked with their prejudices, so blinded by their passions, so eaten up with selfishness and avarice, that it seems almost a miracle to me how grace abounds as it does. It is wonderful!"

" First, however, should not men be brought to form the right conception of God's character? Does not that seem to be the corner stone of all true faith?"

" Assuredly; else we worship blindly, and are but little better off spiritually than if we fell down before our own idols."

" How true that is! *Idols*, indeed! There is where we are still at fault. The world is as full of idols to-day as it ever was during its long history. They may not all be of wood, or of brass, of hay or stubble; yet there are idols enthroned within the secret temple of almost every heart."

"Few live that can deny it," said Amy's friend.

"The whole object of God's care and kindness," continued Amy, "of his providence and discipline, is to draw us away from the follies with which we are surrounded, to the true worship of him. In that worship is happiness. It is the only thing that can satisfy for one moment the cravings of the unquiet spirit, and it is abundant enough to satisfy those inward desires forever. Then how necessary that we get a true conception of the character of our Father from the first! — such thoughts of him as will throw our spirits, so to speak, into an attitude of worship, of gratitude and thanksgiving, the instant our consciousness takes hold upon him! Unless we understand what we are to believe, I do not see how true and joyful believers can ever be expected to abound."

"That is certainly the important step in our spiritual culture, Amy. 'God is love!' Do you think of that often?"

"I think of that *all the time*, Mrs. Parsons! I feel at my heart that this it is that so draws me to him! — that feeds my poor faith so constantly! — that lets into my soul, every day I live, such views as cannot be spoken by lips, nor written for the eyes! — that raises emotions within me such as no description can hope to answer to, and no other soul can understand except by its own jubilant experiences! O, God *is* love — LOVE indeed!"

"If the world would but *think* so!" continued Mrs. Parsons — "if the world would only *believe* this! Then what would take the place of murmurings and complainings but joy and ineffable thanksgiving? What would abound where distrust, and selfishness, and fear now so much abound, but obedience, and trust, and a perfect faith? It is so necessary that we first get a right idea of the character of God, and thus of the nature of our relations to him!"

"There are few trials, I think," said Amy, "that one is called to go through in this life, more severe and searching to the human spirit than this losing of friends. It does seem to me that if the heart is really whole, and sweet, and at peace, *this* is the time when it will all appear."

"Certainly; it must be so. For in so great a mystery as death we seem plunged in a vast abyss: if our faith only lights it up for us with the colors of trustfulness and love, we may be altogether happy even then, and think of our friends as having gone to the better land only a little while before us; otherwise this is a very dark abyss, full of gloom and sorrow. It is only this lack of trust in God that clothes dissolution with such dread."

"So I think, Mrs. Parsons," returned Amy. "We are every one born to die, and we well know it; there is no escape from that law. But death may be robbed of all its terrors. I believe that fear of death is only cowardice — moral cowardice. It seems to argue that God cannot do more and far better for us than he has done already."

21

" What a beautiful world this would be, Amy, if such feelings were general! — if fear was driven out, and only love and trust reigned! "

" Ah, yes, Mrs. Parsons, if only *sin* were conquered! " returned Amy, her countenance lighting with an almost saintly expression. " If we could but whip this monster out of the temple of our souls with whips of scorpions! "

" Yes, that would be the reign of Jesus indeed. That would be the kingdom already come."

" Hasten it on, then! Hasten it on! Let us all work and pray — work and pray continually! There is a mysterious craving within us, that will not be satisfied with the things around us. There is a something in our hearts that bids us everlastingly aspire. If we may only subject our souls to the most perfect filial obedience, and thus subject sin in its turn to the perpetual reign of holiness, then this day of blessedness has dawned."

" It may not dawn in *our* time, dear Amy."

" Ah, no ; yet I have no less faith to believe that the hour is surely approaching. Christ must certainly set up his kingdom on the earth. It will not be such a kingdom as the unbelieving Jews expected, but one founded in truth, and righteousness, and love, and peace. The lion and the lamb shall lie down then together — a beautiful symbol of the universal victory of Jesus! We may not live in the body then, Mrs. Parsons ; yet I do believe that this heavenly vision will gladden our spirits' eyes."

The door opened, and in walked Mr. Parsons. He had

been out calling on his parishioners. After exchanging the usual pleasant salutations with Amy, he drew up a chair exactly before the blazing wood fire, and between his wife and Amy, and thrust out his feet on the hearth to warm them.

"This is a rather raw day, Miss Lee," he said, rubbing his hands and holding them up before the blaze. "I declare, I feel the air more than I have any day this fall, thus far."

"Have you been walking any distance this afternoon?" asked his wife.

"Well, yes; perhaps it *is* a little distance," he replied, laughing. "Yet I shouldn't think it was, if I could have a pleasant day for it. I've been to see one of *your* friends, Miss Lee."

"Ah! and how are they, over at Mrs. Bucclebce's?" inquired Amy.

"O, *there* isn't where I've been! It's at quite another place, and at just the other end of the town."

Amy looked up in his face, and regarded him with a smile of satisfaction.

"I've been up to see Mrs. Tatterags," said he, looking into the fire musingly; "Mrs. Tatterags and all her numerous brood."

"There is really a yard full of them, isn't there?" playfully said Amy.

"O, yes, indeed! yes, indeed! But Mrs. Tatterags seems to have imbibed a little more *cheerfulness* of late. *Once*, when I went there, she found time for little else but

complaints, and regrets, and dissatisfactions; *now*, however, it doesn't seem to be quite so; she has a little sunnier
countenance, and is better disposed to find a bright side
to things, if there *is* one. Miss Lee, I shall give *you* the
credit of all this! There's no telling what your influence
has done for that woman — and, through her, for the whole
family."

Amy looked at Mrs. Parsons and blushed; and just as
she would have withdrawn her eyes, they met those of
Mrs. Parsons, and were fixed upon them.

" There's no need," added Mr. Parsons, " that any thing
be *said* about all this, for I do not suppose that you ever
had such a motive as the love of other people's praise;
you have acted from a higher principle, I know."

" If I have done any good," said Amy ——

" Yes, yes; *if* you have done any good!" broke in the
clergyman; " *if* you have, of course!"

" It is a source of the deepest joy to me," continued
Amy. " It will most certainly bring its own reward along
with it."

" That's what it will!" echoed Mr. Parsons, with a
good deal of contagious heartiness.

" I act only from love. If I can but do any *good*, I
esteem it more a privilege for myself than for those to
whom the service may be done."

The clergyman and his estimable wife exchanged happy
glances.

Amy pursued: —

"In performing a kind office, my benefit is always greater than that of the other party. Not that I set out with the aim to make it so, but just because I do *not* desire that result. In such a kingdom as that of benevolence, he who is the least in motive, in ambition, and in hope of reward, must always be the greatest. Is it not so?"

"You are right, Miss Lee," answered Mr. Parsons. "I only wish that all the world believed as you believe. How soon we should have the reign of contentment and happiness, if these things were really so!"

Mrs. Parsons rose to set out the table, and in a very short time they were enjoying the pleasures of the quiet evening meal.

21 *

CHAPTER XXIII.

THE SNOW STORM.

"I MUST go over to the mountain this afternoon," said Amy one Saturday in December; "for Mrs. Tatterags will really think I have forgotten them all." So after dinner she started off alone, pursuing her usual route by the old bridge.

It was a melancholy day, so far as outward aspects went, with a gloomy sky, and dull masses of clouds blotting out the sun. Any one at all familiar with the promises of the weather would have said it was going to snow; that the air, indeed, was "full of it." But such a consideration did not seem to influence Amy at all, even if it once occurred to her.

The road, after getting out of the habitable part of the village, was lonely and desolate. The sombre color of the sky lent its influence even to the inanimate objects with which her eyes were so familiar. The chill atmosphere made every thing else look cold and forbidding. So different were the old stone walls now by the road side, once ruffled with wild vine leaves, or buried beneath the masses of self-reliant shrubbery! So naked, so bald, so uninvit-

ing, lay the open fields on every hand, stripped of their
green carpets, their thick-standing armies of cornstalks,
and their rustling leaves! The woods up on the mountain's side were gray and leafless. No shade among their
whitened boughs. No foliage to conceal their rugged
stems. No clothing for the jagged rocks, to keep them
out of sight on the hill sides, and to help throw over nature's face a veil of beauty.

When she came to the bridge again, she stopped there
as usual, musing while she looked over the rail. The
stream was frozen as smooth as glass. The surface was
bright and clear, with not a stain from the mud at the
bottom of the river's bed. "O," she thought, "if one
could but understand the mystery of all the life that lies
below! So many things are concealed from us! Where
shall we begin — at what door shall we enter nature's
temple — when we wish to become learners?"

Turning to begin the ascent of the mountain, she almost
involuntarily drew a long breath, as if to gather strength
for the start. Then she plodded on patiently, one foot
before the other, one foot before the other all the time, till
she arrived at the high plain on which she was seated
when Dolly first presented herself. She sat down on a
rock again to rest her, and then hurried on. The air was
very chill, and her walk had made her warm; she feared a
cold, if she should sit down long now.

The moment she came in sight of the Tatterag domicile
she paused to listen. She did not know exactly why she

did so, but perhaps it was habit. Immediately she caught
the confused cries of children, as if some little Babel might
have broken loose. Evidently the younger part of the
family were having a good time of it.

As soon as she knocked on the inner door, the outer
one being left ajar at all seasons of the year, the noise
ceased.

"There!" cried one and another. "Who's that?
Hark, now! Hark a minute, can't ye?" she heard on
all sides.

"O, do shet up!" came a man's voice. "It's enough
to craze any body, an' it don't signify."

"La, Israel!" exclaimed a voice that Amy knew to be
the wife's; "do let 'em have a little play once in a while.
They don't hurt nobody."

Fearing that the youngsters might go at their sport
again, especially after this favorable word from their
mother, Amy knocked once more, and still louder.

"Why!" said Mrs. Tatterags, stepping heavily across
the floor; "somebody's to the door." And instantly she
opened it wide upon Amy. "Of all things in the world!"
exclaimed the astonished woman. "Miss Lee, I do declare! Walk in, Miss Lee; do. We hain't got any too
much room, you see; but we're always glad to see *you*."

So Amy went in, and tried in a single moment to make
herself at home and at her ease. Had she appeared otherwise, in the least degree distant or ceremonious, she
would have excited all their suspicions in an instant, and

counteracted the very object for which she was in the habit
of coming.

"Afternoon, ma'am," saluted Mr. Tatterags from his
seat in the corner of the fireplace, where he was holding
his head with exemplary patience between his knees.

Amy returned his greeting, and little more passed between them ; for, in the first place, Israel Tatterags was
altogether too lazy a man to be expected to make any great
display in conversation ; and, in the next place, he had a
habit of taking himself off out of doors pretty soon after
an arrival. Amy had observed this long ago, and had
become quite reconciled to so singular an arrangement.

Very soon she and Mrs. Tatterags were busily talking.
The latter, of course, held, or labored to hold, her youngest in her arms, whose vigorous kicking, and jumping, and
tossing sometimes took the breath out of her sentences
before she had got quite half through with them.

Amy wished to know if little Dolly needed any more
winter clothes. She had given her a nice woollen frock
already, remade from one of her own warm merinos, and
a pair of shoes, also some stockings ; and with the aid of
Olive, she had knit her a warm hood, comforter, and pair
of mittens. And now she came in to see how they were
all getting on, and if she could, with her small means, do
any thing more. Here is a beautiful picture for those who
ride easily in velvet-cushioned carriages, and whose purses
have never yet shown from the inside that they have a
bottom.

"O, bless you!" answered the mother, in a subdued voice, that betrayed a great deal of feeling; "what are we to do to pay you back for all this? I'm sure I don't see."

"Nothing," answered Amy. "I do what I do because it brings me pleasure. That is all. I wish it made you one half as happy as it does me."

The woman looked inquiringly at her a moment, as if she did not quite understand such a receipt for pleasure as that. Others, besides Mrs. Tatterags, would ignorantly do the same thing to-day.

"You repay me abundantly," Amy went on, "by letting little Dolly come to school." The child had at the first gone up to Amy's side, and stood leaning against her, like a lamb against its mother. "Dolly," said Amy, brushing her hair away gently from her temples, "you like to come to school — don't you? Don't you think she has made some progress since I took her?" she inquired of her mother.

"O, dear! Miss Lee, what can I say to you? You have gone and done so much for her, — so much more than I ever thought 't any body could do, — 't I'm a'most sick thinkin' how poorly the rest appear by the side of her."

"O, well, Mrs. Tatterags, we mustn't get discouraged, you know, simply because we cannot do in one day the work that belongs to months and years. When we find an opportunity to take hold, we should take hold, without any feeling like dissatisfaction that we cannot do more. As we get on, we shall find that the field widens. Work will be given us just as fast as we can perform it — you may be satisfied of that. O, no, Mrs. Tatterags; don't let us get discouraged."

It was a very pleasing way Amy had, and one well calculated to call out the sympathies of a person like this feeble woman, — this speaking of *us*, whenever she spoke only of *her*. It helped the woman to a higher feeling of self-respect, and encouraged the delightful idea of a universal sisterhood.

While, therefore, these two sat and talked about Dolly, about the school, about household matters, and about the general well being and comfort of that noisy little family, the others, who had by this time satisfied themselves with gazing at Amy's dress, features, and general appearance, now fell to their play again with almost redoubled spirit and energy. They would now and then glance around to be sure that their visitor was looking at them, and then drive on with the most increased vehemence.

Did any one, who ever visited where young children chiefly abound, fail to discover that there is a universal tendency among them to "show off" the most when a stranger is about? Whether it is observed or not, it is even so.

The little Tatterags went at it soul and body. One caught another by the ears, extracting any thing but a delectable squeal from the victim. One jumped on another's

back, playing "ride the horse to Boston." Another
climbed upon the table, and after spying his none too
clean countenance in the broken and smoky glass, cried
out from his perch to the others, "See me — see me! I'm
a-lookin' inter the *lookin'*-glass!" and immediately jumped
from the table to the floor with an emphasis that jarred
the whole domicile.

They played menagerie, imitating the not very eupho-
nious cries of the various wild beasts they tried to person-
ate. From under the table roared a savage young lion.
Perched on the rounds of a chair howled an awfully fierce
hyena. A huge elephant — huge chiefly on the map of
imagination — swung his great trunk hither and thither,
youthful ingenuity having substituted a dilapidated trow-
sers' leg for that branch of the animal; and after performing this favorite evolution, the counterfeit animal set up
its appalling cry, "Oof — oof! wank — tank! oof —
OOF!" This brought out the whole series of cages in a
roar of laughter. Amy had been slyly watching the odd
performances, and now she joined in with them with great
gusto. Seeing this, the young animals severally laughed
the louder for a moment, and then hid their heads for
shame in their several cages.

"Them children!" exclaimed the mother, as if to apol-
ogize for their strange conduct.

"O, they are having a nice time of it, I dare say,"
returned Amy. "Let them go on. I like to see children
happy."

"Yes, but they needn't be so noisy, I shouldn't think. Children, don't you make so much noise; you'll drive Miss Lee out of the house." Israel had gone already, but hardly in consequence of the racket. It was his custom, as I said before, to slip out whenever any one else slipped in, as if there might not be quite room enough for two at a time there.

By and by there arose a greater cry, and from all.the throats at once : "See — see ! It snows — it snows !"

"Yes — yes ! It snows — it snows !"

"And bites my toes," rhymed in another.

Amy looked out the low and dingy window, and saw that the snow was falling thick and fast.

"Really, now," she exclaimed to Mrs. Tatterags; "I'm caught out in a storm."

"I'm sorry enough for it," returned Mrs. Tatterags ; "but I guess 'taint a-goin' to snow a great deal. If it does, 'spose you stay up here all night with us." And she could not help a smile as she made the offer. "We haven't any too nice accommodations, I know; but such as we have, you're welcome to 'em, if any body is."

"O, thank you," said Amy; "I do not think I shall have any trouble about getting home. I'm not afraid of snow. But then it would be as well for me to start pretty soon."

"Yes, I should think so myself," replied Mrs. Tatterags. "But I hate to have you go. I don't know why

22

it is, but I like to have you come up here. There ain't
a human face that I'd rather see than yours."

Amy thanked her kindly for her professions of good
feeling. She felt that her reward was already far greater
than she deserved. The affection of this woman was a
source of deep self-congratulation. It more than compen-
sated for all her sacrifices and all her little troubles.

She had much to say additionally to Mrs. Tatterags
before she could take her leave ; and then there were
many things of which she wished to speak to little Dolly.
As yet she had not had much talk with her favorite, con-
siderately putting her off till she should have concluded
with the rest. So that when she did finally rise from her
seat to go, the air was thick with the falling flakes, and
the ground was white every where.

" I'm afraid you can't find your way," said Mrs. Tatterags, as they stood together in the outer door.

" O, I guess so," said Amy, fearing no hinderance.

" It's a-goin' to be a great storm, though, I think, after
all," the woman added, peering as far out as her sight
would allow her into the atmosphere. " Hadn't you better go the other way, down by Mr. Rackett's house, on
this road ? " pointing with her hand in the opposite direction.

" No, I think not," was Amy's answer. " Besides, I'd
like very well, for once, to see how such a storm appears
from this height. I want to get a view down into the
valley."

"Perhaps you will; but I'm thinkin' this snow won't let you see but a dreadful little ways, Miss Lee. I hope you'll go safe, though. Good afternoon, now. Do be careful as you can, and take care o' yourself."

Amy thanked her for her kindly warning, and wished her "good afternoon," and Dolly likewise, who still held her by the hand.

Once through the gate, and out into the open fields, with this fine snow flying and blowing and whirling in her face, and she felt in a moment an enlarging sense of freedom. She swung her arms about in childish delight, and drew long and deep breaths into her lungs. A feeling of sudden invigoration came over her, and she became strong. The strange stillness of nature, and only this rustling of the falling snow in her ears, wrapped her in profound thoughtfulness. Every thing seemed a great mystery around her. The air, filled with the million and ten million flakes, every one dancing and sailing on its own course to the earth, almost invited her to sail away with these winged messengers into its vast and silent abysses. Going through the piece of woods, the path was entirely obliterated. She could hear the snow dropping through the boughs with an almost murmurous sound, like the footfall of angels that were unseen. She paused and listened for the meaning that seemed to reveal itself to her spirit — so still, so solitary, so much away from the reach of all the world. She would sit down a few moments, even in the midst of that steady storm, and enjoy

to the utmost these manifold influences. And in that
wood the light came but dimly; and the curtain of the
snow was fast shutting out even what little light there
was; still she kept her seat, and kept holy companionship
with her thoughts.

After some time she rose. Looking over her shoulders,
she discovered that her apparel was hardly less than a sheet
of snow. She laughingly shook it off, however, and for
a few moments hurried on. But *only* for a few moments;
for as soon as she turned the well-known angle of the
mountain's side, and came in view of the broad plateau,
already deep with the pearly flakes, she looked away into
the mysterious sky, and lifted both hands in delight and
wonder. "O, how grand! how beautiful!" were her
exclamations, as she hastened forward to the edge of the
natural shelf, eager to take into her soul the comprehen-
sive whole of so indescribable a picture. And as soon as
she could find a seat, she gave herself to the contemplation
of a sight that had for her such a mystery and such a glory.
The words spoken to Job came freshly to her mind —
" Hast thou entered into the treasures of the *snow* ? — or
hast thou seen the treasures of the *hail* ?"

In the valley below she could descry nothing. It was a
mass of wheeling and whirling snow flakes. It seemed as
if the view was entirely blocked up. The whiteness of
the snow dazzled her eyes. The longer she gazed, the
more its perpetual falling — falling — falling — bewildered
her brain. She looked upwards into the sky, and nothing

was there but this dim veil of the snow clouds. She
looked off down the valley, or where she thought the
valley should be, and nothing was there but the same perpetually shifting veil. It curtained out the heavens, and
it curtained out the earth. The feathery drops fell on her
uplifted face, and dissolved instantly. She shut her eyes,
compressed her lips, and laughed to feel the storm toying and
playing over her forehead and cheeks. Its melted moisture
seemed to refresh her. Her spirits frolicked like those of a
child, and danced within her as gayly as the very flakes whose
motion appeared such a maze of mystery. It was a new
experience for her. It was a strange hour, full of bewildering delight and joy. She wanted to outstretch her
arms, and grasp the great multitude of unseen ones that
seemed hovering around her. She wanted to shout, to
cry out at the top of her voice, as if mysterious echoes
might return to her from every quarter. O, there was
such a rush of feelings every moment at her heart! There
was such a host of strange thoughts each moment at her
brain! And this was an old-fashioned New England snow
storm; exactly such a one as might be sought for among
the bold hills and mountain heights of Vermont, or the
still bolder and ruggeder elevations of New Hampshire.

Amy was not aware how long she was sitting there, occupied with her excited feelings. She did not know that
the daylight was nearly gone, that there was no twilight
at this season of the year, that much more snow had fallen
since she left the house of the Tatterags, and that the roads

22 *

and pathways were now completely hidden and blocked up. The delay at the house, after she knew that the storm had fairly and fiercely set in, the other stoppage in that patch of woods, before she came out upon this broad white plain —these she seemed to have forgotten. Her mind was so taken up with the storm itself and its thousand great and grand mysteries, she cared and thought little about herself, where she was, or whither she was going. But when her senses came back to her, she looked hurriedly about her, and found that night was fast coming on. The storm increased. the darkness. Gloom was every moment inwrapping her in its folds.

She rose in haste and bent her steps in the direction of the old path. For a little while this was very well. But presently she found all the well-known landmarks, the familiar rocks and trees, entirely disguised or covered up. This was something she had not foreseen; nay, such a thought had not entered her mind. She had no experience in these matters, and innocently supposed she could no more lose her way now than she could in a storm of rain. Yet the heaped snows told no tales of familiar tree trunks, or well-known rocks, or even of the cart track that had led her along so many times in safety. She turned her eyes searchingly towards the spot where she thought the village lay, but there was nothing to be seen but the whirling snows. She looked on one side and the other, and both were alike to her; and in the midst of looking, now one way and now another, she became all at once bewildered, and could not tell which way she had come, or which she was going. It was all confusion to her. She knew not the way *up* the mountain or *down* it. Thus far she had penetrated into this labyrinth, and she could go no farther. If she still persisted in walking, where would her efforts bring her out? Or, if she stood still, how would that be any better? The wind was rising fast, and its swift breaths drove the snow flakes into her face. They cut her cheeks, her eyelids, and her lips with their piercing little crystal arrows. They matted her hair, making it wet and heavy over her temples. She brushed it back with both hands, as if that would help her to see more clearly into the glimmering duskiness. The snows blew into her eyes, and she was forced to close them from pain.

Still she did not think of giving up heart or courage. Her spirits rather rose with the sense of confusion, and out of these innumerable cross-purposes asserted their own supremacy. She gathered her skirts about her with one hand, and resolved to push on and brave the storm as long as she could. Heaven had taken kind care of her till this hour; would Heaven desert her *now?*

It was really encouraging, and would have called forth admiration from any heart, to witness the stout and persistent courage that carried her forward. At short intervals she would brush back her tangled hair with the disengaged hand, and then push on again, searching anew for the road that would conduct her in safety. Her tired feet had all the while been slipping backward, and now they began to

stumble over the rough surfaces of the ground. Next she
felt that she was walking at only a tottering pace, and
faintly realized that her strength was by degrees leaving
her. Had she known just where she was walking, she
might have gone on steadily without exhaustion; but the
bewilderment occasioned by not knowing the path or the
direction, or whether she was going right or wrong, confused her thoughts, misdirected her usual energies, and
left her almost a prey to the many chances that surrounded
her. Feeling thus, she became of course gradually more
and more weak, and less and less able to hold out till she
might chance to reach the road at the foot of the mountain.
Yet sensible as she at last began to be of her unhappy
condition, her heart never grew fretful, nor did even her
thoughts utter a murmur. It was still "*Thy* will!"
even as it had been with her from the beginning. If the
snows were to cover her, and beneath the shroud of their
whiteness she was to go to her last sleep, then the Lord
still did all things well! She should trust with her whole
heart forever!

   She slipped again, fell backwards, recovered herself with
the aid of a neighboring tree, stopped a moment, and
began to reflect what was best to be done. All around
her as far as her sight could reach, wherever she turned
her eyes, into whatever quarter she tried to penetrate,
nothing but a thick tempest of snow. It walled her in on
all sides like a dense fog. She could see no trees in the
distance, no rocks, no road; she was left to the strength

of her limbs alone to extricate her from the fearful situation in which she found herself.

Another effort, another brave sally of the will, and her feet were once more in motion. She made an almost superhuman exertion, and pushed on. But whither? Was she going nearer the true road, or was she wandering away from it all the time? If she could but be certain she was going right, then she felt as if her strength would easily hold out; for this assurance would encourage her. But if she knew not whether right or wrong, the perplexity of her feelings, combined with the ruggedness of the ground, the bewilderment of the storm, and the confusion of her purposes, would very rapidly take the sinews out of her courage, and she would have to give up for weakness and despair.

It grew darker and darker every moment; so dark that she could scarcely see a tree till she came exactly upon it; and she stumbled about over the rocks and stones without either purpose or strength. Her thoughts went back, back to her father. They hovered about the dear friends she had left in the little village. She silently invoked a blessing on them all, for the truth at last dawned upon her that she might never behold them again. Mrs. Gummel was in her mind continually. And so were her dear friend Olive, and Mr. Parsons, and his wife. How they would grieve over the sad event that this day was threatening to bring them! How they would weep to find her body buried beneath the snows, cold, lifeless, and stiff!

She stumbled and tottered on, it mattered but little whither, so she but kept herself in motion. But she could not do even that long. Her sight grew dim, and all things were swimming, and dancing, and whirling before her. Now the dark old trees came round, now the rocks, now the abysses of the sky, and now the rocks and the trees again. She stretched forth her hand blindly, as if to grasp something that she saw. She trembled and shook like an aspen leaf, still battling bravely with the feelings of cowardice and despair. She, a feeble and frail girl, defying, as it were, the tempests out of the deep heavens, staying up her form like a bending reed against their power, and persisting in the face of storm and gloom in seeking her lone path out through the armies of both into final safety.

But it was too much. The powers of nature must give out, though the spirit was yet courageous and strong. She sank down easily upon the soft snow, almost before she was aware of it. Looking about her in the darkness, she faintly realized her hopeless condition. It all flashed over her, though she felt nevertheless that she must be in a dream, that her last hour had come. Instantly she threw herself on her knees, and raised her head in earnest prayer.

"O God, who sendest thy snows upon the earth, turn not away from me in this hour! Enfold me in the everlasting arms of thy love! Save me from all harms, and bring me to thee! O Lord, *thy* will be done! *thy* will be done! Be with me in this dark hour, and receive my spirit! O, let not my faith grow dim in this trying moment! Strengthen my heart by thy love, and take me to thy bosom at last!"

Suddenly she heard a cry — a shout, clear and shrill.

"Holloa! Holloa!"

She erected her head and listened, her eyes wandering every where.

"Who's that? Who's there?" came the voice. It was a man's shout, and help was at hand. God had heard the cry of the orphan, and had never for a moment forgotten her living faith.

She called as loud as she could, once, twice, three times.

Immediately a man's form sprang aside from the pathway, and stooped down to lift her from the ground.

"*Fury!*" was his exclamation. "Why, it's Miss Lee!"

She knew the voice, and could just distinguish the face. Both belonged to no other person than Israel Tatterags.

Without any words, and as if he was suddenly gifted with a new strength, he took her unresistingly in his arms, and hurried with her down into the road, over the bridge, and into the nearest house.

Strangely as it happened, too, she had wandered but a little ways from the path, though to her it was the same as if she had strayed miles and miles away.

CHAPTER XXIV.

A NEW COMER.

THE winter wore away with few or no interruptions. The school continued pleasant and prosperous, the pupils made excellent progress, and all went on harmoniously and to general satisfaction.

Amy's friendship for Olive became deeper and broader continually. Many was the evening, after school was over, that she would go there to take tea and pass the night, sure of a most enjoyable time between supper and the late hour of retiring. Mrs. Bucclebee usually sat with them for a while, offering to make some little conversation with Amy now and then, and then went off to her own room. It was a little noticeable, indeed, that during Amy's whole acquaintance with Olive, and through the entire series of her visits at the house, she had effected no terms of familiarity with the aunt, and knew her not as well as she knew many others of the ladies in the village. Mrs. Bucclebee was a woman of peculiar habits of thought and feeling. Pride was at the helm of her character; and pride never lets in any more of the gentler and lovelier virtues at the door than it can well help.

One afternoon, on returning home from her day's usual
avocations at the school house, and while she was sitting
and talking with Mrs. Gummel as the tea was drawing on
the coals, Mrs. Bucclebee's hired man came past the front
windows and knocked at the door. Amy knew in a moment that he had come with some message from Olive to
herself; and she ran to receive it. The man handed her
a note, saying that he brought it from Miss Olive. Amy
thanked him; and as he turned away, shut the door and
hurried in to get at the contents.

"MY DEAR AMY," they ran: "You must come over to
Ivy Lodge to-morrow after dinner," [the next day was
Saturday,] "and pass the afternoon with me. I have got
company,—you can guess who,—and I know we shall
make out a most delightful afternoon. I must tell you,
too, dear Amy, that I am so happy at this moment, I
desire nothing so much as to have you share my feelings
with me. Come, without fail. We shall be expecting
you certainly.

"Yours affectionately,

"OLIVE."

Amy immediately mistrusted who "the company"
meant; but she was not certain. She and Olive had
enjoyed a great many confidential talks before now; and
it would not be strange if some one of them bore closely
upon this particular matter.

Yet she thought best to speak with Mrs. Gummel about it.

"I have received a little note from Olive," said she; "an invitation to go over there to-morrow afternoon."

Mrs. Gummel merely smiled, thinking nothing else could be called for.

"Do you know whether they have any company there now?" asked Amy. "And do you know who it is?"

"Why, yes; seems to me I *did* see a strange gentleman riding out with Olive this afternoon — just riding through the village street."

"Don't you know who it is, then?"

"No, I'm sure I don't. Who is it, pray?"

"O, that's just what I am to find out myself," answered Amy; and I shall probably do so by obeying this request of my friend Olive to-morrow afternoon. We shall see, I think."

Immediately after dinner, therefore, on the next day, she threw on her things, though not until she had bestowed more than usual care upon her dress, and walked thoughtfully over to Ivy Lodge. It is not to be denied that Amy had curiosity, exactly as every other human being possesses it, and that it was a little piqued by the dark hintings of Olive's note, and that she was rather glad that it was so soon to be gratified; but still she was much more moved with satisfied feelings at the thought of her friend's happiness. If she could by any means add to it in the least degree, that would most certainly be her desire.

Coming to the piazza, Olive ran forward to meet her, as usual, bareheaded and with sparkling eyes. She extended both hands and kissed her.

"I'm so glad you've come!" exclaimed she in a low tone; "for *he's* here at last, and aunt is as full of delight as I am."

Amy knew now in a moment who was meant. Olive had made her a confidant in this matter a long time before.

They stepped briskly across the piazza, Olive chattering busily all the way, and still holding on by Amy's hand. She was telling her what a wonderful surprise it all was, how overjoyed her aunt had been since his unexpected arrival, what he had said about himself and about herself, and how she had described Amy all out to him, exciting his imagination to such a pitch that he insisted on seeing her forthwith.

"*Now*," exclaimed Amy reprovingly, "if I had known this before, I never would have come over here while he staid."

"Wouldn't you? O, wouldn't you?" cried Olive, clapping her hands in great glee. "How glad I am you didn't know it! What fun I shall have yet! O Amy, Amy! Do you know that he is in love with you already, just from hearing my description of you?"

Amy blushed deeply.

They passed in; and Olive led her to her own chamber, where this sort of conversation was still further carried on, while Amy threw off her bonnet and shawl.

"I declare," said Olive, flatteringly, "how very fine
you do look to-day! You are really handsomer than ever,
Amy, I do believe. Just see those cheeks! and those
eyes, now!"

The walk had thrown a beautiful color into Amy's
cheeks, and given increased animation to her eyes; and
it is not to be concealed that she looked exceedingly
interesting, even if one should not be allowed to say —
handsome.

"Olive," she returned, turning round upon her with a
face wreathed with smiles, yet quite serious in one aspect,
"I do certainly hope you love me too well to flatter me.
That is no mark of a sweet and exalted friendship. Pray,
let us be above such things."

"O dear Amy!" said Olive, now going up and putting
her arm about her, "I beg you to forgive me. I meant
nothing at all, only — only that I think you do look so
handsome. And I can't help loving you all the more
for it."

And with these words of affectionate pleading, that no
heart could well resist, she drew Amy to her with her
other arm, and kissed her again and again.

On entering the parlor, Amy first accosted Mrs. Bucclebee, walking over to her and extending her hand. Then
this lady glanced in the direction of the visitor, who sat
opposite, and mentioned to Amy his name.

"This is Mr. Clendenning," said she, nodding at him.
"Miss Amy Lee — Mr. Clendenning."

The gentleman arose, made a very respectful bow, offered to help the young ladies to chairs, and finally resumed his own.

It was not a great while before all were perfectly at ease. Mrs. Bucclebee seemed particularly anxious to keep the conversation a-going, and took quite enough of it upon herself to make up for the two girls besides.

The stranger was a man perhaps thirty-three or thirty-five years old, of a rather dark and foreign appearance, and with a countenance and manners that seemed at once to confess extensive travel and a familiar acquaintance with what is called "the world." He was remarkably intelligent in regard to general subjects; and his answers to the questions put him by Mrs. Bucclebee, for the sole purpose of drawing him out, were given with readiness, fulness, and a not unpleasing flourish of words, phrases, and gesticulation.

Mr. Clendenning — to let the reader into the whole of it at once — was a gentleman of fortune. This fortune he had acquired during a course of years in South America, by trading extensively in the products of the interior. Having finally secured the amount upon which his ambitious spirit early fixed itself, he had returned to his native city and country, as he said himself, "to enjoy it." Many years before he was an acquaintance of both Mrs. Bucclebee and her deceased husband; and he had managed in one way and another to keep up the intimacy, till now, when he was ready to return, he found himself in fact the

23 *

bespoken husband of their pretty niece. He had not
seen her since she was a little girl; but Mrs. Bucclebee's
thoughts had nursed the subject very tenderly, and, without a final meeting, she had succeeded in bringing about
an implied betrothal. Mrs. Bucclebee had merely made a
match ; Olive saw how the matter gratified her aunt, upon
whom she was entirely dependent, and could not refuse
ready assent to whatever proposal came from her. So
while she was yet only a young girl, her rich nature just
beginning to ripen and develop itself, she found that to
all purposes either of choice or pleasure her hands were in
fact tied, and her heart was given away. It would not do
now to rebel ; and she had no intention to do so, either.
She felt that her happiness was altogether in the hands of
her aunt, and that nothing but her word was law.

Amy did not know this at the first ; but she was not a
great while in finding it out. She saw for herself that
this was nothing more than a meddlesome match between
the two parties, and was as thoroughly satisfied that
Olive's aunt was at the bottom of it. And the very first
thing that assured her of this fact was the growing indif-
ference to Mr. Clendenning that Olive could not help
betraying. Her regard was too forced ; there was little
real nature in it, and there must, then, be but little love.

The conversation went on, and before long became general. The two girls occupied themselves with needlework ;
Mrs. Bucclebee took upon herself a sort of general super-
vision ; and the stranger exerted himself to make the time
pass as agreeably as possible.

One thing was quite noticeable — he was continually staring at Amy. Something attracted him very powerfully. Every time her own eyes chanced to wander that way, as she looked up from her work, they were sure to meet the fixed gaze of Mr. Clendenning. Yet he seemed to make but little talk with her, although that might easily be accounted for by the industry of Mrs. Bucclebee in engrossing his attention. But yet those eyes, dark and piercing, expressed much more than words would. They embarrassed Amy very sensibly; for she could not help being perpetually conscious that they were fixed on her, and this conviction would not naturally relieve her of a feeling of undue sensitiveness.

"Then you have had enough of South American life," said Mrs. Bucclebee, wishing to show him off on a subject with which he must be perfectly familiar.

"O, yes, indeed," said he, rather dully. "I desire no more of it, I assure you. Give me the good old quiet life of New England for the rest of my days, and I shall be perfectly satisfied."

And again he directed his eyes at Amy — perhaps directing the remark to her, too.

"I suppose life in South America is a great deal more romantic, more poetic, than it is with us," continued Mrs. Bucclebee. "There is less of this chilling form and cold ceremony — isn't there?"

He smiled.

"Indeed, there's little enough of that any·where in

South America, I can promise you, especially in the interior sections of the continent. No great field for etiquette or rank either, Mrs. Bucclebee, among the serpents and wild beasts in the jungles."

" Serpents ! " exclaimed Mrs. B., with a shudder and a shrug of her shoulders. " O, dear ! What horrid, horrid creatures to think of ! "

" Ah, but you should see a nice full-grown one with your own eyes, Mrs. Bucclebee — say one that is thirty or forty feet long —— "

" O, horrible ! "

" — Coiling up around the stem of a huge tree, and laying his head and neck just over the lowest branch, merely to signify to stragglers and travellers that he is quite ready to receive company. Those are the serpents for you ! None of these little span-long water snakes, that can curl all up like a horse hair in a tumbler of water ; but a genuine, out-and-out serpent, tawny and spotted, bright with yellow and gold, with a tongue that plays in and out of its mouth like a forked flame."

" O, don't — don't, Mr. Clendenning, I beg of you. It makes me crawl to think of them. Ugh ! "

Olive was regarding the gentleman with a very candid, if not credulous expression ; and when her aunt betrayed her terror and disgust by these exclamations, she laughed outright in a ringing voice, as if it afforded her hearty enjoyment. And the more her aunt shrugged her shoulders, the louder she kept laughing ; till at last the tears came into her eyes, and she stopped to wipe them away.

Amy looked up at her, to understand what amused her so excessively; and naturally enough she glanced both at Mrs. Bucclebee and at the visitor.

Those eyes — they were upon her still! She could not help thinking of the eyes of the very serpent he had been describing.

Perceiving her embarrassment, he instantly offered to retrieve the mischief.

"Have you been long in this place, Miss Lee?" he asked her.

"No, sir," she answered; "I am hardly better than a stranger here, I tell them."

"Something like myself, then — ha, ha!"

"She's been here only a part of a year," interposed Mrs. Bucclebee, very patronizingly. "Miss Lee teaches our little village school, I suppose you know."

Amy could not fail to observe the tone in which this was spoken.

"Yes, I *have* heard so," returned Mr. Clendenning, elevating his head somewhat, and facing round as if he were about to open a direct conversation with Amy.

Mrs. Bucclebee, however, was watchful, and meant to allow no such opportunities for social intercourse.

"Did you find all your friends in Boston well, when you arrived?" she interrupted.

"O, yes, ma'am — yes, ma'am," he carelessly answered, slowly turning about again.

"All glad to see you again, of course."

"Ah, well; but if a person is desirous of knowing whether he *has* any friends or not, he ought certainly to go out of the country for a few years, as I have done. One can pretty soon tell when he gets back again."

And in such a strain of general talk the planning aunt kept the visitor well occupied. If he had any thing to say to Olive, Mrs. Bucclebee was right at hand to help add to the interest; if any thing in turn to Amy, that lady was no less alert in directing his attention in quite another way. No such flimsy subterfuges could deceive one as acute as Amy was, and she understood the whole matter at a glance. Yet it subjected her to no sort of perplexity. If Mrs. Bucclebee chose to make herself uneasy on her account, she was quite at liberty to do so. The enjoyment of it would fall on no shoulders but her own.

Tea was announced, and they all walked out. Mr. Clendenning was particularly polite to Amy, both in getting to the table and while the meal was being served. Olive very generously was seating Amy next her friend; but Mrs. Bucclebee corrected her arrangement with the help of a dark frown, and motioned to Amy that Olive didn't seem to understand, that *there* was her seat, "if you please," on the opposite side to Mr. Clendenning. The latter certainly could not have desired any thing better; for now he had an excellent opportunity to look Amy exactly in the face. Amy saw the uneasiness of Mrs. Bucclebee, and from her heart pitied her. Why should *she* be the slightest obstacle to any of that lady's designs?

When they rose from the table, they strolled at their leisure through ·the little rooms, examining the pictures, the books, and the plants that stood shelved in the conservatory ; but at no moment did Mrs. Bucclebee surrender her place at her visitor's side, and not once did she suffer him to engage in a protracted conversation with Amy.

But as soon as the latter began to speak of returning home, — which Mrs. Bucclebee had for a long time been secretly wishing in her heart she would do, — Mr. Clendenning rose to volunteer his escort. Amy thanked him politely, and said she should not be afraid of going alone ; she had done so a great many times. But he insisted, and moved to get his coat and hat. Mrs. Bucclebee was puzzled and perplexed. Still she could not well *say* any thing, for the motive might be too transparent. It was excellent discipline for her.

Mr. Clendenning, therefore, *did* wait upon Amy home ; and the interval of his absence was duly improved by the aunt in instructing her wayward niece how to manage things more shrewdly for the future.

CHAPTER XXV.

QUITE A SURPRISE.

THE stranger remained at Mrs. Bucclebee's during the greater part of the next week, occupying himself with his friends at Ivy Lodge. Yet not altogether there, either; for every afternoon, at about the time Amy dismissed her school, he and Olive either called at Mrs. Gummel's to see her, or else went directly to the school house and walked from there home with her.

It was not to be disguised that he was excessively captivated with Amy, and that he had been from the first. Olive confessed about the whole truth when she told Amy, in her frolicking style, that he was really " in love with her; " and were it possible to suppose that Olive's *heart* had as yet been touched in this matter, the conclusion would be allowable that she would not have still continued to seek *Amy's* society so much, while she could have *his*. I believe that is a general law in these delicate affairs. Each being nothing less than " all the world " to the other, there is no need, and still less disposition, to go in search of sources of happiness outside their own enchanting realms.

But Amy made no sort of advances on her part. She

was aware that the understanding was, that Olive was to be the stranger's wife; whether such a promise had been seriously and sacredly made by *her* she knew not, but she was not forgetful of their mutual relation to one another. For her, therefore, to step in between — but it is foolish to speak of such a thing — Amy Lee was the last one to be suspected of it. Besides, she lacked all *motive* to do so. The stranger was too much blinded by his own eagerness to see that his advances were never met by her. Still he persisted in his purposes, whatever they were, and suffered himself to be deceived by his own false dream. Amy herself could be supposed to know nothing of his secret feelings, and her speech and manners were altogether as free, and flowing, and full of love as they ever were.

It was getting to be late in the week again, and the weather was still cold and uncomfortable. Amy always kept her school room warm, and there she bade defiance to the frost and the shivers. She would have good fires, and the children all enjoyed them. And after she dismissed them for the day, it was her custom often to sit alone over the glowing bed of coals, and give herself to the thoughts that silently set about her. For the last week the regular visits of Olive and her friend had interrupted her, or rather had compelled her to shorten these moments of pleasant musing. But on this particular night, after sitting longer than usual, she discovered that they did not come. So she gave over expecting them, and soon relapsed into a state that bordered very closely on dream-

24

land. It was a quiet hour and a quiet place. No place hardly *can* be more silent than a deserted old country school room at the close of a winter's day. The shadows were thickening, and threw their first duskiness through the windows. Still she sat silent over the coals, and enjoyed the solitude.

She heard no noise whatever, till the door suddenly opened. It startled her so much that she almost stood upright. Her back happened to be towards the door, and she could not see who the intruder was without first turning around. It was Mr. Clendenning.

"Ah! good evening, Miss Amy," said he, shutting the door very deliberately, and advancing to the open stove. "You're all alone here — aren't you?"

"But where is Olive?" she asked, her heart not altogether at rest, in the face of this unexpected call.

"Olive!" said he, affecting much carelessness; "she's at home, I suppose, over at what they call 'Ivy Lodge' — ha, ha! At least, I left her there, and not many minutes ago."

And he drew up the end of a bench to the fire, and sat down without any sort of further ceremony.

"Why didn't *she* come too?" inquired Amy.

"Well," said he, in an easy tone, "she thought she had too much to *do*, to come out with me to-night — one thing and another; I don't know what. Besides, I told her I was only going a short distance, by-way of a little exercise, you know. She didn't mistrust that I was coming over to see *you*, I reckon!"

Amy was astonished. She could not in the moment gather together her thoughts sufficiently to make him a suitable reply. He saw her revulsion of feeling, and hastened to set matters right again as fast as he could.

" Olive is good company," said he, as if to lead Amy away into a criticism of her friend. " I must confess I rather *like* Olive. She's a *good girl*, and knows how to make herself agreeable, when it's necessary."

Still Amy was dumb with amazement.

" I declare, Miss Lee," he went on, with a gesture of impatience, " this must be an *awful dull* place for any one like you. What makes you stay here ? "

Amy could not say any thing yet.

" When I first came into the village I began to wonder how human beings could possibly *live* here ; I *do* wonder how a person like *you* can, Miss Lee — I declare I do."

" Why so ? " she asked.

"O, *because* — I *do* ; I wonder what there is to take up your *time*."

" My *duties* do that," said she.

" Ah ! But in *Olive's* case it seems to be quite another thing. She's quite a different person from *you*, I think ; *any body* would see that."·

Amy wondered what this kind of talk meant. It sounded still worse to her from her being acquainted with the secret relations between her friend Olive and him. She could only reply to his remarks in a general way.

" I'm sure," said she, " I do not see why *I* should be

less easily pleased here than *Olive*." And she looked up in his face for an explanation.

He was hardly disposed to carry that particular matter any farther, however. So he began on another.

" Does your little school here give you any thing like a *support* ? " he asked. " I really don't see how you can live off of it."

" O, yes, sir; it yields me a very handsome little revenue ; quite all I *need*, I am sure."

" Well, some people say, I know, that a body don't *want* any thing more than he *needs ;* but I am not quite prepared to fall in with them. You don't mean to say, Miss Lee, that you wouldn't *be* rich if you could as well as not, do you ? "

She *felt* that his eyes were searching her flushed face, every moment; and she hardly knew, in her unhappy embarrassment, what it *was* best to do.

" There is no wealth like that of a true heart," she answered, so calmly as to be astonished even with herself.

" Certainly — most certainly ! I perfectly agree with you there. There *is* no wealth like that of the heart — every body that *has* a heart will tell you that. I must say I admire one whose nature is rich and poetic as much as *any* man can; and where such a nature is to be found in a *woman*, what is it to be wondered at if the world fairly runs mad after her ? "

There was a pause. Amy's eyes were in the fire. His were on her face. It was a moment of the most trying embarrassment to her.

Yet he was perfectly collected and cool. No one would have supposed that he was in the least degree *interested* in such sentiments as he had just expressed, for he uttered them exactly as he would have read aloud the manifest of a ship, or called off the items in a cargo of South American hides. His coolness piqued Amy, and might offend her. It was patronizing, with an air of impertinence, boastful, and altogether presumptuous.

Finally he began again and in a new place : —

"Miss Lee, I suppose you are not so *perfectly* well satisfied with your present situation as to refuse a good opportunity of changing it ? "

She looked up at him.

"I don't quite understand you, sir," said she, in a tone of inquiry, yet with perfect firmness.

"Why, suppose you had an offer of a better place, I mean — that's all! Wouldn't you accept it ? "

"Indeed, I am quite satisfied where I am, I think. But I should *first* wish to be satisfied if the change *would* be for the better."

"Well, now, see here," said he, leaning forward a very little, as if desirous of being confidential. "A person like *you*, Miss Lee, can't certainly feel altogether resigned to follow so humble an occupation as that of a village school teacher all her days."

"I am very happy," interrupted Amy, "whenever I am discharging my own duties, and making others around me happy too."

24 *

"All that's well enough, I dare say; I won't pretend to dispute it. But I shouldn't conceive that my duties *lay* in a place like this little village, if I were you."

"I am satisfied that at least for the *present* they do," she answered.

"But you won't pretend to say you wouldn't take a wider field, if you *could* ? "

"No; I say nothing about it, sir. I aim to live a whole life in each day, let me be placed any where. I would make that life sweet and full of poetry; for there *is* a poetry in the very humblest and simplest of things."

"True — true, I dare say; only I don't imagine I know as much about such things as you do. But what I was coming at was this: I shall be very candid, as you will see; and you will allow me to get at the matter in my usual business way."

Amy's face burned redly. She could feel the flush all over her forehead, and her ears fairly tingled with the uncomfortable sensation of heat. She knew now what he was about to say. If words would only have come, she would have spoken. But she was dumb.

"Of course," he continued, in the same careless and almost unfeeling way, "of course you wouldn't hesitate a moment to change your situation in life, if you had a good opportunity."

"I do not understand why you feel so positive about it," she interrupted.

"Well, now," he added, not seeming to heed the interruption, " I have an offer to make you. You should know, in the first place, Miss Lee, that I have been a great admirer of yours from the beginning. When I first saw you at Olive's, I fell dead in love with you; and that is all I can say about it. I inquired more particularly about you. They told me you merely taught this little village school; and I was astonished, I must confess; a girl like *you*, Miss Lee, tied down to a wretched little brown country school house like this!"

She was about to say something in reply, but he would not wait to listen, and went on.

" They said, too, that you were *poor*. Now, though I confess that poverty is no *crime*, somebody has well said it was exceedingly *uncomfortable*. So I conclude *your* experience tells you, too."

Again she would have answered him, but he continued.

" Now I am come here to-night, Miss Lee, to offer to take you right *out* of this unfortunate situation. I think you will acknowledge my disinterestedness and my generosity. I am here this moment, then, to ask you to be *my wife*. Just consider what a great *change* this will be for you. Here *I* am with just as much money at my command as I want, and even *more* than I really need for all my pleasures; and here *you* are, a beautiful and accomplished woman, but poor and friendless. Now, in becoming my wife, I make you the sole mistress of an elegant establishment at once. You possess all the grace, the refinement, and the dignity to be at the head of a gentle-

man's household, and would fill such a position — allow me
to say — *superbly*. I have no doubt of that whatever. I
shall very soon set up my own establishment, and I want
a wife. I have come to make you the offer of mistress of
such a place."

Nothing could exceed the impertinence of the man.
Yet he did not seem to be aware of any thing like indeli-
cacy or impropriety. He lacked heart altogether.

" I really must thank you, sir," Amy replied, in a very
firm and decided way, " for your expressions of admiration
for me, but must acknowledge that they are of trifling
worth, after all. As for your application to me to be *your
housekeeper*, I think I must decline the proposal. You
could *hire* you such a person as you want on much more
reasonable terms."

She was cutting, and he felt it.

" No, no ; you don't understand me, I think. I wanted
you to be not only my housekeeper, but my *wife*."

" I perceive that I *did* understand you, sir, and I would
have been inexcusably dull not to have done so. I repeat
— I must *decline* your offer to make me your housekeeper.
I prefer the pursuit of my present calling. It cannot be
near as burdensome to me, and I feel confident that the
situation under you would never yield me any thing like
as much happiness."

Mr. Clendenning was not only wounded by what she
answered in his pride, of which he had a large share, but
he likewise felt considerably irritated. It required all

his self-control to keep him from uttering a really rude reply.

"But then," said he, patronizingly, "see the great change in your circumstances."

"I am not so eager at the present time to *make* any change in them."

"That indeed; but you don't know how soon you may be."

"I am certain that I shall never seek or consent to any such change as *you* have proposed," she replied.

It was evident to her that his self-esteem and impertinence needed correction; hence the sharpness of her last remark. But instead of having the desired effect, it seemed rather to excite his temper. As far as he *dared* show it, therefore, he did.

"Young ladies in *your* situation, Miss Lee," he said, "are not very apt to refuse good offers of marriage."

"I am not a candidate for matrimony, that I know of," she replied; "and if I were I certainly should not step in between my dearest friend and her betrothed husband. That would be more heartless than I feel myself capable of being."

"Then you seem to think Olive and I are already engaged to be married," he said, in affected surprise.

"I have the best reason to think so."

"Well, let me tell you, then, that nothing in the world can be farther from the truth. That's not so, not a single syllable of it. Now, where could such a foolish story as *that* have started?"

She made no answer, willing to let his own thoughts answer him. They would do it the best.

He stopped and reflected. One recollection after another seemed to rise in his mind, each driving the other rapidly across the plane of his thoughts. Now he looked puzzled and perplexed. Again his face flushed, and he showed every symptom of anger. Now he seemed to wish that he could step out of this little village with a single stride, turning his back upon it forever.

And finally he did get up from the bench on which he had been sitting, and wishing Amy a very hasty "good evening," took two or three quite long steps towards the door. As soon as he was gone, so violent and sudden was the reaction in Amy's feelings, she buried her face in her hands and burst forth in a flood of hot tears. The surprise of his visit, the totally unexpected nature of his conversation, the impertinent manner of his proposals, were all quite too much, and for a time her nervous system suffered severely from the shock. When she recovered her usual calmness it was already dark, and she walked home alone and thoughtful. She refused to eat any supper, and shut herself up in her room for the rest of the night, away from every one.

CHAPTER XXVI.

MRS. BUCCLEBEE'S INFLUENCE.

She *had* an influence; and she was not the woman to decline exerting it.

But let me allow my narrative to take its own natural course.

Mr. Clendenning took his departure from her house and from Valley Village the very next day. He was quite abrupt in his leaves-taking, and excused himself by saying that he had forgotten the transaction of business of large importance. So he went away, amid the multiplied and earnest requests of Olive's aunt that he would visit them again very soon, and that the next time he would tarry longer.

For many weeks nothing was heard from him. Mrs. Bucclebee was getting uneasy, and showed the irritated state of her feelings continually. Amy was still a constant visitor at Ivy Lodge in the interval; but of their late company she said little as yet to Olive. She hardly knew, after all, what might be their exact relations to one another; and she did not wish to enter upon a narration to her of this late conference with Mr. Clendenning.

But as the weeks went away, Mrs. Bucclebee's eyes

began to open. She gave play to her suspicions. One
little circumstance after another offered itself to her mind ;
and she was exercising her ingenuity to the utmost to
construct a plain case out of them all against — whom do
you think, dear reader, but Amy?

This, at least, was certain — since the stranger saw Amy
he had showed less attention to Olive. This was quite
enough to begin upon. Of course Amy must have allured
him away. That was the next step. Then what a heartless, false, and entirely unworthy creature Amy must be
thus to deceive her best friend, and all the while under the
profession only of friendship! That was a natural thought
enough, too. Next, if Amy was in the habit of abusing
the confidence of a friend in this cruel way, who could
tell to what extent she would abuse the confidence of the
whole community, and in matters of not half the sacred-
ness that belongs to friendship?

Thus was Mrs. Bucclebee industriously making out a
case against the innocent girl, and daily and hourly for-
ging chains for her future freedom and happiness in that
vicinity. If she could only have looked into the heart
that she so utterly hated, what a reign of far different feelings she would have beheld! Amy was perfectly at peace
with herself, being innocent of any wrong; and however
much she desired to enlighten Olive on the subject of her
late visitor's character, prudence and delicacy combined to
forbid her opening her lips concerning him for the present.

Finally, Mrs. Bucclebee talked with Olive about the

affair herself. She wanted to get at the heart of this strange mystery as soon as she could. She inquired to know if she had been cognizant of any particular intimacy between Amy and her visitor, and if she had been led to suspect that he had any attachment for her. Olive could only blush at hearing such questions put her, and answer them in the most general and unsatisfactory way.

But her aunt's suspicions increased and multiplied. The thought that that poor schoolmistress, as she contemptuously styled her, should come under her very roof, and there undo in a day the plans which she had been carefully perfecting for years, served to irritate a person of Mrs. Bucclebee's temper beyond description; and the necessity that she labored under of keeping this anger of her heart almost entirely to herself in no wise helped calm her inward agitation.

She came to understand, at length, that Mr. Clendenning had deserted her and Olive altogether. It was a fact, and she could not wipe it out of her consciousness. It not only irritated, but it mortified her. The fall of a pride like her pride was a highly notable occurrence. All her darling plans were swept away. All her favorite projects were gone. All her ambitious hopes were frustrated. And only one person could be the author of this fearful mischief, and that person must be Amy. But why Amy? Was it because he at this time visited her, or corresponded with her, or betrayed still any partiality for her? No, perhaps none of these things; yet she was no less the

25

author of the trouble. Even if she cared nothing for the
wealthy stranger herself, was it at all difficult to suppose
that she might be moved with such a feeling as envy, even
if her deceitfulness might not have led her into outright
malice? And thus unhappy Mrs. Bucclebee reasoned with
herself upon the matter; and in this same temper she
talked with her obedient niece about it from day to day.
And Olive wept, while her aunt became more and more
the victim of her own miserable passions.

Amy called at the house one evening after school, quite
as usual, and inquired at the door if Olive was in. The
maid servant answered that she believed she was, and
opened the door wider for her to pass.

But Mrs. Bucclebee heard the inquiry from a neighboring room, and at once sprang forward to the entrance.
Her face was pale with rage, and her manner was the
frenzy of excitement.

" Olive *is* at home," she said to Amy, in a very quick,
fierce voice ; " but she is not to be *seen* to-night."

" Is she sick ? " instantly fell from the old friend's lips.

" Sick ? No ! She's well enough. But she's not to
be seen, I tell you. If you don't know why, perhaps
after a time you will be in the way of finding out."

" Why, Mrs. Bucclebee ! " Amy exclaimed, under her
breath. " What *does* this mean ? "

" *You* should know, miss, if *any body* does. But I wish
you to understand from this time forth, you can't see Olive,
and it will be useless for you to call. I wish the acquaintance dropped."

Amy was thunderstruck. Of this possible event she
had had not the slightest warning. She felt at once weak
in her limbs, and she did not know but she must fall to
the floor.

But presently she gathered her strength again, and put
Mrs. Bucclebee one more question. She was sick at heart,
but she was quite calm.

"This is so very unexpected," said she. "Won't you
be kind enough, Mrs. Bucclebee, to tell me what the *reason* is for this step? What has gone wrong? If any
fault lies with me, let me not delay to atone for it to the
very utmost. I wish you would tell me *all*, Mrs. Bucclebee. I am sure no one could grieve more over such an
occurrence as this than myself."

"No — no," the aunt unfeelingly replied; "if your
own thoughts don't condemn you, nothing would that *I*
can say. Do not think to deceive *me* any longer; you
have deceived *her*, and cruelly wronged her. Let that be
enough. Remember that henceforth your acquaintance
with her ceases. Good evening."

And she fairly shut the door in the poor girl's face.

This was Mrs. Bucclebee. This was the woman of
money. This was the heart where worldly pride and
ambition ruled, and all the passions ran riot in their
power. Only look at the wretchedness of such a character. Only behold the misery, and deceit, and inward
anguish that such unholy feelings so certainly bring forth.

It is hardly possible to describe Amy's situation; she

knew it not herself.   If she was ever thoroughly wretched
in her life, she felt that she was now.   Her last dear
friend thus ruthlessly torn from her, she herself a very
outcast from that dear friend's presence, — O, it seemed
to her that it would have been easier to have Olive
snatched from her by death, than in this rude and cruel
way to feel that their friendship must be sundered.

After composing herself in her chamber as best she was
able, she took out paper and ink, and resolved to address
Olive a note immediately.   If Mrs. Bucclebee was to poison her friend's mind against her, at least she should not
do it without a protest.   The note ran thus : —

"DEAR OLIVE : I do not know what to think or what
to say.   My heart is overwhelmed with grief.   I am ac-
cused of doing you a great wrong, of deceiving you, of
even treating you cruelly ; and yet I know not in what
way.   O, will you enlighten me ?   Will you immediately
recount every one of my wicked acts, that I may hasten to
atone for them all ?

"Your aunt has forbidden our further acquaintance.   I
shall be so sorry for it, and yet I cannot help it !   What
shall I do ?   What *can* I do ?   O, if you will but tell me
what I *have done*.   She will tell me nothing ; only she
says I have wronged you and deceived you.   But how ? —
when ?   Pray, tell me the whole, for I am suffering more
than you know.

"If all this has any thing to do with Mr. Clendenning,

— and I cannot think of any other cause of trouble to her thoughts, — I beg you to set your heart at rest. I have done you no wrong there, though I have long wanted to tell you what I now do. He came when I was alone in the school room, one night, and asked me to be his wife; and as soon as I could recover from my astonishment, I rebuked him for his conduct, and told him of his relation to you. He denied any such relation, and left me in rage. Since then I have neither seen him nor heard from him. Can it be this that has caused such a change in your aunt's feelings?

"I beg you to come to me or write to me at once, and relieve the great anxiety of

"Your ever dear friend,

"AMY."

Little sleep did she get that night, for her great trouble. No one could share it with her. It must all fall on her single heart.

Early the next forenoon she despatched the note by one of her scholars to Ivy Lodge, directing her to leave it there and return without delay. The errand was properly performed; but as soon as Amy reached home at noon again, Mrs. Gummel handed her a little package, which she told her Mrs. Bucclebee's man had brought. Amy took the missive with a trembling hand, and hurried away to her chamber.

With many misgivings she unfolded the bit of newspa-

25 *

per that enclosed the expected note, and threw it hastily
beside her.   Then turning over the letter to read its su-
perscription, she found it was *her own* — the same one she
had sent Olive that very morning.   She looked at the seal
— it had not been broken.

She was sick, and for the moment quite prostrated.
She knew not what to do; nay, she hardly knew where
she was.   The room went round and round.   Her brain
reeled.   Her eyes swam.   She grew blind, and staggered
to the bed, upon which she threw herself.

This was certainly the sorest trial through which Amy
had been called to pass.   She knew too well that her
name and character were in Mrs. Bucclebee's mind asso-
ciated with the meanest suspicions; and she had no assurance that very shortly both would not become subjects of
public vilification.

Alas! it was even so.   Not many weeks afterwards the
reports came round, as such things always do manage to
come, to the ears of Amy herself.   She knew that the
people were all talking about her — not to her praise, but
by way of passing cruel and uncharitable judgments upon
her conduct.   Now hundreds of little innocent circumstances came out, and were illuminated by altogether different motives from any she had ever entertained.   Her
most careless acts were brought up to the standard of a
new interpretation.   Her free, childlike, and impulsive
expressions were one by one dragged like guilty criminals
into the court of other people's prejudices, and through

such trifling witnesses as these she was on almost every side condemned.

Strange, indeed, is the change that a malicious word can work. Most mysterious is the black magic wrought by envy, by hatred, by a wounded pride. Why is it that people believe the worse before they will receive the better? Why is it that a good life for a time offers no obstacle to the wave of prejudice and passion, that will not be hindered in its course till it has swept over the entire character?

Still Amy's faith did not waver. That pure flame never flickered in the least. Her supplications were every day for strength and inward peace, and that the mouths of calumniators might be stopped. She went about her duties at the school room with the same alacrity that had hitherto marked her discharge of them — slighting not the least one of them all in its accustomed round. Her countenance was always cheerful, and as contagious as ever with its sunshine. She attended church with her usual regularity, and tried to forget that the looks of those who once called themselves friends were now turned suspiciously upon her. She overlooked the affected haughtiness and contempt of Mrs. Bucclebee, whenever they happened to meet in the porch or at the door, and felt a real pity for one who could do such a great wrong to her own happiness. She was certain, indeed, that the last change in the world *she* would consent to make, would be a change of places with Mrs. Bucclebee.

The winter at last was over. Spring was come, and
would ere long appear by its many lovely tokens. The
school had been falling off little by little; and that general interest that encouraged her so much at first was sensibly waning and dying out. She made no complaints of
it, however; nor did she cherish any unhappy feelings.
Unquestionably the people of the village had a perfect
right to obey even their own whims, or their prejudices,
in a matter like this; but from that obedience they must
hope to extract their enjoyment. Mr. Parsons stood by
her to the last. That shall be said to his praise. He saw
the trouble, and took every delicate means to hinder its
progress. Still he never openly remarked upon it to Amy,
nor did she to him.

About this time, too, little Dolly stopped coming to
school, on account of sickness. To tell the truth, this was
now a source of greater anxiety to Amy than any troubles
of her own. Perhaps it was a kind Providence that sought
by this means to divert her from too long considering her
own sorrows; for as soon as she became aware of the dear
child's sickness, it seemed to her as if all her heart's griefs
were instantly healed. She had now a new object on which
to concentrate her excited sympathies. Day after day she
toiled up that rugged mountain's side, eager to minister
continually at the bedside of her little friend. She carried her every nicety that she and Mrs. Gummel together
could devise. She sat by her, talking cheerfully and encouragingly, and telling her how soon now the beautiful

spring would burst upon them, when they would once
more ramble over the flowery fields together.

At last the school term closed. Amy said nothing of a
new engagement to any one, and nothing was said to her.
It was enough for her that the popular feeling had set in
such a strong current against her. She might be able to
stem it in time, but the motive was altogether wanting.
There were hardly enough pupils in at the close of the
term to warrant the ceremony of the usual examination,
and so it was dispensed with. She felt that she had lost
her influence for usefulness any longer there, and made up
her mind that a removal would very soon be necessary.
Many are the hearts that would have been troubled grievously at such treatment as this; but however much she
may have regretted the unhappy occurrence, her lofty sense
of innocence carried her through without murmuring. If
others did wrong, it was not a wrong done *her*; they could
injure only themselves. They could take nothing from
the peace that she enjoyed; they robbed no hearts save
their own.

At the last she did talk the matter over with Mrs. Gummel, and then with Mr. and Mrs. Parsons; but she opened
her lips concerning it to no other human being. They
admitted with sorrow that public feeling was much as she
described it, and were loath to agree with her that her
usefulness and happiness had both come to an end in that
place — at least for a time.

But Mrs. Gummel made Amy promise to stay certainly

a month longer with her, now that her duties at the school
were over, and during that period to remain only as her
guest. There were several reasons, besides Mrs. Gummel's
friendship, why she should accept the proposal ; and she
did so gratefully. She was now free to go and come as
she chose, and was glad in her heart to remain still longer
in the pleasant country to welcome in the spring.

CHAPTER XXVII.

THE PITCHER AT THE FOUNTAIN.

DOLLY grew worse. She was suffering from a complication of troubles — the foundation having been laid by a violent cold which she had taken during the winter.

Being quite at her leisure, Amy had a great deal of time to devote to the child. She went over as soon as she could in the morning, carrying what comforts she was able to provide, and late in the afternoon she left her. The most of the time she was at the bedside; but she was constantly offering to be of service to the anxious mother, and trying to assist her in various ways about her domestic arrangements.

While sitting one afternoon by Dolly, the child awoke very unexpectedly, and began talking freely with her kind friend. Dolly had greatly changed in her appearance since she first became the recipient of Amy's partiality. She was now more refined in her expressions, and had learned more graceful manners. Amy saw at the beginning that all this was in her nature, but it was overlaid and buried by the rubbish. She only needed better influences, and her life would soon become as sweet as her own childish breath. Such influences were brought to bear upon her ; and she was now the object equally of the affection and the admiration of all the town.

" Miss Amy," said she, looking very composedly in her friend's face, " I have such strange dreams."

" You shouldn't give yourself any thought about your dreams, dear child," answered Amy.

" But how can I help it ? I don't believe I shall ever get well now, Miss Amy.

The latter looked at her in surprise. " Why do you think so ? " she calmly asked her.

" O, I'm sure I don't know ; but *I never shall.* And what will become of my dear mother when I am gone ? "

The child threw her blue eyes up at the rough boards that answered for the ceiling overhead, and Amy saw that tears immediately came into them. The sight touched her heart.

" I wish my mother was more like you, Miss Amy," she continued. She don't like to hear me talk about dying; but *you* aren't afraid to die — are you, Miss Amy ? "

" There is nothing to be afraid of, dear little one. We are still in the hands of the same loving Father. No, I *hope* I am not afraid of death. We must all die at some time ; and none of us can tell when. It is best to be in a state of mind always to bear so great a change with calmness."

" I know mother will miss me so much, though. I wonder who will help take care of the children when I am gone."

"God will provide," said Amy; "he is able to do all things. We must trust in him. If we do not love him as we should, then we shall always be murmuring at what he does. We shouldn't complain at the prospect of death, my child; for we know that through death we enter into a far better life than this."

For a few moments little Dolly was thoughtful. Her eyes sought the face of her friend, and went over it in affectionate search again and again. The bedroom was most scantily furnished, and the out-door air was not altogether prevented from entering at the cracks. There was only a small strip of a rag carpet before the little bed, on which stood both Amy's chair and the plain pine stand of cups and vials. There was a half curtain to the solitary window, made of checked stuff, whose original colors had long ago faded out of sight.

While Amy still talked with her, and from time to time read most comforting and inspiring passages to her out of the Bible, the door opened slowly, and she heard a heavy tread behind her. Looking round, she saw it was the sick child's father. Since her illness, it was touching to behold the power she held over his rugged heart. He seemed now more a child than herself. He would weep at the slightest cause, and his countenance expressed a perpetual sorrow. He came into Dolly's room now very often, and sat down on the edge of the bed, and there looked at her for many minutes without speaking. And he would take her hand in his, too, and with the other toy

affectionately and dotingly with her long and beautiful
locks — the great sorrow pulling grievously at his heart
strings the while.

This time, after first accosting Amy in a remarkably
kind and grateful way for *him*, he took his usual seat on
the bedside, and placed his little one's hand between both
his own.   How small and white hers looked in his!

" Do you feel any better, sister ? " he asked her, stooping down closer and studying the expression of her eyes.

" O, I can't tell, father," she answered ; " but I am sure
I shan't live ; I know I shan't live !   You mustn't feel so
bad about it, though.   I'm not afraid to die, dear father."

He could not answer her.   The tears rushed to his eyes,
blinded him, and rolled slowly down his rough cheeks.

" O, you mustn't cry for it, father.   Kiss me now, and
let me see that you love me."

" I do love you, my little lamb," said he in a tremulous
voice, stooping down and kissing her.

" Now, if I die," she went on calmly, " there will be no
use in crying — will there, Miss Amy ?   Tears won't bring
me back, dear father.   But if you love God, you will live
with me again.   Do try and love God, father."

" O, I *know* I am wicked, Dolly.   I *know* my heart ain't
right at all.   I feel how bad I am every day of my life.
But I can't be any better.   How can I ?   What shall I
do ?   I'm nothing but a dreadful poor man, with all these
children to love, though I can't seem to do nothing for
'em.   What shall I do, Dolly ?   Can't you tell your
father, now ? "

"You must pray, dear father. I say my prayers every day; and Miss Amy says we ought to pray in our hearts every hour. I love to pray; but once I didn't know how. Miss Amy taught me; and I am always so happy for it afterwards."

There was a pause. Amy could distinctly hear the deep and unquiet breathings of the father, who still sat on the bed, and held his little one's hand.

"I wish I knew how to pray," said he, sorrowfully.

"Don't you?" asked Dolly. "Can't you say what Jesus told us to say — 'Our Father, who art in heaven'? O, do *try*, father. Do learn to pray. It will make you so happy."

"I'm afraid I'm too wicked, sister," and he slowly shook his head — "too wicked."

"No one is too wicked, father." She put out her other hand from under the clothes, and now clasped his with both her own. "It's a good sign, too, when you feel so, for then God will give you what you ask. That's the way the heart begins to feel how poor it is. When you feel so, then God is near you. But you must pray, dear father; and then you can feel how good he is. O, I am so happy when I pray."

Amy had a great deal that she wished to speak, and she could have spoken from a full heart indeed. But it was far sweeter to hear this little child talk thus to her father, and to behold how her tender words drew him to the truth.

"When I die," continued she, "I want you always to think of me, father. Will you promise never to forget me?"

"Darling," said the affected man, speaking in a broken voice, "do you think I ever *can*? But you *won't* die — no, you *mustn'* die."

"O, do not say that. God will do what is best. He knows better than we do. And I shall see Jesus, too — my own blessed Jesus. O father! I wish he was as dear to you as he is to me. Miss Amy told me all about him, and how good he was, and how he died only for love to me — and for you, too, dear father; for *you*, too. He has given me a new heart, and I am happy. I do not fear death now. Once I thought it was such a dreadful thing to be buried under the ground, and I used to cry when I thought much about it; but it isn't *I* that will lie there; I shall live in a more beautiful world than this is, dear father; I shall be with my dear Jesus. He has made my heart so glad here, I know he will do a great deal more for me when I am with him. No, indeed; I'm not afraid to die. I only thought how sad 'twould be to leave you, and mother, and all the rest here behind; and that made me sad. But Miss Amy says I mustn't feel that way; for God is a good Father, and he will take care of us all."

He released one of his hands, and began toying with her locks, that were showered over the pillow.

"Poor thing!" he whispered; "it's hard to think of it."

"O, no, dear father; only it's hard for you to be contented under it. Isn't that it? Do you feel all the trust in God, and all the love for the dear Jesus, that makes me so happy? O, if you did — if you did! I *wish* you would try, father!"

This talk continued a long time. Amy saw it made a deep impression on the father's heart, and she rejoiced. A little child should yet lead this lion heart with nothing but the silken thread of love.

When at length Amy took her leave of the child, which of late had always been a protracted and tearful scene, she came upon the mother in the adjoining room, who stood with her apron at her eyes weeping and lamenting.

"O, no," said Amy, "this will not do; this is not right, now. Come; cheer your heart, or nothing will go on well. Tears won't do, Mrs. Tatterags, you know."

"Will she live?" the woman sobbed out, her eyes swollen and red with weeping. "O, do tell me if you think poor little Dolly will live."

"There is but One who knows," answered Amy. "He holds the secrets of life in his hand. Trust him forever. Do not lose confidence in him. Love him continually. Pray to him, Mrs. Tatterags; pray continually. And even then, if dear little Dolly dies, you will feel it is all for the best, and you will be happy. Pray, do not set up your own heart against the overruling providence of our Father. He keeps the very sparrows, you know the Bible tells you,

26 *

and not one even of them falls to the ground without his
notice. Shall he not, then, care for all of us ? "

With such words of kindness and comfort she went
away. As her feet plodded down the mountain, however,
she had secret misgivings that her little friend's end was
fast approaching. She talked much about her to Mrs.
Gummel when she got home again; and by her simple
narrations of what she heard and saw at that humble
house, she moved that good woman to tears.

Mr. Tatterags himself came down on Saturday, as Amy
was not able on that day to go up to see the sick one, on
purpose to bring her a message. Her heart beat a great
deal faster as she stood before him in the door, for she did
not know but the dear little one had gone. The color all
left her face.

" Dolly sent me here a-purpose," said the father; " and
what could I do but come? The poor lamb! I would be
glad to walk a good many miles for her, if I only thought
'twould make her get well."

He paused to check his rising feelings, and then went
on : —

" She wanted me to ask you, — and she whispered it
into my ear, too, as if 'twan't quite right to do it, and I
don't hardly think it is myself, — she wanted me to ask
you if you'd come and stay with her all day to-morrow."

" Certainly I will," quickly answered Amy.

" To-morrow's Sunday, you know; and she says she
don't know as she'll see you at all another Sunday. If

you'd only come up and stay with her to-morrow, Miss Leo, 'twould be a great favor done to *us* as well as to *her*."

" I certainly will. I will be there early. You must kiss little Dolly for me, and tell her I will be there early. How is she this afternoon ? "

He hesitated, looked down at the ground, and then looked all around him.

" She ain't any better," he finally answered. " We think she's a-failin'."

He could say no more, but turned immediately away, thanking Amy with a quick half bow. But she saw that he dashed away the tears with the back of his hand as soon as he got on the grass again; and that was enough.

Such a morning as that next morning had not risen in a great while. The sun shone clear and bright, and already many of the birds were at their early songs in the maple boughs. The time seemed, indeed, hallowed.

Soon after breakfast Amy put on her things, took a few little comforts and dainties in her hand, and set out for the humble residence of the Tatterags. Her thoughts by the way were alternately of her little friend on her sick bed and of the glory of the morning. As she crossed the old bridge, the running water below was a stream of living melody. While she toiled slowly up the mountain, the chorals of the joyous birds were a source of the sweetest serenity to her feelings. She sat down to rest herself a few minutes in the usual place upon the terrace, and there her soul worshipped God anew in the contemplation of

that most beautiful landscape. All things tended to in-
spire her. There was the village below sleeping and
dreaming in the blessed sunlight of that Sabbath morning.
There was the gleaming river twisting through glen and
meadow, and finally spreading out in a broad and beautiful mirror below. And the far-off hills, too, hemmed in
the picture like a solid framework — the blue and misty
heavens coming down to kiss them with the lips of crim-
son and purple clouds.

But inspiring as the scene was, it could not hold her
long there. Her *heart* was not yet at the end of its journey ; she rose, therefore, and went forward.

The moment she came in sight of the house of Mr.
Tatterags, she saw the father standing in the little yard
before the door, bareheaded, with his hands in his pockets,
and looking down in deep thought to the ground. When
he heard her footstep at the gate, he gazed at her in
silence, and appeared to be unable to speak.

" Good morning," said Amy, pleasantly as ever. " How
do you all do up here this beautiful morning? How is
my little Dolly ? "

He shook his head sadly, and again threw his eyes upon
the ground.

" She's no better," said he, almost in a whisper.

" No better ! Isn't she ? Let me go in and look at
her at once."

Amy hurried past him, and he turned and followed
along after. She reached the room where Dolly lay, and

found the mother at the bedside, with several of the children. The mother looked pale and anxious, and the children frightened and uneasy. As Amy entered, the former was bending down over Dolly, asking her if she didn't feel any better. She made some answer which Amy did not hear; and then Amy caught the low sound of her own name. The little one spoke of her.

"I'm here," she instantly cried, stepping forward so suddenly as even to startle Mrs. Tatterags considerably. "I'm right here at your side, my darling," and she stooped over and kissed the sick lips, with a heart overflowing with love and sympathy.

Dolly threw up her arms around the neck of her friend, and seemed in that single moment to be altogether happy. She strained Amy to her, as if she would nót again let her go.

Mrs. Tatterags was still calm, though by no means resigned to the worst. The doctor was there the afternoon before; and though he tried to revive their courage, he could not hold out to them a great deal of hope. He endeavored by gradual and gentle means to break to them the whole meaning of his fears, and to prepare their minds for the very worst that might come.

"She's not so well this morning," whispered the mother, as Amy again stood up to speak with her.

"I don't know," answered the latter. "Perhaps she may show better symptoms before the day is out."

She looked and saw now the father, listening at the

door, that stood ajar, and seeming to concentrate all his
feelings into that one moment of agonizing apprehension.
It was unhappy, indeed, only the sight of the woe that
was invading this humble little household.   Amy turned
from it at once, and began to talk cheerfully with the child.

"Do you know what a beautiful morning it is, Dolly?"
she asked her, glancing towards the window. "It is Sunday, too."

"I can see the sun a little from here, Miss Amy," said
she. "Sunday, is it?   Why, so 'tis.   I don't believe I
shall be here another Sunday."

"O, don't talk so, Dolly — *don't*," pleaded her distressed mother.

The father ceased from his pacing the floor of the next
room, and listened again with aching eagerness.

"I always wanted to die Sunday when I did die," continued she.

"Why so?" asked Amy, desiring to exhibit calmness
to the mother even when talking of such a matter as death.

"Because it's a holy day," answered Dolly; "and I
know that Jesus will be nearer to me then than he is on
the other days."

"No; he is no nearer then than he always is.   He is
at the door of your heart every hour, asking to come in."

"It *seems* so; I can't help *thinking* it's so," said the
child. "O, to go to God on his own Sabbath, Miss Amy!
But you mustn't cry when I am gone.   Mother, I shall
always be near you, and shall love you more than I ever

did here; for I shall know how to love better in the other
world — won't I, Miss Amy?"

It was a sad, and yet it was a profitable scene, which
was passing in that dwelling on this Sunday in spring.
The family did nothing and thought of nothing except
what related to Dolly. The forenoon lapsed; and during
the passage of those sacred hours Amy could see that she
was very rapidly failing. Once the mother called her out
into the next room, and tearfully asked if she *could* live;
but Amy could not hold out to her a false hope; and she
answered that the dear little one might pass away before
the sunset, even as her own heart seemed to desire. She
begged the poor woman to put trust in God, explaining in
her loving words how dear all his children are to him, and
how his fatherly care surrounded each one of us continually. She labored to increase her feeble faith, and told
her that with more of this she would be happy. The loss
of her darling would be no affliction; it would be her own
greatest gain.

As the afternoon set in, Amy saw that it would not do
to leave her alone for even a minute. It was too evident,
by this time, that she might at almost any instant drop
away. Still she held her faculties all complete. Her reason never became shadowed, and her mind did not wander.
She lay and regarded them all; and though she was visibly growing weaker and weaker, yet she had expressions
of affection for them every one. The children hardly
knew how to understand her; but the parents were wholly

overcome. They could not bring their hearts to it, for the old flint had never been broken. Grief might yet subdue. Heaven's ordering would be the best.

At about four o'clock, she looked up at them from out her large eyes, — so expressive at this time, — and exclaimed in a low voice, —

"O, I *know* I'm going to die. I can't live any longer. Jesus is calling me home, mother. O, won't *you* go, too? I am dying *now*, Miss Amy. I *know* I shall go soon. O, I can't breathe. Open the window, father."

They sprang to do as she requested; and Amy raised her head upon her arm, and gently fanned her face — that poor, pale face, with the locks blowing on either side of the temples with every current of the wind.

She looked unspeakably grateful to them all.

"O, you have been so good to me, *dear* Miss Amy!" said she, speaking with difficulty, and very low. "You have done so much for me! I *hope* you'll come to me in heaven. I know we shall meet there ; and mother, too ; and father ; and all the rest."

Now they stood with their aprons and their hands to their eyes, weeping aloud. Amy alone was calm and self-possessed.

"*Don't* cry, mother — O, *don't* cry. What is there to cry for? Jesus is calling me, and I hear him. I shall be so much *better* now, and so much happier. O, don't cry because I am going to die."

Then she closed her eyes, and appeared to slumber.

Her breathing was quick and faint. It could hardly be distinguished at all. Amy's arm was still lovingly beneath her.

There was a long silence, and it was crowded with suspense. The whole of the family were still at the bedside, looking on, and Amy like an angel there to bring sunlight into the gloom of their sorrow.

"Is she breathing?" asked the mother, alarmed to see no signs of life.

Amy put down her ear to her lips.

Just at that moment there was a motion and a whisper, very faint, yet wholly perceptible.

"Dear Jesus!" she exclaimed, as if already she had taken the voice of a young angel. "O *dear* Jesus! I am going home."

Still Amy listened. But there was no more sound; no more voice; not a lisp, or a whisper.

She put her ear still closer. No breathing now. She was gone. Her auburn locks were showered over the pillow, and she lay a corpse. But the gentle young spirit was in heaven.

27

CHAPTER XXVIII.

BACK TO BOSTON.

AMY sat at her chamber window. It was the evening before she was to leave the town and her few dear friends. Though she regretted the manner and the motive of the person who had been influential enough to work this sudden change in her life, she nevertheless made no complaint, and felt no disposition to murmur. Whatever was ordered she felt certain to be for her good; and under all circumstances, therefore, she was cheerful.

She thought of where she should be the next day at that time, how much she would miss her old friends here at Valley Village, and what new feelings would possess her in her changed way of life again. That afternoon she had been over to bid farewell to Mr. and Mrs. Parsons. Not without tears could she speak the last words to them, for they were really near her heart. They *hoped* she would not quite forget them, though Amy knew too well that that was impossible. They insisted that she should come back again to Valley Village at some future day, and stay with them just as long as she liked. They parted from her with many expressions of real affection, and

(314)

loaded her with their best and kindliest wishes, and with their most earnest blessings.

Olive she could not see. There was no last word to be had with her. A high barrier had been interposed between her heart and the heart of her dear friend; and though nothing was plainer than that the two girls still loved one another devotedly, yet every thing like contact was most carefully prevented. Amy could hardly keep the tears out of her eyes, as she thought of this needless and unhappy state of things. She knew that her own heart was free from guilt. She felt only pity for the wilful cause of the wrong, and deep sympathy for the other sufferer.

Yet it was very sad, after all, to think of leaving Olive under such circumstances. It cast a cloud over the whole future.

And then, too, the sudden death of little Dolly was a great weight at her heart. It seemed to her as if one by one the idols had been wrested from her embrace, and she were now told by a voice above her head — "Go; you have reaped your harvest here; there is a still wider field for you, where you can do greater good." And she prepared to obey the voice, trusting alone in the providence and love of the good Father.

Mrs. Gummel rose very early on the next morning, and knocked on Amy's door to wake her; but Amy was up before her. The stage drove through the village street, and up to the door, pretty soon after breakfast; and while the driver was busy at strapping on the baggage behind,

Amy and her friend were weeping and exchanging farewells in the little entry.

" Now, you *will* write me, won't you ? " begged Mrs. Gummel, still holding her hand.

" Certainly — certainly ; and you will let me know how *you* get on, too ; and tell me all about this dear old place, when you write. I *do* love this spot, though I must leave it."

" Remember, now, that I was the first person here whom you knew ; and you have been with me from beginning to end ; and poor little Henry —— " But Mrs. Gummel choked, and could say no more.

Amy pressed her hand in token of sympathy.

" God has taken him," said she, in a tremulous whisper.

Then Amy proceeded again, and for the last time, to thank her for her great kindness, and called down the richest blessings of Heaven on her head. She told her not to forget, either, that while this life was certainly a time to be well improved, wherein we were to try and en-joy the whole wide range of our faculties, yet it was not *the entire* life ; there was a vaster, and a grander, and a much more beautiful one wrapped in the folds of a mys-terious future.

And with such words the two friends parted ; for the stageman immediately called out that all was ready, and after a last embrace she hurried up the steps into the coach. The door slammed in her face, and the driver mounted to his seat. Amy bent forward to take a last look, and there still stood Mrs. Gummel in her little door, her cheeks streaming with tears. Amy waved her hand, and the wide world lay between them.

Her thoughts were indeed various, while she rode over the country turnpike; and up from the mass of these crushed feelings arose the fragrance of a sweet and enduring piety. These changes could not reach the centre of her serenity. They were good for her soul's health, because they both kept it in active exercise, and impressed upon it the lessons of trust and humility; but they never affected that deep and quiet feeling of peace that reigned in the heart of her being, and radiated sweet joy in all directions to the circumference.

That whole day was passed in travelling. Late in the afternoon she descended from a hack to the sidewalk before Mrs. Dozy's door, and was immediately greeted with much warmth by that lady, who had hurriedly run down the stairs for that purpose. What a joyful meeting it was! Good Mrs. Dozy could say nothing — she only took Amy by the hand, and led her in silence straight up the stairs. They were all glad to see her again, and offered their congratulations at her return with great freedom. Sitting down in a circle around her, before she could even disrobe herself of her travelling garments, they began to put her questions without number.

"But look here!" finally exclaimed Mrs. Dozy, her thoughts coming to her; "the child must be starvin'. Do

27 *

let's go and get her something to eat." And no sooner
said than done.

After Amy had been rested a little, and had partaken
of supper, and "got a good cup of tea," — as Mrs. Dozy
said, — she manifestly felt better. She began the history
of her last year's experience to them, and finished it, detailing, however, only such items of it as she thought
prudent, or capable of interesting her eager listeners.

When Mrs. Dozy showed her into her room — the same
room that she had occupied with her poor father, and the
one for which, too, she had written — a sudden wave of
desolate feeling washed over her heart, and she burst forth
in a flood of tears.

Mrs. Dozy was silent. She understood those sacred
emotions too well herself to offer any interruption to their
full and free course.

To Amy the old gloom still seemed to remain. The
room was dark and dreary with it. She looked about in
every corner, and her thoughts were of him who was gone.
That dear father! though his face was hidden in the darkness of the grave, yet it seemed to look out every where
dimly into her own. She could not speak for some time.
The old memories crowded too thickly about her.

Once reinstated, however, in the ways of the former
retired life here, and matters moved along without any
particular obstruction or change. Amy went out again, as
soon as she was well settled, to hunt up music scholars.

She resolved to return to her old avocation when she came
back to Boston, sure of finding a suitable support in its
pursuit.

Accordingly she engaged about it without further delay.
First, she called on all her former pupils. Some she found
had moved away, some were already under the secured
tuition of others, and some were glad to return again to
the instructions of their old teacher. They all welcomed
her back with great sincerity, exclaiming how much better
she looked now than when she went away, and expressing
the hope that Boston was always to be her home.

Among the new pupils that she obtained, there was one
young girl named Mary Braggins. Her father was a merchant in Boston, of high standing, of very considerable
wealth, and with but one other child besides herself. This
other one's name was Ellen. She was many years older
than Mary, and at this day seemed rather to exercise a
maternal government over her. Perhaps Ellen was twenty
or twenty-two years of age — a trifle older than Amy
herself.

Mr. Braggins was a widower, and lived in good "style,"
his eldest daughter willingly holding herself responsible
for any shortcomings in that matter of which he might be
convicted. Ellen was ambitious enough for them all. She
had been petted from her youngest days; and from a little
pet gradually — and not *very* gradually, either — she came
to be a great *ruler*. We often hear of such transforma-
tions, even if we do not see them·

In the matter of Amy's qualifications, no one had so
busy a part to take as Ellen. She assumed the office of
examiner at large and in particular. Not that the betrayal
of care about an arrangement that was sensibly to affect
the culture of her young sister was a matter of such
special importance to her thoughts, but rather because
she felt herself called upon to exercise authority at all
times when the opportunity offered, and especially so when,
as in the present case, she could seem to lift herself at the
expense of the feelings of another.

But Amy was engaged as the music teacher of little
Mary, and felt certain that she should like her pupil as
they got on together. And so the event proved. Mary
was a promising scholar, and applied herself with earnestness. Amy was much encouraged with her industry, and
at all times spoke in the most flattering terms about her
to Ellen. The latter, too, could not well help seeing for
herself the child's progress, and was apparently quite satisfied. And thus at once grew up, first an acquaintance,
and then a friendship, between the girls, that promised
much future satisfaction and pleasure. Ellen's assumption
of authority seemed gradually to yield before the perpetual gentleness of so lovely a heart as Amy's. She gave
over her airs of patronage altogether, and essayed milder
and more attractive means. The refinement and exalted
purity of Amy put her former ways to the blush completely. And in very spite of herself, she found at last that
she was being drawn to the heart of the humble music

teucher by a silent and secret power, against which there was no resistance.

Ellen Braggins was a beautiful girl, and gifted with a fine education. She possessed a brilliant intellect — quick, subtle, and strong — and manners well calculated to attract those in whose society she might be thrown. Though her father kept a housekeeper, yet she considered herself at the head of the establishment, and went about from the top to the bottom of the house with all the authority of style that could set well on the shoulders even of a proprietor.

She was in the habit of receiving considerable company from time to time, some of which Amy happened to meet on the occasions of her own professional calls. Amy could not fail to observe Ellen's great freedom with them, and sometimes she was even made to feel the humiliating position in which a trifling remark of the other would place her. It only meant that she should not venture to think of assuming too much familiarity with the visitors, and especially that she should never offer to place herself on a footing of equality with the youthful mistress of the house. Aside from this, Ellen never showed Amy any thing but the kindest and politest treatment, and in private she did not disguise her desire to make a confidant of her. Amy affected to be blind to her more offensive manners, and forgave and forgot all, that they might meet on the ground of one single sympathy that both had in common. Yet at no one time did she consent to part with her self-respect. But she bore it with so much sweetness, so much grace, and gentleness, and humility, that it was wonder enough that Ellen was not made a convert to her influence in even a greater degree than she really was.

The new calling was highly agreeable, and made Amy many new friends. Though she had been brought to it again through sorrow and sadness, yet it yielded her heart a revenue of satisfaction beyond any thing that she had dared to expect.

CHAPTER XXIX.

A PICTURE OF TROUBLE.

PASSING through a retired and narrow street one afternoon, on her way home from the day's labors, Amy saw a crowd of men, women, and children gathered on the sidewalk before a dingy door, and a little way off, a young girl weeping bitterly. The child was bareheaded, barefooted, clad in the cheapest and coarsest garments, and sat down on the curb stone, bewailing her wretchedness in a tone that challenged Amy's pity in a moment. Going directly up to her, therefore, she asked her what was the matter.

"Father's got hurt! O, father's got hurt!" she cried, not offering to look up and see who was questioning her.

"Where is your father?" Amy asked hurriedly. "Where do you live?"

"In there — in the-e-r-e!" the child mournfully drawled out, giving way still more to her trouble. And as she spoke, she also pointed in the direction of the door around which the people of the neighborhood were gathered.

Amy went without any hesitation to the spot, and moved as to pass in. Those who stood about the entrance, with such pale faces, and talking in such ominous whispers,

immediately made way to give her room, casting strange
glances after her, as if to inquire who she could be.

The entry was long and narrow, and the walls in any
other than a cleanly condition. On the floor had at some
past time been sprinkled sand, which now exhibited all
the variety of colors that in the interim it had imbibed.
Amy followed the remnants of the crowd along, and so
climbed a flight of dirty stairs. Through the door on the
left, at their top, she saw a collection of people, and knew
that there was the place where this misfortune was to
be seen.

Going in, therefore, she observed a pale-faced man
stretched out upon the bed, who now and then threw his
arms about restlessly, and kept moaning and groaning
continually. His eyes were wild, she could see as she
approached nearer, and at times they were fixed for a moment or more in his head, expressing a great deal of suffering. He would bite his lips with fierceness, and in his
agony gnash his teeth.

The surgeon had been there to bind up his wounds, but
had now gone. At the bedside stood a thin, anxious-
looking woman, bending over him to catch every syllable
he uttered, and now and then turning around to wring her
hands for her great grief. There were likewise other
women in the room and about the bed, with eager and
bloodless countenances, staring hard at every one who
came through the door, and staring particularly at Amy
since she had entered. They would run over her person

with their inquisitive eyes, and then whisper one with the other about where she could have come from and who she could be.

On the opposite side of the bed was sitting a young man, closely attentive to the slightest movements of the sufferer, but whose face expressed quite as much anguish as that felt by the most distressed one there. He would study the features of the man on the bed, and then relapse into his own individual look of friendlessness and misery. Amy asked herself if indeed all the woe of the world was crowded into this cribbed little chamber.

"What is the matter?" she asked of the woman at the bedside, in a whisper.

The latter looked through her rolling tears into her face, holding up her apron.

"O, he's had a buildin' fall on to him. He's my own *husband*." And then she put her apron to her eyes and wept aloud.

Amy said and did what she could to pacify the poor woman; but the more she exerted herself, the more the distressed creature increased her sobs. It was a pitiful sight.

All the time she was engaged with the wife of the poor man, Amy observed that the eyes of the young man opposite were upon her. He could not well avoid hearing what passed between them. If so, it certainly must have been that which so deeply seemed to interest him.

"He's all our dependence," cried the wife. "We can't

28

get along from one day to another without his work; and now jest see what he is! — both of his wrists broke, so the doctor says, and his hip all put out, so't he can't walk for weeks and months agin, if he *ever* does. O, dear! O, dear! What *shall* I do! What *shall* we all come to!"

Amy asked her how many children they had to provide for.

"There's six of 'em — God bless the poor little things! They're without any father now, and I'm sure I don't know what's to become of 'em. O, *dear!* O, the good gracious! What *shall* I do! What *shall* I do!"

Some of the children hereupon came crowding in, all crying as hard as they could cry, and scarcely one of them knowing for what. Amy could not help regarding them with the profoundest pity.

"They must be provided for," said she to the woman.

"Ah, but who's going to do it for me? Shall I go and make 'em all little *paupers*, and my own *children* too? Would you like to do such a thing as that yourself, sweet lady, when you know you've never had to beg for one of 'em yet a day?"

Amy well understood the poor mother's feeling. It *was* hard to think of handing over her children to the care of the city authorities, and it certainly was an alternative of which the woman had never before thought. Well might it distress her to have it brought home to her heart.

In a few minutes, however, Amy had been around among the other women collected there, and arranged with them to take four of the children, under the promise of a small amount of pay for every week. She learned, too, that they all lived either in the same or the adjoining building, and therefore the separation would not be a matter of any regret. They would have as good care as if they were to be with their mother, and their little shadows would not yet be thrown across the threshold of any poorhouse. After making these arrangements, she asked the afflicted mother if they were satisfactory to her. The latter lifted up both hands and called down the choicest of Heaven's blessings on the "dear young lady's" head. Amy then put some silver in her hand, and bade her be of good heart, and hope all the time for the best.

And turning about to take another look at the sufferer on the bed before her departure, she observed that the eyes of the young man opposite were still fixed on her with marvellous intentness.

"He will soon be easier, I hope," he remarked, dropping his gaze to the bed. "Poor man! I pity him."

Amy looked at the wounded man, and all the time that she looked, she could not help wondering what could be the tie that held that young stranger to this unfortunate laborer. And the longer she thought upon it, the more she was puzzled and perplexed.

He was quite twenty-four, with a fine face, though it was shadowed by an anxious expression. His dress was plain and neat, though in good taste and excellent condition. He had dark eyes and eyebrows, black hair, and

features that stood for signs of a most earnest and sincere
expression. Some of the time he leaned his head upon
his hand, and then he looked exceedingly sorrowful.
Without doubt he had seen grief, perhaps great grief;
that each lineament of his face seemed to express. He
evidently did not belong there either; there appeared to
be no natural relationship between him and any one of
those present. They regarded him as a stranger, and
some of the women addressed him distantly by the title
" Doctor."

Amy took her leave, and comforted the distressed
woman by telling her she would come again to see her on
the next day.

The walk home was as if she were in a vast solitude, so
much did her thoughts isolate her from all things around
her. If her eyes were upon the ground, or on the brick
walls of the houses, or passing searchingly over the faces
of those she was every moment meeting, it was the same
to her; she knew not who passed — she recognized no faces
— she was hardly sure whether it was buildings, trees, or
sky on which her eyes were riveted.

Only a few minutes after she entered her room again,
and as soon as she had laid off her things, the door bell
rang, and the girl showed some one up stairs into the parlor. Immediately she knocked on Amy's door, and told
her that a gentleman wished to see her in the other room;
yet the girl's face betrayed no little uneasiness, as if she
was not sure that all was right.

"Who is he?" Amy asked her. "Did he give you his name?"

"No, ma'am," answered the girl; "and he didn't know *yours* neither. He *said* he didn't."

"Didn't know my name! Whom did he inquire for, then?"

It was Amy's turn to be astonished now.

"He only said he wanted very much to see the young lady that boarded here, and that jest come in. That's all he said to *me*, ma'am. But he looks nice, and I guess he's good. I'd go in and speak to him, Miss Amy."

So she went. But the thoughtful maid voluntarily remained a minute or two in the entry, not knowing but she might in some strange contingency be needed. And after vainly waiting as long as she thought it necessary, she relinquished her post at last and hurried down stairs.

As soon as Amy entered the parlor, she saw with much surprise that her visitor was the young man whom she had but just left sitting at the injured man's bedside. A thousand thoughts rushed across her at this unexpected revelation. She was possessed with wonder, with curiosity, with a kind of sympathy, and, it must be confessed, with a very dim and indistinct thought of fear.

She looked calmly in his face. There sat that same expression of sad friendlessness, perhaps a little heightened now.

"Pardon me," said he, rising and making a most respectful bow; "I know I am doing wrong; I know I have

28 *

no sort of right to expect that you will listen to me; but
a wretch like myself is apt to forget every thing but his
wretchedness, and to do what he never would at other
times."

He paused. Amy sat down and waited to hear his
errand.

" You must think it very strange that I have followed
you home; but if you could read the volume of misery
that is bound up in my heart, you would at least forgive
me. I saw your face at that bedside of suffering, and in
a moment I felt that I knew you. I felt that it was you
alone of all other human beings who could understand my
deep, deep miseries. Forgive me if I am too bold, or if
I intrude in the least upon you at this time. I will go out
into the street again if you wish me to go; but O, let me
beg first to let you into the secret of my sufferings.".

She could not directly answer him, as he paused again
in expectation of an answer; but the slight motion of her
head was sufficient to give him encouragement to go on.

A very trifle did his face light up at this sign of sympathy, and he proceeded.

" You saw me at the bedside of that unfortunate man.
I was there because I witnessed the misery of his family.
Seeing that, I felt that there were others in the world fully
as wretched as myself. I went along with the crowd that
followed him into his own house. Never had I seen his
face before, and I did not know that I should ever see it
again. Perhaps when you first saw me sitting there at

the bedside, you thought I was a relation. I am not, unless suffering makes us relatives. It often does beget strange connections in this world, such as we would not at other times be willing to believe possible."

Alas! how very true did Amy's own experience tell her that all his sad words were!

Again he hesitated. His own sense of delicacy and propriety could not but teach him that he had come with an uncommon errand. Nothing, too, but his quick perception had suggested to him that he was likewise addressing an uncommon person.

"Then you are *not* related to this poor family," said Amy, encouragingly.

"O, no; no, I do not even know their names. I was drawn there only by the strong magnetic power of sympathy. I thought I had found those who might be even as wretched as myself; and wretched indeed I am, my own bleeding heart every moment tells me."

The water rushed to his eyes. Amy regarded him with a look of tenderness and pity. He caught that look, and his sorrows seemed to lift their heavy cloud.

"Shall I tell you this that so crushes my life? *May* I tell you what my trouble is?"

She could merely nod assent, for his distressed manner had so wrought upon her sympathies as to choke her utterance.

"Six years ago," said he, "the world was full of joy and promise for me. I was then innocent and happy. My

heart was clean. I did not know iniquity. I had not
then stained my hands with it. O, *what* a change from
that time of hope !

" My parents are respectable, and I have enjoyed good
advantages in my youth. Alas ! they were *too* good.
They were much better than I deserved. I have wronged
those who have helped me. Mine has been the crime, and
I feel every day that mine must be the atonement.

" When I was only fifteen years of age I was put into
the counting room of a Boston merchant, to learn under
him the rudiments of a business education. As I had a
decided taste for such pursuits, I made progress in my situation very rapidly. I was promoted as fast as I could
be, and perhaps much too fast for my own good. Each
succeeding year found me in an improved position, and in
the receipt of a better salary. I was prospering beyond
either the expectations of my friends or myself.

" The gentleman with whom I was engaged was a man
of stern and lofty mercantile principles, though he possessed the heart of a woman. I respected him and I tried
to love him ; but he seemed to keep his love for others
than those whom he employed in his office ; he never lav-
ished any of it on *me*.

" But let me be brief. In an unhappy hour I came
under the influence of others whom I should have shunned.
Only think of it ! I had no home, no friends here in the
city, no one to whom I could look for direction and sympathy. What is the wonder then that the most vagrant

and accidental influences surrounded and finally controlled me!

"I was tempted, and by others; and I fell. My crime was *forgery*. My victim was my *employer*. He who had made me what I was, and created for my heart those delightful prospects that it took such a deep, deep pleasure in — *he* was the one I wronged. And from the day of my crime till this day I have not ceased to repent the deed for which I have suffered so much.

"I was tried, or rather, I confessed the charge brought against me, and received a lighter punishment in consequence. My youth likewise plead loudly for me; and so did the peculiarity of my temptation. I was sent for three long years to the State Prison, and I have been out not yet quite a month."

Amy could not help shuddering at listening to the ending of his recital. The State Prison was a gloomy place, and called up yet more gloomy associations. She looked at him in wonder. He, so young, so frank and ingenuous, of such refined and gentlemanly manners — *he* the graduate of the State Prison! Could it be possible? O, how deeply, in that one moment of his final confession, were her sympathies all moved for him! His sadness was no mystery now. It was not strange at all that he should have gone with the ragged crowd into that humble abode, and there tried to make his own wretchedness feel light by comparison with that which he witnessed. Nothing marvellous was it, either, that his heart should have bound-

ed with an impulse of living joy at beholding the free and
disinterested kindness of this stranger girl, who came in
only to do good, to bind up the wounds of broken spirits,
and drop words of cheer and comfort into wretched hearts.
Not strange that that youthful stranger's sympathy should
have attracted him even to the threshold of her own home,
and to opening to her the secret anguish that was preying
upon him like a vulture.

"Forgive me!" he pleaded again. "I do not know what
I am doing, in bringing this great trouble of mine to you,
and you a stranger. Forgive my presumption, I beg you.
I thought I might get sympathy — get advice — get some
little regard — O, if only *ever* so little! No one cares for
me. No one has a syllable for me. No, no, I am nothing
but an outcast — a wretched, wretched outcast."

There was wonderful pathos in his words. Amy was
thrilled with the sound of them. She saw plainly the
sufferings to which he was a prey. She understood the
nature of the terrible disease that was threatening the
health and the life of his soul. And making a great
effort to control her feelings, she went on with her reply.

She expressed the deepest sympathy for his unfortunate
condition. She begged him not to give over to despair,
but to live in patience and hope. What though the whole
world were joined against him — there was nothing to
hinder his finding a friend in God. She pointed to him
the way. She showed him how his trials would all prove
themselves to have been his best teachers, if he would but

read their lessons aright; they might be sad lessons, and very hard ones, but their use and meaning were not to be mistaken. And she besought him to throw off his thoughts of fear, of mortification, of disgrace, and to remember that his soul was great, and full of strength yet, and wholly immortal. It would not be manly to despair. He owed a debt to himself, that he would never be excused from discharging. It was his duty to forget all that had happened, to place himself in the attitude of perfect humility before his Maker, to be disregardful utterly of the whip that pride was flourishing over his head, and to gather a new strength, and a new hope, and a new life from the promise that God in his great goodness makes to us all alike — the bond and the free, the innocent and the guilty.

Her words manifestly touched him as no words had since his release from imprisonment. He seemed to bow right down under them without a single murmur, and in his heart to exclaim, "You have saved me! You have saved me! There *is* something for me to live for yet!"

CHAPTER XXX.

DESPAIR.

AMY went to the house of the distressed poor family several times after this first visit, and almost every time she found the young stranger there. He always greeted her with unaffected cordiality, though his countenance never seemed to be free from the shadow of his great sorrow. Sometimes he walked along home by Amy's side, conversing with her upon his feelings and his situation. Her words appeared to do him a great deal of good. There was a new courage in them for him. They were the words of a trustful, true, and thoroughly brave spirit.

He was in the habit, too, of soliciting her advice respecting the improvement of his circumstances, and received it, when offered, with every expression of gratitude. He felt that she was stronger than himself; that her thoughts were readier to devise, and her will was more prompt to execute; that she commanded him as if he were a mere child at her feet; and that her strength of spirit was incomparably superior to his own. Twice she had pressed gifts upon his acceptance, so that he could not find the strength or the courage to refuse them. She knew his

needy condition, and her woman's heart did not hesitate
to perform its heavenly duty. She did not wait for future
opportunities to be doing good with her limited means,
but went about it without any hesitation now.

For several days it happened that she had not seen
him, though she called very regularly at the poor man's
dwelling. He had stopped going there altogether. Her
thoughts were busy in trying to conjecture what could
have become of him. She was beset at times with the
most unhappy fears lest an untoward fate might have
overtaken him. Into every face that she met on her way
along the street she looked with an eager and excited
interest, hoping at the last by a happy accident to recognize his own. But her search was vain.

It was a balmy day in the very last of the spring, and
all her daily duties were over. She felt as if she would
like a little recreation and fresh air, and so walked over
to the Common. The moment she passed between the
iron posts, and stepped upon the broad, smooth mall, a
sense of freshness and freedom stole into her heart, and
she felt in that instant the inflowing tide of an almost new
existence. The broad trees swung their branches over her
head, forming an arbor wherever she went. The shadows
of their green leaves were scattered over the ground,
making all about her the picture of a most fanciful mosaic.
From over the grass-crowned knolls came breaths of fragrance, and breezes from the water, that seemed to search

her very heart. Her eyes caught the vision of the leaping spray of the fountain, and sparkled with pure delight.

Slowly she wandered along, occupied chiefly with her thoughts. Without knowing how far she had been walking, she discovered at length that she had completed the entire circuit of the Common. Already she was approaching the little burying ground — that saddening, yet most pleasant spot, within the large enclosure; and in obedience to the instincts of her nature, she slackened her pace to one of more deliberateness. Her eyes roamed among the crowded hillocks, and took a sweet and melancholy delight in the fresh green grass that was creeping silently over them.

She chanced to throw a glance at one of the benches near by, and saw a person whose manner and posture particularly impressed her. He sat facing the place of the graves, and with his back turned to the passers. His head was down, and his eyes were on the ground. Something led Amy irresistibly nearer to him. He heard the approaching footsteps, and half looked up. The movement seemed altogether mechanical, and might have been the habit of his fear.

In an instant she recognized the face. It was that of the friendless outcast who had told her of his woes.

She walked to the bench very deliberately, and stood beside him. He looked up. His face expressed both sorrow and fear. It was a very strange look, but it was the true betrayal of the feelings that then ruled his heart.

"I had thought I might never see you again," said Amy, kindly and cheerfully. "I wondered what had become of you."

He shook his head sadly.

"No one in the wide world knows my agony," he answered in a hollow voice. "I have told you more than I ever told any one else, and may God reward you for your sympathy. I know you would do for me what no one else would; but even all that cannot hold me up. I am sinking down every hour. How long I may hold out, O, who can tell? I do not know that myself. The very recollection of your kindness only gives me the deeper despair. From the pure heights of your sympathy I look down into the abyss of my own misery, and shudder — O, my very flesh creeps. God help me! If I was only good! If I could but find relief!"

Amy saw that the great drops of perspiration were standing thickly on his forehead, and that his hands were tremulous with excitement.

"I am sorry," said she, as calmly as possible, "that you will not yet submit to the Power that holds all these earthly dispensations in his hands. Can you not believe that out of this temporary evil much lasting good may result? Can you not in trust put the dark Past behind your back, and live only in a peaceful, holy, and prayerful Present? Rouse yourself now; shake off the weight of this morbid fear; open your soul to the sweet influences that are all around you; and resolve that with one manly

effort you will be free.   I know that you have suffered ;
but that surely can be no reason why you should expect
always to suffer.   Why will you let only wretchedness
into your heart ?   Why will you not try and form a league
with hope, and let despair go forever ? "

"O, if you could look into my heart, and there read
all !   If you could understand just *how* I am made to suffer every day ! "

"I do try to read your feelings," answered Amy, sym-
pathizingly.

"I know you do ; I know you do ; but still you cannot
see the whole.   Only this day I have gone through with
what I never thought I could, and what I would sooner
die than go through again."

Amy looked at the wild expression of his face with
perfect astonishment.

"I have been, this very afternoon," said he, lowering
his voice till it sounded in that place even sepulchral, " to
the house of the man I once wronged.   I resolved to go
and tell him all my feelings, and to ask him to forgive me.
He was not at home himself, but I was shown in.   His
daughter came into the room.   I had known her before
my fall, and I was blessed in the consciousness of her love.
I had not seen her since the occurrence that publicly
branded me as a criminal.   You may not believe me when
I tell you of the wild joy with which my heart leaped up
to greet her again.   I was almost beside myself.   It seemed
to me a happy providence that had brought me to *her*

before I saw her father. I felt that my brain was swimming, and I could not see the objects in the room distinctly ; yet I rose to greet her as I used to greet her in
the old days that are gone, and to beseech her to forgive
me the terrible wound I had given her feelings. She
stood like a statue, fixed in the attitude of astonishment
and anger. All the better feelings of my heart set back
in one mighty tide of revulsion ; and my anger, my broken pride, my humiliated spirit, and my strong despair
fairly overwhelmed me. I could have died in that moment, and felt that death was a welcome gift. She stood
there and spurned me. She cast my guilt cruelly in my
face. She asked me how I dared enter their house after I
had been the inmate of a prison. She heaped upon me
all the words of burning scorn that she could command,
and finally ordered me from the room and the house.

" At that moment her father came in. Now, I thought,
I could find one corner of a heart that might pity me.
Ah, if you could only have seen how the manner and the
look of that man suddenly changed. First he looked at
me, and then at his daughter. He was about to ask how
I came there, when she interrupted him. She told him
of my daring presumption, and that she had already ordered me to leave the house. Then he turned full upon
me. " Why did you not go, sir ? " said he. I approached
him, feeling that I owed him a greater debt than I could
ever hope to repay, yet trying at the same time to feel
that I was still a *man*, and still possessed a priceless soul.

29 *

With as humble words as I could command I begged him
to pass over my fault, and to assure me that at least I had
his forgiveness. That would do much to calm my feelings, and to make me happy. If you could have heard
his language! You certainly must have thought that the
house at that moment held a murderer, and that he was
almost insane in his exertions to expel him. He turned
upon me like a fury. With the fiercest language he up-
braided me with my crime, and then asked me how I
dared show myself again to him. He waved his arm to
me with a show of commanding authority, and bade me
leave his presence. It was of no use for me to plead. It
was foolish for me to stand there and try to employ reason, or persuasion, or even petition. I bowed my head ;
and as I went out, in my heart I felt that for the whole
world I would not change places with him. May God
forgive him — and forgive *her* too! O, if they only knew
the depth of wretchedness into which their words have
plunged me !

"I came out into the open air, and I thought I might
feel better. I tried to silence these loud accusations of
my feelings — to quiet this frenzied beating of my heart
— to cool this feverish throbbing of my pulses. But every
moment only adds to my misery. I *cannot* live — I do
not *wish* to live. I have come here to die — to pass away
out of this shadow of my troubles — here, in sight of these
graves — and be forever free."

And while he spoke, he drew forth a vial from his vest
pocket, labelled " Prussic Acid."

"O, no," gently said Amy, sitting down now at his side, and taking it unresistingly out of his hand; "O, no, indeed; don't think of *that*; it would not be *manly;* it would certainly be *cowardly*. Only stop and *think* a moment. Your life does not belong to you to take; it is the property of another. He will ask it as soon as he has wrought out his work through you here. Let *me* keep this stuff. You are not well now; but you will be better soon. I have great faith in your lofty manhood, and I believe that you will not disappoint me. Here," — and she took out some money from her purse, — "you shall not want so long as my poor means can supply. Take this from *me*, and do not forget my words, or my friendship."

He would not receive the gift into his hand; so she thrust it into his pocket.

"It isn't much," said she; "but it will keep you from downright want."

"Heaven bless you, my *best* friend!" he exclaimed, clasping his hands prayerfully. "O, to *think* of it! — to think that in all this crowded city, where there is so much wealth, so much pretended sympathy, so much vaunted charity, you alone of its tens of thousands are ready to extend help to a sufferer like me! I would not have believed once that such things are true. I would not once have thought that love, and charity, and tenderest sympathy are to be found in hearts that the proud world knows nothing of. Heaven bless you! Heaven bless you! I will live now, if only for the sake of a noble woman like you. I will try and raise myself from this awful pit into which my own crime has thrown me."

"Live rather for *yourself*," said Amy, in her singularly bewitching voice. "You have a soul that a single crime like this should not be allowed to destroy. Do not throw away your better self merely because you may have fallen too readily into temptation at the beginning. You do not yet know the priceless value of your faculties. You do not comprehend the vastness and the grandeur of your destiny. And now to give up every hope, every aspiration, every noble effort, all the riches of a heart whose wealth is yet unexplored, all the deep, deep satisfactions that this life, if truly lived, is able to yield on every side, — to give over all these, because, in an unfortunate hour, you yielded to a temptation that drew after it a public disgrace, is without reason or faith. You *must not* do it. You must raise yourself *above* these feelings, and put them beneath your feet."

"O, if others would talk to me about it as you talk!" he groaned out.

"Mind not what *others* say. Possess only your own soul. No one can injure you but yourself. You can find no such foe to your peace any where as you will find in your own breast. Again I beg you, do not be troubled about the speech of others. Some talk idly, meaning nothing at all. Some talk with malice, and they are to be pitied for the blindness that their passions create. Some are mere echoers of what they hear others say. They are not to be cared for. Do not be troubled at *the most* that people can say. Do not think to live to the opinions, or the speeches, or the whims of others, but find only the centre of your own individual being, and there reside with calmness and hope. O, if you will but make yourself at one with God — will only put forth your own purposes in perfect harmony with his purposes — will pluck out pride, and fear, and an unmanly cowardice from your heart, and throw your whole life into the circuit of the divine laws that move within and around us all — you *cannot* but be happy — you *must* be happy! This anxiety about what the world says, and what the world thinks, will vanish away like a mist in the morning. You will come up into a clearer, and a rarer, and a purer atmosphere. You will rather draw the world to *you*, for very shame at the conviction of its own meanness and inferiority. Men will not point the finger of affected scorn at you as you pass; they will secretly pray for the possession of that indescribable beauty and that priceless peace that so openly adorn your life."

He groaned again; but his face wore a jubilant and a heroic expression.

"And you will look at your trials, your temptations, yes, even to your past disgraces, with an undisturbed spirit, feeling that out of all these many tribulations, and these manifold woes, you have come into a kingdom where they are not admitted. You will thank God forever for every thing he sends you, because you will believe from the depths of your heart that all comes for your highest good. *This* is life — *this* is the true life here. Others will behold it, and the dark corners where their passions and fears were wont to lurk will be illuminated with its steady light. Come; let us not think of the past any longer. Let us live in a better present from this moment forward."

" You have saved me ; O, you have saved me ! " he cried, clasping his hands together, while the tears rolled down his cheeks. " God reward you ; *I* never can."

In that moment Amy felt that she would not have changed places with the mightiest potentate that is throned on the face of the earth.

CHAPTER XXXI.

CARRYING A MATTER HOME.

THE very next afternoon, after little Mary Braggins's music lesson was over, and while Amy was preparing to take her departure from the house, the door of the room opened, and Ellen came in. She accosted Amy in a very friendly way, and sat down not far from her, as if to engage her in a few minutes' conversation.

Their remarks rambled off from one topic to another, without any definite purpose, taking in all things, from the last piece of music Mary had learned to play, to that threadbare topic, the weather. It was a beautiful day, and the windows were opened to let in the fresh air that came every where with its fragrant blessings.

Speaking of one thing and another, Amy finally happened to allude to the family of the poor man who had been hurt by the fall of the building. Without meaning to make any boast of her own charity, she was detailing the manner in which her sympathies had been excited; and she went on to say that she had called on them regularly ever since the day of the accident, and done what little she could for them.

Ellen put her many questions respecting them, appearing greatly interested ; and after Amy had satisfied her
with answers to all of them, she rose and went out of the
room.   In a few minutes she came back, and placed in
Amy's hand some bank bills.

"I wish you would dispense these among them," said
she, "just according to your own judgment.   You know
exactly what they need."

Amy looked both surprised and joyful.

"But hadn't you better go and perform this kindness to
them yourself?" she asked.   "I will gladly show you the
way.   You will make their hearts thus ten times happy."

But Ellen chose to be an unknown almoner.   She said
she was perfectly willing that her friend should have all
the credit.

Amy answered that *credit* was not what she desired.
The true reward of a good deed was the inward *satisfaction* that never failed to accompany it.

Yet Ellen insisted that she should carry them her offering *this* time, and at some other she would be very glad
to accompany her on her errand of kindness.

Amy could not make *this* case of trouble known without
likewise alluding to another ; that singular one which had
there, by the strangest accident in the world, been revealed
to her.

"I found," said she, her face betraying by its heightened
color the interest her heart took in the subject of her narrative, — "I found a young man, a perfect stranger, sitting

at this poor laborer's bedside, watching by him as tenderly as if he were his own father."

"And he was a *stranger*?" questioned Ellen. "Wasn't he *related* at all to this poor man?"

"No, he had not even *seen* him before. I did not know who he was, or where he came from. But there he sat, over that sufferer, and watched him with all the anxious tenderness of a son."

"How strange! I declare, there is something like a little *romance* there — isn't there? Was he well dressed? or did he appear to belong to that same class of people?"

"Yes, he was quite well dressed — neatly and tastefully, though not at all *richly*. But his countenance betrayed him better than any garments could. That was refined and saddened. Its expression was very interesting indeed. I could not help studying it closely."

"How *strange!* isn't it?" a second time said Ellen. "But did you ever see him there at the man's bedside again?"

"Day after day I met him there, always in the same place — always bending over the sufferer with the same look of tender solicitude; till one day I missed him."

"And never saw him again?" quickly asked Ellen.

"O, yes; I saw him afterwards; but it was not till several days had elapsed."

"Pray, where did you see him *then*? How did you find him?"

Ellen's feelings manifestly were deeply enlisted in the

narrative of her friend. She folded together her arms
very tightly, and looked eagerly in Amy's face with great
impatience.

"Indeed," said she, "I confess I am quite interested in
this person. I wish I could *see* him, and know *more* about
him. Where did you say you saw him the *next* time?
What did he say about himself?"

"I saw him sitting on one of the little benches on the
Common," said Amy, "near the old burying ground. He
was sad and downcast enough."

"Poor fellow! I pity him! What *was* the matter?
What was his great sorrow? Did you ever learn?"

"O, he told me, — for I went up and accosted him, —
he told me that he was in very great distress ——"

"So *poor*, I suppose."

"No; but distress of *mind*. He cared nothing for
poverty, and said that was the last thing that troubled
him."

"What a brave spirit!"

"You shall better judge whether he was then so very
brave or not. He said, as I put him one question after
another, that he could not live, and did not know as he
wished to. Life had no charm for him. His heart was
burned to dry ashes with the fierce flames of his passionate
sufferings."

"Poor creature! Lost all his friends, I suppose. Or
perhaps the one heart he had loved now repulsed him and
scorned him."

"Yes, that was the last blow from' which he had suffered," said Amy.

"Did he — did he confess to you as much as *that* ?" quickly asked Ellen, her face turning pallid with the remembrance of her own cruelty (though *she* did not deem it so) to one who had once so loved her. "Did he tell you *that* ?" she repeated, with some excitement.

"Yes; and even more — more than I ought to tell you, I think, and more than I *can* tell you. You can infer what his wretchedness was from what I have already narrated."

"O, yes, indeed; yes, indeed. Poor creature! How few there are in the world," she moralized, feelingly, "who know any thing of the distress of others! How very, very few there are !"

And she threw her eyes down upon the floor, and seemed lost in thought.

"But I made one discovery," continued Amy, "that startled me. He drew from his pocket a vial containing deadly *poison*, and said that he had taken his seat there by that burying ground to destroy his life."

Ellen shuddered, caught her breath in horror, and lifted up her hands.

"He went there to commit suicide !" she exclaimed.

"Yes. He was tired of life — his friends had all deserted him — he was entirely alone in the world — there were no prospects before him — and he had no living hope in his heart; and he had resolved to get rid of his trou-

bles, he told me, in one brief moment. The treatment of
her whom he loved had more immediately driven him to
this resolution. So he confessed. He could have borne
every thing else but that, — penury, distress, friendlessness, beggary, even, — so *she* would not cast him away.
His heart appeared to be utterly gone. His spirits were
wholly broken. He could scarcely lift his head and look
me directly in the face. I pitied him as I never pitied
a wretched sufferer before."

"I should have thought you would, indeed. But did
he say nothing to you about his early life? Did he not
tell you of his troubles — of what had brought all this
grief upon him? Was that all kept to himself?"

"No; he confessed every thing to me. He said he had
nothing in the world to keep back."

"Indeed!" exclaimed Ellen.

She moved uneasily in her chair, betraying the eagerness she really felt to get at the entire story. Something
whispered mysteriously to her heart that this history held
a lesson in its brief pages for *her*. Something told her of
a wrong that she might herself, in a hasty moment, have
done another, for which no sort of recompense had yet
been made.

"He was quite young, you say?" she inquired again,
as if to make herself sure on every point.

"Yes, not more than twenty-four or five; and his face,
it seemed to me, hardly confessed to as much as that.
Early in life, he said, he was put into the service of a

merchant in this city. He went along with great promise, and received promotion very steadily. He was liked by his employer, and he had many friends. He gave his heart finally to his employer's daughter, — the child of that merchant, who was a proud man, though the very soul of commercial honor, — and he felt happy in being assured of her love. Time passed lightly, and each year seemed to open to him new prospects. But suddenly he fell ! "

" *Fell !* " exclaimed Ellen, under her breath almost.

" Alas, it is too true! He had not strength to withstand temptation."

" What did he do ? " Ellen inquired very rapidly, her face alternately flushing with heat and turning white like marble.

" He confessed it all to me. It was not a tale that under other circumstances I would have liked to hear, but I was very deeply interested in him. Being in the midst of temptations that he could not resist, he gave up to them at once, and became a criminal by committing forgery."

" How strange ! " gasped Ellen, clutching hold of the back of her chair.

Amy could not but observe her excitement now with surprise.

" *Forgery !* " again exclaimed Ellen, in a falling voice.

" It's a crime that usually brands a person with a pretty
30 *

deep mark, so far as the opinion of the public is concerned," said Amy.

"Yes, indeed," answered Ellen, fetching a very long
and difficult breath. "Yes, indeed."

"But what has followed since his liberation from prison
has interested me more than all the rest. It appears that
he loved the daughter of the merchant with whom he had
been placed — the daughter of the man whose name he so
wrongfully counterfeited ——"

"Is it possible! is it possible!" interrupted Ellen,
starting forward in her seat. "Can it be that —— "

"And not long after obtaining his freedom, and not
very long ago was it, either, he went to the house of that
merchant, determined first of all to ask his forgiveness,
and then to beg to be forgiven by her whose heart he had
so wronged beyond the power of reparation, but whom he
still loved as he could not again love another."

"Went to *see her!*"

"The father, he said, was not at the moment in; but
the daughter came into the room, and at once recognized
him. He was ready to throw himself a suppliant at her
feet — humble, repentant, and quite heart-broken. He
would have performed almost any office, however menial
or servile, if only by the means he could be assured of her
forgiveness and favor. To her hand and her heart he felt
that he had forfeited all right. All he besought was her
forgiveness. He knew that he had wronged her, and how
much he had wronged her. Though he yet loved her better

than his own life, still he would never think or dare to
be loved by her in return. With these feelings, humble
and contrite from the bottom of his soul, he stood in that
girl's presence, waiting to hear one single syllable from
her lips that would drop a balm like that of forgiveness.
But she knit her brow, and spurned him angrily. She
asked him how he had dared to enter a house upon which
he had brought nothing but disgrace by his conduct and
connection. She cast his late act of criminality in his
teeth, and ordered him out of the room.

"At that moment her father came in. Since the day
when the young man had been convicted of his crime in
the public court room he had not seen the merchant once.
But they recognized one another in an instant. Before he
could say for what he had come there, his old employer
angrily bade him instantly leave the house. There was
nothing to be answered to this — there was no earthly
alternative but to go. And without a syllable of protest
or murmur, feeling that his severe punishment was all deserved, yet heart-broken, and lost to the strength of any
further hope or resolution, he went out the door in silence,
and procuring poison, resolved at once to destroy himself.
I found him, by a good providence, just at this most unhappy crisis of his life, and my words and my spirit, under
God, had the power to arouse him to a new purpose. He
blessed me as we separated, and said that I had saved his
life — that henceforth he would *live*, if only to do honor
to the single heart that had shown him sympathy when
he most needed it."

Amy paused. She had finished her pathetic recital. But as she looked over at Ellen, she discovered that her head was bowed down, and her face was buried in her hands. She sobbed and moaned most tearfully.

"What *is* the matter? what *is* the matter?" quickly inquired Amy.

"O, Heaven forgive me! *I* have been false, and *you* — you, a *stranger* — have been true!"

And she threw herself at her length upon the sofa, and wept as if she would not be pacified.

The young man was the clerk of her own father; and *hers* was the heart that had in that terrible crisis spurned him!

CHAPTER XXXII.

ONCE AGAIN.

FROM this time forth the visits of Amy upon Ellen were voluntarily multiplied. She went to the house when any thing rather than a music lesson summoned her. Ellen loved her society now, and their talk was at every visit protracted and confidential. Of course it was chiefly of the one whose name, hitherto quite unknown to Amy, had been mixed so intimately in with the affairs of the family.

One morning Amy sat alone in the parlor with her friend, who now seemed to look up to her loftier and purer character for very guidance in her complicated troubles, when the door opened from the hall, and a gentleman was ushered in by the servant.

From the manner in which he came forward and accosted Ellen, it was manifest that he was an old friend and acquaintance, and admitted without much ceremony to the privileges of the house. Though Ellen received him with much cordiality and frankness, yet there was perceptible in her manner a certain self-possessedness, if not reserve, that seemed altogether new to this present occasion. Amy herself could not help remarking it.

Scarcely had the gentleman gone through with his greeting, when he threw his glance over to where Amy was
sitting, and Ellen stepped back to perform what is generally called an "introduction."

" This is my friend, Miss Lee, Mr. Clendenning," said
Ellen, in all simplicity and sincerity.

At first he drew back peremptorily.   Then his familiarity with the iron customs of a false society came to his
relief, and he even passed to the other extreme of feeling,
and walked up to Amy, offering her his hand.

She rose, respectfully bowed, said not a word by way
of salutation, and persistently kept her hands at her side.
This was indeed chilling.   Ellen observed the gentleman's
sudden embarrassment, and was perfectly amazed at Amy's
manner, for it was totally unaccountable.   Yet she could
not speak.   No syllables of hers were allowed to interpose
in a situation so unexpected.

He recovered himself the best way he was able, and
went and sat down not far from Ellen.   Yet he was by no
means at his ease.   Even *his* assurance was not broad
enough and long enough to cover the chagrin of this moment.   Still he did the best he could.   No one would be
likely to envy him, however, let him do the best he might.

So he began — to Ellen only, of course — about the
weather.   What a lovely morning it was !   How inspirit-
ing all the world out of doors looked and felt !   What a
life there was in every thing !   What fragrance in the atmosphere, though it bathed only brick walls, and drew

through no passages but the stony streets! How changed men's faces seemed that morning, and how changed the countenances of the ladies too! And so on in this way, till he could the better collect himself, and the better be prepared for a conversation of a higher character.

"Ah!" exclaimed he, rattling on gayly and unconcernedly, "have you been to the Opera yet, Miss Braggins?"

She told him that she had not, though she certainly designed to go soon.

"Yes; very fine performance last evening — *very* fine." A glance at Amy, and a glance back again quicker than the first. "You *must* go, Miss Ellen, I assure you. *Really*, you don't know what you lose. Have *you* attended yet, Miss Lee?"

Nothing could surpass the cool effrontery of his manner, as he put this interrogatory.

"No, sir," said Amy, with quite as much distinctness as the occasion required; "I never attend the Opera."

For a moment he was staggered; but he got over it again as soon.

"If I had thought of it last evening," said he, turning to Ellen, "I should surely have called for you. I am sorry. How is your father this morning? He keeps his usual stock of robust health on hand, I conclude. Is he at his counting room as much as he used to be — say a great many years ago, when — ha, ha! — when you and I, Miss Ellen, were a good deal *younger* than we are now — ha, ha!"

Ellen could not reply to all his questions at once; so she satisfied herself with answering his last one. She told her visitor that her father, she believed, confined himself to his business as closely as he ever did.

"Just his way!" exclaimed Mr. Clendenning, throwing up his head. "Always his way! I declare I wonder when he will think there's no more work for him to do."

Ellen answered that he would never be likely to wish for the time to come when he would have nothing to do; for industry was all that kept him happy.

"Indeed," said the visitor, affecting a careless, if not a somewhat patronizing air, "industry is a very good thing — I may truly say, a most excellent thing; that is, provided one doesn't let the thing push him into mere drudgery. I don't think any one can do much without it; that is, long at a time; but *too much* of a good thing — *you* know the old adage, Miss Ellen — ha, ha, ha!"

It was hardly possible to imagine any thing more hollow, artificial, and conceited than this laugh. With all the charity that Amy possessed, it was difficult for her to banish the supreme disgust that she so thoroughly felt.

"By the by," he added, with full as much complacency as ever, "what ever became of that young *clerk* of your father's who took it into his foolish head one day to forge his name? Let me see: he went first to State Prison — didn't he?"

It seemed as if Ellen's heart for a moment had ceased to beat. She felt a rising and a choking sensation in her throat, and knew not but she must fall forward upon the floor. But she controlled herself. Amy's face now was deathly pale, for her sympathy in this trying moment for her friend was very quick and very strong.

"Yes, he did," Ellen made out to answer, with a great effort.

"Strange sort of an operation *that* was!" said he, half sneeringly. "Why, I should have thought the fellow was *a fool*. Do you know where he is *now*?"

"He is in town, I believe."

She was hardly able to answer it, but she did. Amy saw the fearfulness of her trial, and determined herself to put a hasty termination to it.

"Ellen," said she, in a low and musical voice, that even drew the eyes of Mr. Clendenning full upon her, "where is little Mary this morning? I haven't seen her."

"O, yes," answered Ellen, rising from her seat and stepping to the door. "I will call her. She is in the house."

And she went out of the room, leaving Amy and Mr. Clendening there alone.

Amy instantly reached for a book that lay near at hand, and the gentleman, without once deigning to extend her any further notice, rose and began a stroll around the room, looking musingly at the pictures on the walls, and idly humming a bit of an air from the last opera that had enchanted him. Though he immediately threw aside the very pretences of a gentleman by offering such a marked slight to Amy, yet she was in her heart very thankful that

31

he did not attempt any further advances. And here and
there he wandered about, humming in that familiar and
thoroughly contemptuous manner, till Ellen and Mary
made their appearance.

"Ah, here's my little Miss Mary!" he exclaimed, as
she entered, taking Amy's first salutation from her lips.
"How does she do this pleasant morning?"

Mary went and received the proffered hand, smiled
pleasantly enough to drive away all evil feeling from any
one's heart, and immediately hastened to the side of her
friend and instructor.

Amy sat and interested her with her questions and remarks, leaving Ellen and Mr. Clendenning to have their
conversation all to themselves. The latter did not fail to
improve the opportunity to the utmost. He even tried to
make amends for his earlier embarrassment, and engaged
the attention of Ellen very deeply by his earnest and interesting narratives. She almost forgot the peculiarity of
his manner when he had first entered, and listened with
as much intentness apparently as she would have done at
any other time.

Thus the moments slipped away. Mr. Clendenning
was, in truth, waiting for Amy to take her departure.
There was nothing that he was more anxious for. He
was afraid of leaving her behind, to have the opportunity
of saying the *last word*. The mean-souled are just those
who are troubled about such matters, and usually the
only ones.

But Amy had no thought of going; certainly not till after he had. And thus the case at length stood.

But he was finally obliged to yield; and as he offered Ellen his hand again at parting, he threw a glance at Amy, that expressed all the rage, scorn, contempt, and threats which he was forced to keep pent up in his bosom. Yet he could not refuse to bid Amy good morning likewise, for by betraying his anger he knew he would be very sure to forfeit the esteem in which he was held by Ellen.

The moment he was gone, she dismissed little Mary from the room, and at once began to interrogate Amy concerning the strange conduct of her visitor.

"Now, I have perfect confidence in you," said she, "and I want you to be frank with me. Let me ask you a few questions. You have *seen* Mr. Clendenning before?"

"Yes."

"When was it, pray?"

"At the time when I lived in the country; only last winter, while I was teaching school out there," promptly answered Amy.

"But something unpleasant has passed between you before. What was it? I wish you would tell me."

"I will — I will be as frank with you as you have desired. I had a very dear friend there, whom it was expected he was to marry; and while I knew this very well, and he must have *known* I knew it, too, he came over to my school room one afternoon, while I was alone, and offered to make me his wife."

"And engaged already!"

"Yes, I had the best reason to believe that."

Ellen's face flushed instantly, and her eyes sought the
floor. One would have known she was troubled, by seeing
how busily her foot kept drumming.

"The hardest of it was," continued Amy, "that though
I of course spurned his unmanly offer, I lost by the means
my best friend. For he left the place the very next day,
and nothing was heard from him afterwards. I was supposed to be the mischief-maker, and by the force of the
prejudice that soon began to spread among the people, I
was compelled to surrender my school and leave the village. From there I came here, and this morning I have
seen him for the first time since."

"And *that* accounts for your reserve towards him, then?
I think it's all plain enough *now*."

"I bear him no anger nor ill will," said Amy; "but I
cannot consent to countenance his conduct by any fictitious
appearance of further friendship. Certainly he shall not
deceive *you*, through any instrumentality of *mine*."

It was enough. The explanation sufficed to open the
eyes of Ellen, and to place her on her guard for the future.

When the two girls separated that morning, tears were
swimming in the eyes of both. Amy's goodness and gentleness was doing its perfect work. But with the heart
of Ellen, her story of the sufferings of that friendless
·young man — friendless utterly but for the quick and
noble sympathy of Amy — was working with a wider and

a deeper effect than aught else. She felt the reproach of her own feelings, till it became an ever-present torture to her. It was a bitter thing to think of, too, that Amy alone, and a stranger besides, should have been the one to arrest him in his unhappy course, and to lead him gently away to the path of patience and peace.

31 *

CHAPTER XXXIII.

RECONCILIATION AND PEACE.

IT was indeed the work of a true and noble heart that finally brought about a better understanding between Mr. Braggins's family and the unfortunate clerk; but Amy's was the heart through whose patience, and gentleness, and love it was all effected.

She might even have been surprised herself to discover how fast the proud and heartless prejudices were melting away, and how the sunlight of higher views and a more charitable feeling was stealing in and driving out the darkness of the passions; but the surprise was so intimately related to joy itself, that it added a new strength to the labors of her day, and welcome and happy dreams to the slumbers of her night.

Mr. Wilde — such was the young man's name — she now saw daily, and from him learned with much delight the progress of the reconciliation. Looking into his face, or listening to the tone of his conversation now, she could not but remark the changed air of satisfaction that was the characteristic of both.

Of course Mr. Clendenning's further friendship was discarded by Ellen, and that, too, without a great deal of ceremony. He felt that his own mean acts were very rapidly finding him out. Go where he would, it soon seemed to him as if his heartless character had preceded him. Like a shadow, it was always cast before him; till presently Ellen ceased to hear any thing further about him; and it was generally supposed that he must have betaken himself to a locality where he was not as well known. Unquestionably his pride had suffered the most, for that was the point at which he was the most vulnerable. As soon as that was destroyed, there would be better hopes of his reformation.

Mr. Braggins at first was most wilfully opposed to listening to any thing like a proposal to receive his former clerk into favor again. It seemed as if he could not be made to move from his position. He was a man of exceedingly strong prejudices, which he even reckoned to be at times the only safeguard that could be set about his chilling morality. He was correct enough, and exemplary enough; nobody would think of denying that; but he was wanting in warm and glowing charity: he lacked the heat of a love that is needed at all times to make us loved again.

Only through his idolized daughter Ellen, therefore, could Amy ever hope to make her influence reach his heart. And she kept at her work of gentleness patiently and continually, happy in the deep faith that she freely entertained for the ultimate perfection of blind, weak, and uncharitable humanity.

Little by little be began to relent. The crime of his clerk refused forever to stand out before him in such colossal proportions. He could not but think that if men were so apt to nurse prejudices, and so given to cramp their souls with the iron memories of long-gone wrongs, there would be little need to hope for charity and forgiveness at the hands of the common Father; for until we release others from the thraldom of our evil thoughts, we cannot expect to be free from a far worse thraldom ourselves.

Ellen prevailed on him to admit the delinquent into his library one evening, and the directions were properly given. Through Amy, of course, they were carried to him. There was no other means of communication then than herself. Very soon afterwards he was the glad recipient of them. He hurried to his employer's room, and threw himself at once upon his knees before him.

" I have need of your forgiveness," said he, " for I am wretched and unhappy. I have wronged you deeply, though the wrong I did my own soul was greater. Overlook my fault. It has brought me a bitter, bitter lesson, that I shall never forget. I ask for nothing more. Of course you cannot receive me into your business again ; and I do not expect it ; I must earn my bread elsewhere. I may be considered henceforward an *outcast ;* yet I will try and carry the soul of a *man*. Your forgiveness, sir, is all I ask."

The manner of the young man entirely disarmed the rigid heart of the wealthy merchant of its weapons of prejudice, and exposed him to the most gentle influences. Immediately he begged him to rise from his position of entreaty, and to accept not only the assurances of his forgiveness, but of his personal favor also. In addition to this, — now that generous feelings had found an outlet, it was difficult to stop their outgushing, — he freely offered to receive him back into his counting room again, and even pressed him to accept the proposal, when he found that the young man hesitated. And well might he hesitate ; for he was wholly overcome with surprise.

But the noble work was done. A prejudiced nature had had its hard flintiness broken, and a humble, repentant, half-broken spirit was raised again to its own level of native dignity. What a change ! What a blessed deed to be performed by one poor, friendless, but brave and generous heart — the heart of a true and trustful girl !

Verily might the proud world, and the selfish world, and the scornful and false world, take a lesson from a deed like this. Verily might it be taught that the endeavor of one honest, sincere, truthful, and glowing heart is mightier by far than the vaunted power of armies and navies. Of a truth do such great and good souls have their reward ; and this is the reward — that deeds of

virtue and nobleness never, never fail to enrich a thousand
fold the souls of which they are conceived.

Matters having been thus amicably adjusted, Amy cast
about her to see if there might not be some way by which
she could enlarge her income, and so put it within her
power to do more good.   Opportunities offered themselves
on every hand, and she felt that there was no need to
make any great exertion to hunt them out.   They came to
her faster than she could find the means to provide for
them.   But she. studied the science of economical management with much assiduity, and so accomplished vastly
more than she had at first dared to propose.   Actual won-
ders, in the way of philanthropy, seemed to unfold themselves beneath her skill.

Still she kept thinking the matter over more industriously.   She sought to make others happy.   That was
her own greatest happiness.

At length she hit upon the thing exactly.   It was a
project that commended itself, too, entirely to her *heart* ;
and that was its foremost recommendation for her, too.
She bethought herself of trying the field of authorship ;
not that wider field, over which the more brilliant intel-
lects glitter like the stars in the sky, but the more modest
and unnoticed corner usually devoted to the amusement
and instruction of the juveniles ; yet not any less dignified, and not any less noble, than the other.   Amy esteemed it even a *holier* calling.   And so indeed it is.

Therefore she sat down at once, and acted singly and

resolutely upon her thought. Her heart was equally brave
and self-reliant at all occupations, and in the face of all
obstacles. She labored with all her might, putting her
soul into her work. The first manuscript was finished.
She carried it to a publisher — timidly, it is true, yet
hoping against all sorts of discouraging fears. A publisher she had conceived to be an awful being, clothed with
attributes such as belonged to the possession of no other
living potentate. But how great was her disappointment,
and how very agreeable it was, likewise, when she saw him
blandly bow her into his apartment, and as blandly promise
to read her manuscript at the earliest possible day !

Of course it was accepted. Such an effort *must* be good,
because it came from a single, sincere, and great heart.
That stamp would insure it favor every where; and bear-
ing, too, the stamp of the heart of a true woman.

That manuscript is in press. It has not yet seen the
light. And Amy is waiting to know if she may rely
on such a source for the further spread of her kind charities; content, however, to abide whatever may be the
event.

Not long after the consummation of this new relation between Mr. Braggins and his clerk, Amy was
put in receipt of a long letter from her friend Mrs.
Gummel, of Valley Village, who dwelt sadly still on
the loss of her society; and likewise of one from both
Mr. and Mrs. Parsons — the good minister and his wife.
These were very dear tokens to her of former friend-

ships, that still glowed and flamed upon the altar of her heart. They carried her thoughts back to the other places and other persons, and rejoiced her with the fresh recollection of objects on which her nature might feed to the last limit of her days.

CHAPTER XXXIV.

AND THE LAST.

Thus was Amy at this time situated. Her heart was full of faith, her life was full of love. She was now fairly entering upon life. All its prospects and promises — thousand-hued ever to the dreaming eyes of youth —were rapidly opening to her. She had known sorrow and she had tasted joy. To a nature as deep as hers, neither would be likely to bring a very superficial experience.

We leave her where we love to leave one whom our eyes have watched fondly and gratefully — exactly in the midst of her labors, surrounded with all her multiplied and multiplying duties, drinking deep draughts of satisfaction from her good works, and perpetually enriching her soul with the secret and countless graces that flow out from humility, and faith, and obedience, and love. All these things made her strong. Hers was not a coward's heart. She knew nothing like fear. Her cheek never turned pale at the sudden thought of consequences that till that moment were unknown. She was not driven out of her even course by surprises of any kind. With her all was perfect peace, and serenity, and happiness.

32

(373)

Ah, how few know what a great work one single soul
like this can perform in the world! How few understand
the thousand and ten thousand influences that radiate like
the golden sunlight from a pure heart like hers, flooding
many and many a dark corner with its cheerfulness, arousing
other hearts all around by its own grand example, awaken-
ing faith where only doubt, and distrust, and perhaps despair were before, and working out to the very last hour
of existence that perfect work which brings a deep peace
passing all understanding! Blessed are these few brave
and true souls, whether men or women, for theirs is a
heavenly kingdom already. Blessed are their rich and
exalted natures, for they breathe an atmosphere where the
fogs of selfishness, and fear, and envy, and passion cannot
come.

She did not sit down and grudgingly begin to calculate
when she should get through her work, and when she
might begin to enjoy the fruits. She wrought and enjoyed both together. She did not strain her gaze sadly
into a dead and silent past, nor try to look doubtingly
into the shadows of a future that no human eye may
pierce; but she lived only in the present, that single
bright thread of living light, which is eternally shooting
across the deep gulf of the past, and eternally throwing its
one golden ray over the broad heaven of our consciousness.
She did not live for a show, but for the grand reality.
Life with her was no mere spectacle; it was a plain and
divine fact. To her the soul was greater than all else.

And believing only in this sublime truth, and throwing herself obediently and joyfully into the protecting arms of the good Father, who will not forget for a moment even the least of his children, she wrought and lived, wrought and lived, making each day a new existence, and blessing God devoutly that such a glorious existence was never to have an end.

O, the nobleness of such a life as this! How it brushes away with a single sweep all the cobwebs of falsity and untruth, of surface and unreality, from before the soul's vision, and brings it clearer and truer views of the exceedingly excellent glory into which every human soul may yet be ushered!

Ere long she received another letter from Valley Village. She broke the seal and found it was from Olive Adams. It could not but surprise her a little, for since she had left the village she had not directly heard a word from her friend.

The letter communicated the intelligence of the sudden death of Olive's aunt, and besought Amy to come out to Ivy Lodge at the earliest day possible. Olive wanted her to give up her music teaching, at least for a time, and renew the sweet old friendship again. She promised her a pleasant home, and all the comforts that her abundant means would furnish. Descanting but lightly upon the unhappy causes of their separation, she nevertheless by her manner of writing assured Amy of her continued affection, and her anxiety for a speedy reunion.

And with this unexpected letter in her hand, sitting thoughtfully at her window in the quiet boarding house of Mrs. Dozy, the past and the present mingling the multitude of their associations and their memories all around her, we will leave her alone. Only let us pray that *our* faith and *our* obedience may through life be as single and sincere as hers.

Lightning Source UK Ltd.
Milton Keynes UK
UKOW031726021212

203059UK00009B/278/A